AF168179

Lecture Notes
in Business Information Processing 563

Series Editors

Wil van der Aalst , *RWTH Aachen University, Aachen, Germany*
Sudha Ram , *University of Arizona, Tucson, USA*
Michael Rosemann , *Queensland University of Technology, Brisbane, Australia*
Clemens Szyperski, *Microsoft Research, Redmond, USA*
Giancarlo Guizzardi , *University of Twente, Enschede, The Netherlands*

LNBIP reports state-of-the-art results in areas related to business information systems and industrial application software development – timely, at a high level, and in both printed and electronic form.

The type of material published includes

- Proceedings (published in time for the respective event)
- Postproceedings (consisting of thoroughly revised and/or extended final papers)
- Other edited monographs (such as, for example, project reports or invited volumes)
- Tutorials (coherently integrated collections of lectures given at advanced courses, seminars, schools, etc.)
- Award-winning or exceptional theses

LNBIP is abstracted/indexed in DBLP, EI and Scopus. LNBIP volumes are also submitted for the inclusion in ISI Proceedings.

Maximilian Schreieck · Ilan Oshri ·
Julia Kotlarsky · Oliver Krancher
Editors

Bridging Digital Sourcing, Platforms, and Ecosystems

16th International Workshop, DSPE 2025
Obergurgl, Austria, March 4–7, 2025
Revised Selected Papers

 Springer

Editors

Maximilian Schreieck (ID)
University of Innsbruck
Innsbruck, Austria

Ilan Oshri (ID)
University of Auckland
Auckland, New Zealand

Julia Kotlarsky (ID)
University of Auckland
Auckland, New Zealand

Oliver Krancher (ID)
IT University
Copenhagen, Denmark

ISSN 1865-1348   ISSN 1865-1356 (electronic)
Lecture Notes in Business Information Processing
ISBN 978-3-032-04511-9   ISBN 978-3-032-04512-6 (eBook)
https://doi.org/10.1007/978-3-032-04512-6

Preface

This volume brings together a curated selection of articles presented at the *Digital Sourcing, Platforms, and Ecosystems Workshop*, held in March 2025 in Austria. The workshop convened leading scholars and practitioners to explore the evolving intersection of digital sourcing strategies and platform-based ecosystems—a nexus that is increasingly shaping the future of organizational design, value creation, and technological collaboration.

The workshop was conceived as a response to the growing need for integrative thinking across disciplines that have traditionally operated in silos. Digital sourcing, with its focus on how organizations acquire and manage digital capabilities, and platform ecosystems, which emphasize the orchestration of value through interconnected actors and technologies, are converging in practice but often remain disconnected in academic discourse. This event aimed to bridge that gap by fostering dialogue, sharing empirical insights, and developing conceptual frameworks that illuminate the synergies and tensions between these domains.

This book is the result of a rigorous and collaborative academic process that began with 20 initial submissions. From these, 9 papers were selected for invitation based on their originality, relevance, and potential impact. Each invited paper underwent a thorough double-blind peer-review process, receiving feedback from two independent reviewers prior to the workshop. During the workshop, authors also benefited from interactive discussions and constructive critiques from participants, which further enriched their work. The final chapters presented in this volume are revised versions of these papers, incorporating both pre-workshop reviews and insights gained during the event.

This volume opens with an introduction developed by three of the co-organizers of the workshop, serving as a foundational chapter that outlines emerging directions for future research. With a particular focus on the intersection of sourcing and platform ecosystems, the chapter aims to stimulate scholarly dialogue by proposing conceptual linkages and identifying key questions that merit further exploration. It reflects the collaborative spirit of the workshop and sets the stage for the contributions that follow. The other articles in this book reflect the richness and diversity of the discussions held during the workshop. They span topics such as platform governance, sourcing strategies in multi-sided markets, digital capability building, ecosystem orchestration, and the role of data and AI in shaping sourcing decisions. Each contribution offers a unique lens on how organizations can navigate the complexities of digital transformation through both strategic sourcing and ecosystem engagement.

Collectively, these works emphasize the importance of rethinking traditional boundaries—between firms and platforms, between buyers and suppliers, and between internal capabilities and external partnerships. They highlight how digital sourcing is no longer merely a procurement function but a strategic lever for ecosystem participation and innovation. Likewise, they show how platform ecosystems are not just technological infrastructures but dynamic arenas for co-creation, competition, and value distribution.

We hope this volume serves as a valuable resource for researchers, practitioners, and policymakers seeking to understand and shape the future of digital sourcing and platform ecosystems. The insights herein are not only timely but foundational for building resilient, adaptive, and collaborative digital enterprises.

July 2025

Maximilian Schreieck

Ilan Oshri

Julia Kotlarsky

Oliver Krancher

Organization

Workshop Chairs

Maximilian Schreieck — University of Innsbruck, Austria
Ilan Oshri — University of Auckland, New Zealand
Julia Kotlarsky — University of Auckland, New Zealand
Oliver Krancher — IT University of Copenhagen, Denmark

Honorary Workshop Chair

Leslie P. Willcocks — London School of Economics, UK

Contents

Bridging the Information Systems Literature on Digital Sourcing, Platforms, and Ecosystems

Maximilian Schreieck[1] (iD), Oliver Krancher[2] (iD), and Ilan Oshri[3(✉)] (iD)

[1] University of Innsbruck, Innsbruck, Austria
maximilian.schreieck@uibk.ac.at
[2] IT University, Copenhagen, Denmark
olik@itu.dk
[3] University of Auckland, Auckland, New Zealand
ilan.oshri@auckland.ac.nz

Abstract. This chapter bridges two foundational streams in Information Systems (IS) research: digital sourcing and digital platform ecosystems. Historically treated as distinct, these domains are increasingly converging due to shifts in technology, organizational strategy, and ecosystem dynamics. Digital sourcing has evolved from cost-efficiency and capability access toward innovation and agility, while digital platforms have matured into orchestrated ecosystems enabling third-party value creation. The chapter outlines key theoretical foundations shared across both streams and identifies three core areas of convergence: governance, relationships, and knowledge and innovation. The chapter proposes future research directions, including hybrid governance models, algorithmic orchestration, and integrative learning frameworks, and lays the groundwork for a unified perspective on how organizations leverage external actors and technologies in the digital age. This conceptual bridge offers a foundation for advancing theory and informing practice in increasingly platform-based and sourcing-dependent ecosystems.

Keywords: Digital Sourcing · Digital Platform Ecosystems · Multi-Sourcing · Governance · Orchestration

1 Introduction

Digital sourcing, and digital platforms and ecosystems are two key literature streams in IS research [see these MISQ Research Curations on both topics for an overview of both streams: 1, 2]. While both streams explore how organizations leverage external actors and technologies, they have largely evolved in isolation, with little overlap or integration.

Yet in practice, the boundaries between sourcing and platforms are increasingly blurred. The rise of digital platforms has transformed sourcing practices: organizations now rely on crowdsourcing platforms [e.g., 3, 4] and enterprise software platforms as vehicles for obtaining information systems (IS) resources and capabilities. These models depart from traditional dyadic client–vendor relationships, requiring new governance and relational mechanisms. At the same time, sourcing requirements and practices influence

M. Schreieck et al. (Eds.): DSPE 2025, LNBIP 563, pp. 1–14, 2026.
https://doi.org/10.1007/978-3-032-04512-6_1

platform design and governance. For instance, enterprise clients sourcing information technology (IT) via platforms often demand solutions tailored to their specific contexts, prompting platform owners to find new ways to balance standardization with customization [5, 6]. These developments reflect deeper infrastructural and combinatorial shifts in digital sourcing, as organizations integrate platforms into increasingly modular and distributed sourcing configurations [7].

To better understand these developments, we argue that a conceptual bridge between the digital sourcing and the digital platform ecosystem literature is needed. This book compiles contributions from the 16th Digital Sourcing, Platforms, and Ecosystems Workshop (formerly the Global Sourcing Workshop), covering research on digital sourcing, digital platforms and ecosystems, and work at their intersection. In this introductory chapter, we sketch potential connections between the two streams. We begin with a brief summary of the two literature streams, followed by an exploration of their commonalities and differences in three core areas that cut across both fields: governance, relationships, and knowledge and innovation.

1.1 IS and Digital Sourcing Research

IS sourcing broadly refers to the study of how organizations acquire IT-related services and capabilities across organizational and geographic boundaries. IS sourcing has been a central theme in IS research since the 1990s. Early studies responded to a growing trend among firms to outsource IT functions to third-party providers. This trend was fueled not only by cost-reduction goals—as often emphasized in popular discourse—but also by the desire to access external capabilities, adapt to technological change, and improve strategic focus [8–10]. Thus, sourcing was concerned with efficiency and value creation from the outset, depending on the sourcing context and governance model.

Over time, IS sourcing evolved from a narrow focus on single-vendor outsourcing of IT infrastructure or application services to more complex arrangements such as multi-sourcing [11, 12], concurrent sourcing [13], crowdsourcing [4], and offshoring and nearshoring across national boundaries [14–16]. These developments reflected growing inter-organizational and geographical complexity, introducing new coordination and control challenges. In parallel, research increasingly examined how outsourcing relationships can foster innovation [17]. More recently, the term digital sourcing has been introduced to capture how sourcing practices adapt to broader shifts in the digital age—such as the emergence of platform-based infrastructures, API-driven modularity, and malleable technologies—and how these practices increasingly support innovation, agility, and digital transformation [7].

Research on digital sourcing draws on a range of theoretical lenses. Foundational work relied on economic theories such as Transaction Cost Economics and Agency Theory to explain sourcing decisions and governance choices in the presence of opportunism and incentive misalignment [18–20]. In parallel, knowledge-based perspectives—including the Resource-Based View, Knowledge-Based View, Capabilities Perspectives, and Information Processing View—have explained how knowledge asymmetries, absorptive capacity, and coordination demands affect sourcing performance [11, 14, 21, 22]. More recent studies have drawn on Paradox Theory and Affordance Theory to explore the tensions and possibilities that arise when outsourcing is used not only for efficiency but also for innovation in dynamic environments [23, 24].

1.2 Digital Platforms and Ecosystems Research

Research on digital platforms and ecosystems represents a key IS stream that has emerged in the early 2000s as online businesses created the first successful digital platforms (e.g., eBay and Google). Digital platforms can be defined as "open, participative infrastructure" that create "value for all participants" (Parker et al., 2016; Van Alstyne et al., 2024). This broad definition comprises subtypes of digital platforms such as transaction platforms that focus on intermediating transactions between buyers and sellers (e.g., eBay, Amazon) and innovation platforms that provide a technological foundation for third-party applications (e.g., Google Android, Apple iOS, Sony PlayStation) [25, 26].

Typically, digital platforms are the foundation for ecosystems of actors that interact with the platform. We broadly define digital platform ecosystems as the set of actors (organizations and individuals) that co-create value on a digital platform [27–29]. Ecosystems allow the platform owner to coordinate multiple actors through orchestration rather than dyadic contractual agreements [30]. For example, Google and Apple have created flourishing ecosystems around their mobile operating system platforms, Android and iOS. Third-party developers can join the ecosystem and develop third-party applications, without Google or Apple tasking them with developing specific apps. Google and Apple, as platform owners, apply governance mechanisms such as code checks and feedback systems, such as reviews and ratings by end users, to ensure that third-party applications fulfill the quality requirements [31].

Research on digital platforms and ecosystems is grounded in modularity, orchestration, and ecosystem theories, drawing on these theories to shape our understanding of the architecture of digital platforms and the governance of digital platform ecosystems [32–35]. For example, Parker and Van Alstyne [36] describe how companies become "inverted" by opening up to third-party developers, shifting value creation from inside the organization to the ecosystem. When doing so, companies must design open architectures and boundary resources supporting third-party development [37, 38].

Increasingly, researchers draw on affordance, capabilities, and tension perspectives [6, 38–41] to understand how digital platform ecosystems, as sociotechnical systems, evolve. For example, when incumbent companies transition towards digital platform strategies, traditional IT governance modes conflict with the more open platform governance mode, creating tensions within the company [6].

Considering the two literature streams of digital sourcing, and digital platforms and ecosystems, we identify similar research themes and commonalities within these themes (Table 1). Overall, both digital sourcing, and digital platforms and ecosystems consider that organizations increasingly interact across organizational boundaries to create value and innovation. While both literature streams build on distinct core theories, both now draw on theories addressing sociotechnical tensions and innovation processes.

In the remainder of the chapter, we will review commonalities of the two literature streams along the themes of governance, relationships, and knowledge and innovation. Then, we will provide an outlook on future research at the intersection of digital sourcing, and digital platforms and ecosystems research.

Table 1. Overview of the main research themes and commonalities of the two literature streams: digital sourcing, and digital platforms and ecosystems.

Dimension	Digital Sourcing	Digital Platforms and Ecosystems	Commonalities
Overall			
Core Focus	Traditionally focused on cost-efficiency and access to capabilities [15, 42–44] Recently reframed as a lever for strategic innovation [23, 45, 46]	Aimed at scaling innovation by enabling third-party value creation [47–49] or providing a marketplace for third-party apps or other products and services [26]	Both view external engagement as a source of value creation and innovation
Theoretical Foundations	Historically based on Transaction Cost Economics (TCE), Agency Theory, Resource-Based View (RBV), and Information-Processing Theory [11, 42, 50] More recent work introduces Paradox Theory and Affordance Theory to address tensions in innovation-focused outsourcing [23, 24]	Grounded in modularity, orchestration, and ecosystem theories [32–35] Increasingly using affordance, capabilities, and tension perspectives [6, 38–41]	Both fields now draw on theories addressing sociotechnical tensions and innovation processes
Governance			
Governance Forms	Combines formal (contracts, SLAs) and relational mechanisms (trust, collaboration) [50–52] Innovation requires flexible governance [23]	Blends architectural, rule-based, and relational governance [32, 38, 53] Must balance control and openness [54, 55]	Both manage tensions between control and autonomy in evolving environments
Control Locus	Client-led control through contracts and oversight [14, 15]. Some shift to joint governance in multi-sourcing [11]	The platform owner controls through APIs, rules, and technical standards [32, 38]	Both rely on centralized coordination with decentralized execution

(continued)

Table 1. (*continued*)

Dimension	Digital Sourcing	Digital Platforms and Ecosystems	Commonalities
Participation Logic	Vendors are pre-selected via formal processes; some shift to more dynamic participation. [52, 56]	Complementors join voluntarily but follow platform governance [49, 57]	Both use entry conditions and constraints to align contributions
Relationships			
Structure	From dyadic to multi-vendor and hybrid models [11, 12]	Multilateral networks of complementors, users, and services [48, 49]	Both need coordination across distributed actor networks
Power Dynamics	Clients typically dominate, but specialized vendors may hold sway [12, 14]	Platform owners dominate, though complementor power can grow [58, 59]	Both involve asymmetric but dynamic power relations
Value Logic	Shifting from efficiency to co-innovation [45]	Focus on generativity and ecosystem-wide value [47, 60]	Both rely on external partners to co-create value
Knowledge and Innovation			
Knowledge Interaction	Involves knowledge transfer and integration; success depends on absorptive capacity [11, 21, 61]	Emphasizes knowledge recombination through APIs, SDKs, and design interfaces [38, 62]	Both must support cross-boundary knowledge flows and mutual learning
Interfaces and Boundary Resources	Enabled via contracts, intermediaries, and governance tools [63, 64]	Supported by technical artifacts like APIs, SDKs, and developer portals [38, 60]	Both use boundary resources to coordinate and innovate across organizational borders

2 Governance

2.1 Governance Forms

Governance has long been a core concern in both digital sourcing and digital platform ecosystems. In digital sourcing, governance arrangements typically combine formal mechanisms—such as contracts, service-level agreements (SLAs), and penalties—with relational mechanisms such as trust, shared norms, and collaborative routines [50–52]. Empirical studies have found both complementary and substitutional relationships between these mechanisms. For instance, formal contracts can support relational governance by clarifying expectations and reducing ambiguity, thereby fostering trust—a complementary effect [50, 63]. However, under certain conditions, strong reliance on formal control may crowd out social norms or intrinsic motivation, leading to substitutional effects [52]. This insight suggests that achieving flexibility in innovation-oriented sourcing contexts typically requires a balanced mix of formal and relational governance. Specifically, relational mechanisms alone may be too fragile, while formal mechanisms alone may be too rigid. A balanced configuration helps organizations navigate the tensions between control and adaptability common in dynamic, innovation-focused environments [23].

In digital platform ecosystems, governance likewise blends formal and informal mechanisms but is operationalized through architectural, rule-based, and relational forms. Architectural governance is enacted via platform modularity and boundary resources such as application programming interfaces (APIs) and software development kits (SDKs), which define permissible actions and enable third-party innovation [32]. Rule-based governance includes platform policies, developer agreements, and certification requirements, while relational governance covers community norms, communication channels, and trust-building activities between the platform owner and ecosystem participants, including review and rating systems [31, 38, 53]. A defining challenge in platform governance is managing the trade-off between control and openness [54, 65, 66]. Too much control can stifle innovation and discourage participation, while too little control can lead to fragmentation or a decline in quality. Benlian, Hilkert [55] identify several dimensions of perceived openness—such as access, transparency, and reciprocity—that complement more technical or rule-based aspects of governance, again pointing to the need for a hybrid governance approach in dynamic ecosystems.

Taken together, governance in both digital sourcing and digital platform ecosystems involves managing tensions between control and autonomy. In sourcing, autonomy may manifest in the relational flexibility and discretion granted to vendors. In platforms, autonomy is reflected in the freedom of third-party developers to create, modify, and distribute applications. In both settings, hybrid governance models that combine economic and social mechanisms—whether through contracts and trust, or APIs and community norms—enable organizations to navigate changing environments and sustain value creation.

2.2 Control Locus

The locus of control—i.e., where decision-making authority resides—has been a key consideration in both digital sourcing and digital platform ecosystems. In digital sourcing, control has traditionally been client-led, with clients exerting authority through formal contracts, service specifications, and oversight mechanisms [14, 15]. This centralized control reflects the client's accountability for service delivery and risk mitigation, especially in classical outsourcing arrangements. However, more recent sourcing configurations such as multi-sourcing and concurrent sourcing have introduced greater interdependence among multiple vendors and internal actors, leading to calls for more distributed or joint governance models [12]. In these settings, clients increasingly share decision rights and coordination responsibilities with vendors or integrators, often supported by cross-organizational roles such as the guardian—a boundary-spanning actor responsible for ensuring coherence across sourcing arrangements [11].

In digital platform ecosystems, control is exercised differently. Platform owners establish control through architectural and rule-based mechanisms, such as defining APIs, access protocols, and participation rules [32, 38]. These mechanisms define how third-party complementors can interact with the platform, while generally leaving it to the complementors to decide what to build. Thus, control is indirect: platform owners govern the how—that is, the conditions of participation—while granting autonomy over the what. This contrasts with outsourcing, where clients often govern both the how and the what of third-party activities.

Despite these differences, both domains rely on centralized coordination with decentralized execution. Whether through client oversight or platform architecture, a focal actor defines the structural and procedural terms under which others operate. However, the degree of autonomy afforded to external actors varies considerably: vendors typically act under client direction, while complementors operate more independently within a predefined platform structure.

2.3   Participation Logic

The logic of actors entering and participating in digital sourcing and platform ecosystems differs substantially. In digital platform ecosystems, complementors typically join voluntarily, guided by platform-level governance mechanisms such as interface standards, APIs, and entry constraints [49, 57]. While participation is voluntary, platforms shape complementor contributions through entry rules, certification processes, or performance-based incentives that align third-party activities with the platform owner's strategic objectives.

In contrast, vendor participation in digital sourcing ecosystems is typically pre-structured through formal selection processes. Classical sourcing models involve upfront selection of a limited number of vendors based on contractual arrangements. However, newer sourcing configurations reflect a shift toward more dynamic participation logics. For example, Lioliou and Krancher [52] show how a client firm orchestrated a multi-sourcing model based on "micro-tendering," where vendors continuously bid for work packages rather than being tied to fixed contracts. This model creates a quasi-marketplace that allows the client to dynamically allocate work based on evolving needs, while still exerting governance over vendor contributions. It builds on the insight from Wiener and Saunders [67] that clients increasingly function as market orchestrators, creating "visible hand" environments in which vendors are simultaneously required to compete and cooperate—what the authors term forced coopetition.

These shifts blur the boundary between sourcing and platform governance. As Hurni and Dibbern [68] argue, advanced multi-sourcing arrangements resemble innovation ecosystems in which vendor contributions are not only coordinated but also co-evolved. In such settings, participation becomes less static and more emergent, as vendors join, exit, or change roles based on value-added contributions rather than fixed contractual positions. This dynamic participation logic closely mirrors platform governance mechanisms while retaining the client's central role in shaping outcomes. Thus, both sourcing and platform ecosystems rely on mechanisms to constrain and align third-party contributions—but differ in whether participation is pre-structured or voluntary, and whether governance stems from contracts or platform rules.

3 Relationships

The relational dynamics in IT outsourcing and digital platform ecosystems reveal both convergences and divergences in how actors interact, coordinate, and co-create value. While both domains involve inter-organizational collaboration, the structural, power, and value logics underpinning these relationships differ in meaningful ways, offering fertile ground for future research.

In IT outsourcing, relationships have traditionally been dyadic, structured around formal contracts between a client and a vendor. These relationships are often hierarchical, with the client exercising control over deliverables, timelines, and performance metrics. However, the rise of multi-sourcing and concurrent sourcing has introduced more complex relational configurations, involving multiple vendors, intermediaries, and internal stakeholders [11, 12]. These models necessitate coordination across distributed actor networks and have led to the emergence of boundary-spanning roles such as the "guardian," who ensures coherence and alignment across sourcing arrangements. Power dynamics in outsourcing remain asymmetrical, with clients typically holding decision rights, although specialized vendors may exert influence through domain expertise or strategic capabilities [14].

In contrast, digital platform ecosystems are inherently multilateral. Relationships are formed among platform owners, complementors (e.g., third-party developers), and end users, often without direct contractual ties. Platform owners orchestrate these ecosystems through architectural and rule-based governance, while complementors voluntarily engage to create add-on services or applications [32, 49]. The relational structure is more fluid, with actors joining or exiting based on perceived value and alignment with platform norms. Power dynamics are similarly asymmetrical but more dynamic: platform owners set the rules and control access, yet successful complementors can gain influence through innovation, user adoption, or ecosystem dependencies [58].

Despite these differences, both domains share a shift in value logic—from transactional efficiency to co-innovation. In outsourcing, this shift manifests in collaborative engagements where clients and vendors jointly develop solutions, often leveraging shared knowledge and capabilities [45]. In platform ecosystems, value is co-created through generativity, where complementors build on platform resources to deliver novel services, often in response to user feedback or emerging market needs [47].

Understanding these relational nuances is critical for theorizing the evolution of digital ecosystems. As organizations increasingly rely on external actors for innovation and agility, the ability to manage complex, dynamic relationships across sourcing and platform boundaries will become a key strategic capability.

4 Knowledge and Innovation

There are numerous areas of commonality in knowledge and innovation processes between digital sourcing and platform ecosystems. For one, both literatures have taken an interest in how learning develops between key actors. In the classical sourcing literature, there has been extensive research on knowledge processes (e.g., knowledge transfer, knowledge sharing) that point to learning between the client and the vendor in dyadic and mediated settings [21, 69], and between vendors in multi-sourcing settings [52]. The focus of the sourcing literature has been to understand how a vendor develops capabilities and what mechanisms have been serving as boundary spanners that enable capability acquisition and development. Among the various mechanisms mentioned in past studies are codification of knowledge and knower [21] and knowledge sharing norms within a vendor ecosystem [52, 70]. A key assumption in the sourcing literature is that the vendor and the client are expected to develop a shared understanding of the domain, procedures, and objectives to ensure the success of the sourcing engagement [71].

The platform ecosystems literature has also taken an interest in learning processes. At the core of this interest is the understanding of how the platform owner and complementors develop capabilities. A key assumption in the platform ecosystems literature is that complementors are autonomous actors who engage with the platform with limited contractual obligations [72]. As such, unlike in the sourcing literature, platform ecosystem studies do not assume shared understanding between the platform owner and complementors, but rather the utilization of platform boundary resources (e.g., APIs) that link the platform and the add-on services. Thus, complementor learning can be structured via training (e.g., technical aspects), but also can be experiential by sensing emerging end-user needs and further developing their add-on services. Similarly, platform owners focus on learning through experimentation with new services, but also by observing complementors' add-on services as information that enables them to better appropriate value and orchestrate their ecosystem of complementors and services.

Both sourcing and platform ecosystems are anchored in the idea that learning and knowledge processes are key to achieving success from their respective ecosystems and partnerships. Yet, in sourcing settings, the objective of the learning is to create shared understanding between the parties to ensure a seamless service delivery, while in platform ecosystems, it is to co-evolve and expand the ecosystem's value co-creation. Nonetheless, there are similarities in learning mechanisms and knowledge processes deployed in both sourcing and platform ecosystems settings.

5   Future Work

As digital sourcing and platform ecosystems may converge in some specific settings, future research must address the evolving complexities and tensions that arise at their intersection. Building on the themes of governance, relationships, and knowledge, we propose several avenues for future inquiry.

Governance.   Governance in digital sourcing and platform ecosystems centers on managing the tension between control and autonomy. In sourcing, governance blends formal mechanisms like contracts and SLAs with relational mechanisms such as trust and collaboration, requiring a balanced mix to support innovation and adaptability. Platform ecosystems similarly combine architectural, rule-based, and relational governance, with a key challenge being the trade-off between control and openness to maintain ecosystem quality and participation. Across both domains, hybrid governance models—integrating economic and social mechanisms—are essential for sustaining value creation in dynamic environments. We therefore propose the following avenues for future research:

- How can ecosystems be orchestrated effectively when dyadic sourcing relationships and loose ecosystem ties co-exist?
- What governance challenges arise when platform owners act as both orchestrators and sourcing providers (e.g., AWS, Salesforce)?
- What role do algorithmic or AI-driven governance systems play in mediating hybrid sourcing and ecosystem relationships?

Relationships. These relational dynamics suggest several avenues for future research. First, how do relational structures adapt as sourcing and platform models increasingly converge—e.g., when platforms serve as sourcing vehicles or vendors act as complementors? What hybrid models emerge, and how do they balance formal control with voluntary participation? Second, how do power dynamics evolve in ecosystems where traditional sourcing hierarchies meet platform-based autonomy? Third, what mechanisms support trust, coordination, and mutual learning in these hybrid environments, especially when actors operate under different governance logics?

Knowledge and Innovation. Both digital sourcing and platform ecosystems emphasize the importance of learning and knowledge processes for ecosystem success. In sourcing, learning is typically structured around developing shared understanding between clients and vendors, with mechanisms like codification and knowledge-sharing norms supporting capability development. In contrast, platform ecosystems assume autonomous complementors who utilize experiential engagement, and thus learning, with users. Despite differing assumptions, both domains deploy mechanisms that facilitate cross-boundary learning and innovation, offering opportunities for integrative research. Some of the questions that can guide future research are:

- What hybrid learning models enable mutual capability development between clients, vendors, and complementors in sourcing-platform ecosystems?
- How do boundary resources (e.g., APIs, SDKs) function as knowledge bridges in hybrid ecosystems that combine sourcing and platform governance?
- What role do user feedback and community norms play in shaping learning outcomes across sourcing engagements and platform ecosystems?

6   Conclusion

This chapter has explored the evolving intersection between digital sourcing and digital platform ecosystems, two foundational streams in information systems research. While historically distinct, these domains are increasingly converging in practice, driven by shifts in technology, organizational strategy, and ecosystem dynamics. Digital sourcing has expanded beyond cost-efficiency to embrace an ecosystem structure, innovation, and agility, while platform ecosystems have matured into complex, orchestrated environments that enable third-party value creation with some evidence of contractual relationships between the parties. Both streams now grapple with similar challenges around governance, relationships, and learning. We take the first step towards bridging these literature streams and hope that, as digital sourcing and platform ecosystems continue to evolve, their convergence offers fertile ground for advancing theory and informing practice in the digital age.

References

1. Kotlarsky, J., et al.: MISQ research curation on IS sourcing. MISQ Res. Curation 2018–2022 (2018)
2. Van Alstyne, M., et al.: MISQ research curation on platforms & ecosystems. MISQ Res. Curations (2024)
3. Taylor, J., et al.: Procuring services through IT crowdsourcing: the role of IT administration and IT flexibility. J. Inf. Technol. **39**(2), 288–316 (2024)
4. Leong, C., et al.: Platform leadership: managing boundaries for the network growth of digital platforms. J. Assoc. Inf. Syst. **20**(10), 1531–1565 (2019)
5. Sarker, S., et al.: Exploring value cocreation in relationship between an ERP vendor and its partners: a revelatory case study. MIS Q. **36**(1), 317–338 (2012)
6. Schreieck, M., Wiesche, M., Krcmar, H.: From product platform ecosystem to innovation platform ecosystem: an institutional perspective on the governance of ecosystem transformations. J. Assoc. Inf. Syst. **23**(6), 1354–1385 (2022)
7. Krancher, O., et al.: Digital sourcing: A discussion of agential, semiotic, infrastructural, combinatorial, and economic shifts. J. Inf. Technol. (2024)
8. Lacity, M.C., Hirschheim, R.: The information systems outsourcing Bandwagon. MIT Sloan Manag. Rev. **35**(1), 73–86 (1993)
9. Grover, V., Cheon, J., Teng, J.T.C.: A descriptive study on the outsourcing of information systems functions. Inf. Manag. **27**(1), 33–44 (1994)
10. Loh, L., Venkatraman, N.: Determinants of information technology outsourcing: a cross-sectional analysis. J. Manag. Inf. Syst. **9**(1), 7–24 (1992)
11. Oshri, I., et al.: An information processing view on joint vendor performance in multi-sourcing: the role of the guardian. J. Manag. Inf. Syst. **36**(4), 1248–1283 (2019)
12. Krancher, O., et al.: Bilateral, collective, or both? Formal governance and performance in multisourcing. J. Assoc. Inf. Syst. **23**(5), 1211–1234 (2022)
13. Tiwana, A., Kim, S.K.: Concurrent IT sourcing: mechanisms and contingent advantages. J. Manag. Inf. Syst. **33**(1), 101–138 (2016)
14. Dibbern, J., Winkler, J., Heinzl, A.: Explaining variations in client extra costs between software projects offshored to India. MIS Q. **32**(2), 333–366 (2008)
15. Gopal, A., et al.: Contracts in offshore software development: an empirical analysis. Manage. Sci. **49**(12), 1671–1683 (2003)
16. Mani, D., Barua, A., Whinston, A.: An empirical analysis of the impact of information capabilities design on business process outsourcing performance. MIS Q. **34**(1), 39–62 (2009)
17. Gambal, M.J., Asatiani, A., Kotlarsky, J.: Strategic innovation through outsourcing – A theoretical review. J. Strat. Inf. Syst. **31**(2), 101718 (2022)
18. Aubert, B.A., Rivard, S., Patry, M.: A transaction cost approach to outsourcing behavior: some empirical evidence. Inf. Manag. **30**(2), 51–64 (1996)
19. Poppo, L., Zenger, T.: Testing alternative theories of the firm: transaction cost, knowledge-based, and measurement explanations for make-or-buy decisions in information services. Strateg. Manag. J. **19**(9), 853–877 (1998)
20. Karimi-Alaghehband, F., et al.: An assessment of the use of transaction cost theory in information technology outsourcing. J. Strat. Inf. Syst. **20**(2), 125–138 (2011)
21. Kotlarsky, J., Scarbrough, H., Oshri, I.: Coordinating expertise across knowledge boundaries in offshore-outsourcing projects. MIS Q. **38**(2), 607–628 (2014)
22. Karimi-Alaghehband, F., Rivard, S.: Information technology outsourcing and architecture dynamic capabilities as enablers of organizational agility. J. Inf. Technol. **34**(2), 129–159 (2019)

23. Aubert, B.A., Kishore, R., Iriyama, A.: Exploring and managing the "innovation through outsourcing" paradox. J. Strat. Inf. Syst. **24**(4), 255–269 (2015)
24. Kotlarsky, J., Rivard, S., Oshri, I.: On a supplier's paradoxical practices: the case of technological innovations in outsourcing engagements. In: Thirty-Seventh International Conference on Information Systems. Dublin (2016)
25. Gawer, A.: Bridging differing perspectives on technological platforms: toward an integrative framework. Res. Policy **43**(7), 1239–1249 (2014)
26. Cusumano, M.A., Gawer, A., Yoffie, D.B.: The Business of Platforms: Strategy in the Age of Digital Competition, Innovation, and Power. Harper Business, New York (2019)
27. De Reuver, M., Sørensen, C., Basole, R.C.: The digital platform: a research agenda. J. Inf. Technol. **33**(2), 124–135 (2018)
28. Ceccagnoli, M., et al.: Cocreation of value in a platform ecosystem: the case of enterprise software. MIS Q. **36**(1), 263–290 (2012)
29. Gawer, A.: Platforms, Markets and Innovation. Edward Elgar Publishing (2008)
30. Jacobides, M.G., Cennamo, C., Gawer, A.: Towards a theory of ecosystems. Strateg. Manag. J. **39**(8), 2255–2276 (2018)
31. Goldbach, T., Benlian, A., Buxmann, P.: Differential effects of formal and self-control in mobile platform ecosystems: multi-method findings on third-party developers' continuance intentions and application quality. Inf. Manag. **55**(3), 271–284 (2018)
32. Tiwana, A., Konsynski, B., Bush, A.A.: Platform evolution: coevolution of platform architecture, governance, and environmental dynamics. Inf. Syst. Res. **21**(4), 675–687 (2010)
33. Tiwana, A.: Platform synergy: architectural origins and competitive consequences. Inf. Syst. Manag. 1–20 (2018)
34. Wareham, J., Fox, P.B., Cano Giner, J.L.: Technology ecosystem governance. Organ. Sci. **25**(4), 1195–1215 (2014)
35. Baldwin, C.Y., Woodard, C.J.: The architecture of platforms: a unified view. In: Gawer, A. (ed.) Platforms, Markets and Innovation, pp. 19–44. Edward Elgar, Cheltenham, UK and Northampton, MA, US (2009)
36. Parker, G.G., Van Alstyne, M.W., Jiang, X.: Platform ecosystems: how developers invert the firm. MIS Q. **41**(1), 255–266 (2017)
37. Tiwana, A.: Platform Ecosystems: Aligning Architecture, Governance, and Strategy. Morgan Kaufmann, Burlington, Massachusetts (2014)
38. Ghazawneh, A., Henfridsson, O.: Balancing platform control and external contribution in third-party development: the boundary resources model. Inf. Syst. J. **23**(2), 173–192 (2013)
39. Huber, T.L., Kude, T., Dibbern, J.: Governance practices in platform ecosystems: navigating tensions between co-created value and governance costs. Inf. Syst. Res. **28**(3), 563–584 (2017)
40. Schreieck, M., Wiesche, M., Krcmar, H.: Capabilities for value co-creation and value capture in emergent platform ecosystems: a longitudinal case study of SAP's cloud platform. J. Inf. Technol. **36**(4), 365–390 (2021)
41. Helfat, C.E., Raubitschek, R.S.: Dynamic and integrative capabilities for profiting from innovation in digital platform-based ecosystems. Res. Policy **47**(8), 1391–1399 (2018)
42. Dibbern, J., et al.: Information systems outsourcing: a survey and analysis of the literature. ACM SIGMIS Database **35**(4), 6–102 (2004)
43. Larsen, M.M., Manning, S., Pedersen, T.: Uncovering the hidden costs of offshoring: the interplay of complexity, organizational design, and experience. Strateg. Manag. J. **34**(5), 533–552 (2013)
44. Cheon, M.J., Grover, V., Teng, J.T.C.: Theoretical perspectives on the outsourcing of information systems. J. Inf. Technol. **10**(4), 209–219 (1995)
45. Oshri, I., Kotlarsky, J., Gerbasi, A.: Strategic innovation through outsourcing: the role of relational and contractual governance. J. Strat. Inf. Syst. **24**(3), 203–216 (2015)

46. Kotlarsky, J., et al.: Editorial: understanding strategic innovation in IT and business process outsourcing. J. Strateg. Inf. Syst. 251–254 (2015)
47. Förderer, J., et al.: Does Platform owner's entry crowd out innovation? Evidence from google photos. Inf. Syst. Res. **29**(2), 444–460 (2018)
48. Hein, A., et al.: Value co-creation practices in business-to-business platform ecosystems. Electron. Mark. **29**(3), 503–518 (2020)
49. Saadatmand, F., Lindgren, R., Schultze, U.: Configurations of platform organizations: implications for complementor engagement. Res. Policy **48**(8) (2019)
50. Poppo, L., Zenger, T.: Do formal contracts and relational governance function as substitutes or complements? Strateg. Manag. J. **23**(8), 707–725 (2002)
51. Goo, J., et al.: The role of service level agreements in relational management of information technology outsourcing: an empirical study. MIS Q. **33**(1), 119 (2009)
52. Lioliou, E., Krancher, O., Oshri, I.: The complementary and substitutional effects of forced and emergent mechanisms in multisourcing. J. Strateg. Inf. Syst. **34**(1) (2025)
53. Hurni, T., et al.: Complementor dedication in platform ecosystems: rule adequacy and the moderating role of flexible and benevolent practices. Eur. J. Inf. Syst. **30**(3), 237–260 (2021)
54. West, J.: How open is open enough? Melding proprietary and open source platform strategies. Res. Policy **32**(7), 1259–1285 (2003)
55. Benlian, A., Hilkert, D., Hess, T.: How open is this platform? The meaning and measurement of platform openness from the complementors' perspective. J. Inf. Technol. **30**(3), 209–228 (2015)
56. Kotlarsky, J., Rivard, S., Oshri, I.: Building a reputation as a business partner in information technology outsourcing. MIS Q. Manag. Inf. Syst. **47**(2), 901–922 (2023)
57. Kude, T., Dibbern, J., Heinzl, A.: Why do complementors participate? An analysis of partnership networks in the enterprise software industry. IEEE Trans. Eng. Manage. **59**(2), 250–265 (2012)
58. Hurni, T., Huber, T.L., Dibbern, J.: Power dynamics in software platform ecosystems. Inf. Syst. J. **32**(2), 310–343 (2022)
59. Kude, T., Huber, T.L.: Responding to platform owner moves: a 14-year qualitative study of four enterprise software complementors. Inf. Syst. J. **35**(1), 209–246 (2025)
60. Heimburg, V., Schreieck, M., Wiesche, M.: Complementor value co-creation in generative AI platform ecosystems. J. Manag. Inf. Syst. **42**(2), 491–528 (2025)
61. Krancher, O., Dibbern, J.: Knowledge transfer in software maintenance outsourcing: the key roles of software knowledge and guided learning tasks. Inf. Syst. Outsourcing Era Digit. Transformation 147–181 (2020)
62. Förderer, J., et al.: Knowledge boundaries in enterprise software platform development: antecedents and consequences for platform governance. Inf. Syst. J. **29**(1), 119–144 (2019)
63. Huber, T.L., et al.: A process model of complementarity and substitution of contractual and relational governance in IS outsourcing. J. Manag. Inf. Syst. **30**(3), 81–114 (2013)
64. Krancher, O., et al.: The governing mechanisms of successful multisourcing projects. In: Willcocks, L., Oshri, I., Kotlarsky, J. (eds.) Transformation in Global Outsourcing: Towards Digital Sourcing of IT and Business Services, pp. 19–60. Springer International Publishing, Cham (2024)
65. Eisenmann, T.R., Parker, G.G., Van Alstyne, M.: Opening platforms: how, when and why? In: Gawer, A. (ed.) Platforms, Markets and Innovation, pp. 131–162. Edward Elgar, Cheltenham, UK (2009)
66. Ondrus, J., Gannamaneni, A., Lyytinen, K.: The impact of openness on the market potential of multi-sided platforms: a case study of mobile payment platforms. J. Inf. Technol. **30**(3), 260–275 (2015)
67. Wiener, M., Saunders, C.: Forced coopetition in IT multi-sourcing. J. Strat. Inf. Syst. **23**, 210–225 (2014)

68. Hurni, T., Dibbern, J., Huber, T.L.: Emerging innovation ecosystems: the critical role of distributed innovation agency. Inf. Syst. Outsourcing Era Digit. Transformation 101–143 (2020)
69. Jarvenpaa, S.L., Mao, J.Y.: Operational capabilities development in mediated offshore software services models. J. Inf. Technol. **23**(1), 3–17 (2008)
70. Ji, Y., Du, W., Pan, S.L.: Vendor capabilities development in blockchain sourcing: a parallel play approach. J. Inf. Technol. **39**(2), 270–287 (2024)
71. Oshri, I., Henfridsson, O., Kotlarsky, J.: Re-representation as work design in outsourcing. MIS Q. **42**(1), 1–23 (2018)
72. Engert, M., et al.: Sustaining complementor engagement in digital platform ecosystems: antecedents, behaviours and engagement trajectories. Inf. Syst. J. **33**(5), 1151–1185 (2023)

Digital Sourcing Within Digital Platform Ecosystems: A Complementor Perspective

Dragos Vieru[1]([✉]) [iD], Stefan Klein[2] [iD], Albert Plugge[3] [iD], and Simon Bourdeau[4] [iD]

[1] TÉLUQ University, 5800 Rue Saint-Denis, Montréal, QC H2S 3L5, Canada
dragos.vieru@teluq.ca
[2] University of Münster, Schosspl. 2, 48149 Münster, Germany
stefan.klein@uni-muenster.de
[3] Nyenrode Business University, Straatweg 24, 3621 BG Breukelen, The Netherlands
a.plugge@nyenrode.nl
[4] Université du Québec À Montréal, 405 Rue Sainte-Catherine Est, Montréal,
QC H2L 2C4, Canada
bourdeau.simon.2@uqam.ca

Abstract. This multi-case study explores the digital sourcing practices of two complementor firms within two digital platform ecosystems (DPE) owned by Microsoft and SAP, respectively. We draw on organizational ambidexterity and social mechanisms as lenses to analyze how the two complementors address the paradoxical practices of exploration and exploitation within the context of their respective DPE. Our analysis suggests that the identified social mechanisms illustrate how each complementor engages in digital sourcing to create new ideas with other DPE actors that will nurture capability development (exploration) and transform these ideas into practice (exploitation). We identify two modes of ambidexterity, whereby one capability is used to improve the other, i.e., *'exploration-for-exploitation,'* an orientation towards continually improving the quality of the service delivery, and *'exploration-through-exploitation,'* an approach of project-driven learning.

Keywords: Digital platform ecosystems · Complementors · Social mechanisms · Organizational ambidexterity

1 Introduction

Research on digital platform ecosystems (DPEs) has received significant attention in the literature over the past decade [36], particularly in topics such as network effects and value creation and capture [9]. The academic literature reveals that complementors in DPEs are primarily addressed from the platform owner's perspective [19, 49]. In their review of the literature on DPE, Hein et al. [24] recommend that more research be conducted on the role of complementors, as little is known about how they can influence value-creating mechanisms.

Complementors represent external actors that join the DPE and create complementary products for platform users through digital sourcing [24]. Following Engert et al.

[15] and Baiyere et al. [4], we define the process of providing digital products or services, such as software development, cloud computing, or data analytics, as digital sourcing. Examining the practices of complementors on a digital platform is inherently connected to the digital sourcing literature, as both focus on how external entities contribute to and derive value from digital ecosystems through collaboration, resource sharing, and technological integration. DPEs are ideal for digital sourcing due to low entry barriers, direct market access, and network effects. However, as Krancher et al. [29] suggest, the digitalization of services and the shift to platform-based service delivery introduce new challenges for client firms. With services hosted on a platform, client firms must now bridge the gap between their digital systems and those offered by the complementors through the platform.

In this context, complementors can leverage digital platforms to reach and serve a large and diverse customer base, benefiting from the platform's core functionality and reputation [47]. They face two essential challenges. First, they must develop complements (complementary services/products) that contribute to the platform's core. Hence, complementors sustain owner and client relationships to explore new ideas and foster capability development [8]. Second, they need to ensure the quality of existing complements. This corresponds to exploiting existing products and services [24]. If a complementor is unaware of balancing exploitation and exploration, this may hinder their role within the DPE. This is even more important in highly dynamic environments, such as the business management consulting industry, which is characterized by increasing requirements to develop new services that satisfy customers' changing demands [10] and technology-driven short innovation cycles [48], with an inherent emphasis on project execution, quality, and delivery.

Balancing exploitation and exploration practices represents the core tenet of organizational ambidexterity (OA) [18]. The emergence of OA can be described as a process encompassing a series of individual and collective practices and events that unfold over time within a specific organizational context [21]. Although most organizational ambidexterity research focuses on the firms' organizational level [35], a less analyzed path for firms to develop ambidexterity is engagement in collaboration with external actors [27]. It has been shown that "inter-organizational coordination is achieved through social mechanisms, that are, governance mechanisms based on social relationships and networks" [6].

Research on inter-organizational relationships (IOR) has undergone a significant shift over the past twenty years. Instead of concentrating on specific technologies, IOR researchers focus on collaboration and the knowledge that users possess and share about technologies [16, 28]. Thus, this line of thought highlights the importance of identifying the mechanisms that enable partners to cooperate effectively and fully utilize their shared technological tools. Rooted in the dynamics of relationships and the recursivity of action and its context [21], the concept of social mechanisms seems appropriate for use in research on the field of DPE, both conceptually and as the basis for a methodological strategy [3].

We consider social mechanisms as being processes composed of actions, events [20], and "chains or aggregations of actors confronting problem situations and mobilizing more or less habitual responses" [24, p. 368]. DPE literature provides limited guidelines on giving directions for the exploitation and exploration of new technologies (i.e., complements on a DPE) [31]. As more research is needed to better understand how organizations develop ambidexterity in the context of DPE while engaging in digital sourcing practices, the goal of this research is to explore how complementors balance practices of exploitation and exploration based on the following two research questions:

RQ 1: How do complementors within a digital platform ecosystem provide digital sourcing to the other actors on the platform (owner, clients, other complementors)?
RQ2: What are the social mechanisms for developing organizational ambidexterity on a DPE?

We drew on organizational ambidexterity and social mechanisms as theoretical lenses to answer the research questions. We conducted a multi-case study of two business management consulting firms, one German (Noventum) and one Canadian (XRM Vision), for which balancing exploitation (essential for the financial bottom line) and exploration (a differentiator among other DPE complementors) has become part of their identity and mission. Our research contributes to the theoretical understanding of ambidexterity in DPEs. It provides practical insights for complementors striving to leverage digital sourcing for sustained innovation and growth.

2   Theoretical Background

2.1   Digital Platform Ecosystems and Complementors

Derived from biology, the term ecosystem in an economic context generally refers to a group of interacting firms that depend on each other's activities. According to Ceccagnoli et al. [7], a platform ecosystem comprises the platform's sponsor and all complement providers that enhance the platform's value to consumers. Platforms are a key component of many technological systems, providing a foundation for other related products, services, and technologies to be built upon [17]. The increasing prevalence of digital technology has expanded the significance of platforms in the IT domain [46]. Digital platforms are distinct from applications due to their ever-changing environment, an increasingly diverse user base, and the frequent introduction of new technological features and services [23]. As such, platform designs must consider principles that cater to the requirements of multiple distinct user groups.

According to Boudreau & Hagiu [5], digital platforms are technological entities that facilitate value creation by utilizing socio-technical means to orchestrate an autonomous ecosystem. This ecosystem comprises platform owners, stakeholders, complementors, and digital-platform-specific applications [40]. Complementors represent external actors that join the DPE and create complementary products for platform users through digital sourcing.

Complementors in a DPE may explore emerging technologies provided by technology suppliers while exploiting existing technologies simultaneously [38]. Research suggests that complementors should focus on products that the platform leader is unlikely to offer, thereby contributing to the innovation of the platform [11]. This platform characteristic, generativity, is defined as the "overall capacity to produce unprompted changes driven by large, varied, and uncoordinated audiences" [24, p. 89]. At the same time, complementors must ensure the expected quality of existing services, which involves leveraging existing products and services.

Connecting to the platform allows complementors to create complementary innovations and access the platform's customers directly or indirectly. Examples include independent business solutions vendors affiliating with the IBM Power platform [43] and developers producing video games for specific consoles [9]. A digital platform ecosystem represents a system that comprises a platform owner that implements technical, business, and social mechanisms to facilitate value creation on a digital platform between the platform owner and autonomous complementors [24].

Complementors that explore new opportunities often utilize mechanisms such as sensing and seizing through business model design. These mechanisms correspond to complementors' dynamic capabilities to respond to technological developments [1]. In parallel, complementors must ensure the expected quality of existing digital sourcing services, which corresponds to leveraging existing products and services. This corresponds to the concept of organizational ambidexterity, which can be achieved through both intra- and inter-organizational relationships.

2.2 Organizational Ambidexterity Through Intra- and Inter-organizational Relationships

Defined as simultaneous actions undertaken by firms to address two dissimilar situations simultaneously, to explore and exploit, organizational ambidexterity (OA) represents the ability of an organization to compete in markets where efficiency and incremental improvement are valued and to also compete in markets where flexibility and experimentation are needed [26]. Exploration is linked to activities that create and discover new opportunities [27], while exploitation is described as enhancing current operational quality by leveraging existing organizational resources [35].

When achieving organizational ambidexterity, most research focuses on the organizational level or below [35]. However, a growing body of work examines how interorganizational relationships (IORs) can be leveraged to achieve this goal. Several studies on technology alliance diversity have shown that collaborating with different types of partners can lead to new knowledge combinations and improved innovation outcomes [42, 45]. This has led some researchers to suggest that organizations can balance conflicting activities by engaging in interorganizational relationships [25]. In open innovation processes, organizational boundaries are often more fluid, and firms work closely with different actors in their environment to generate new ideas. However, partnering firms must establish an organizational design to pursue alignment and adaptation [44].

The pertinence of OA in the context of ecosystems for IOR is emphasized by Haghshenas and Østerlie [22], who found that ecosystem actors not only explored new opportunities in entering the DPE but also sought strategies to exploit and further strengthen their existing capabilities and position within the ecosystem. We conjecture that complementors will engage in exploration activities with the platform owner and other complementors, as well as in exploitation and exploration activities with their clients.

2.3 Social Mechanisms and Organizational Ambidexterity: A Complementary Perspective

The dynamic interplay between organizational ambidexterity (OA) and social mechanisms is central to understanding how complementors navigate the tensions between exploration and exploitation within DPEs. While OA provides the conceptual framework for balancing these dual imperatives, social mechanisms are the operational enablers that facilitate this balance through structured inter-organizational interactions.

Social mechanisms broadly refer to the processes, structures, and interactions that facilitate coordination, knowledge exchange, and governance within and across organizations [3, 21]. They unfold in time and emerge from the narratives of events [3], practices, and interactions that cause the outcomes of the inter-organizational integration process [6]. Social mechanisms can be categorized into relational mechanisms, which concentrate on interpersonal and inter-organizational relationships, and structural mechanisms, which relate to formal governance structures, regulations, and institutionalized coordination efforts [6].

First, relational mechanisms—such as trust, reciprocity, and repeated interactions—enable complementors to explore new opportunities while maintaining stable exploitative relationships with platform owners, clients, and other ecosystem participants [6, 12]. These relational ties lower uncertainty, allowing firms to experiment with new solutions while ensuring a commitment of resources to ongoing service delivery. In a network arrangement, such as a digital platform, social capital and embeddedness within network relationships promote knowledge sharing and innovation, while ensuring continuity in business operations [30, 39]. In platform ecosystems, relational mechanisms enable complementors to establish strategic partnerships, engage in coopetition, and develop long-term collaboration strategies that foster ambidexterity [37].

Second, structural mechanisms such as governance frameworks, platform policies, and role definitions shape how organizations engaged in inter-organizational arrangements transition between exploratory innovation and exploitative efficiency [24, 27]. These governance structures regulate access to platform resources and create structured learning opportunities that enable complementors to refine existing solutions while experimenting with novel offerings [40]. In the context of OA, structural mechanisms provide predefined pathways for exploration and exploitation, allowing complementors to innovate within clear boundaries while leveraging platform resources for efficient service delivery [24].

By embedding ambidextrous capabilities in structured social interactions, complementors enhance their ability to adapt, co-create, and maintain competitive differentiation within a DPE. Thus, instead of treating OA and social mechanisms as separate constructs, we suggest they should be viewed as mutually reinforcing, where social mechanisms offer the coordination, trust, and governance structures essential for sustaining ambidexterity in complex digital platform environments.

3 Research Method

In the context of a DPE, collaborating organizations are best analyzed through a process of theorization that focuses on how decisions and actions at different levels of analysis mutually shape each other [32]. Due to the complex role of complementors in DPEs, we adopted an explanatory theory-building approach from cases [14]. This methodology is suitable because it highlights the social construction and demonstrates how our theorization operates within a particular context [14]. We followed Eisenhardt's [13] recommendations. We anchored our problem definition and preliminary construct specification in the extant literature. Based on this literature, we constructed our data collection instruments following abductive logic (inference to an explanation). After entering the field, this was followed by a "flexible and opportunistic" [13, p. 533] data collection approach and an inductive within-case and cross-case data analysis.

3.1 Sampling and Data Collection

To select a complementor, we used two main criteria. We sought complementors that had no conflicting role as platform owners. Noventum provides SAP-based tailored business solutions to its banking clients. Likewise, XRM Vision is a Customer Relationship Management consulting firm specializing in digital sourcing services, including the design and implementation of Microsoft Power Platform (MPP)-based solutions. Second, we selected complementors with a high degree of autonomy and independence from the platform owner. In doing so, we identified emerging OA dimensions and mechanisms implemented by a complementor as part of a DPE collaborative initiative.

We used a two-phase approach. We began by collecting publicly available data (website information and whitepapers) related to the DPE, which helped us understand the core relationships within each ecosystem. In the second phase, we conducted semi-structured interviews based on an extensive interview guideline (or protocol) designed to contribute to the consistency and reliability of the results. The interview protocol covered the following topics: 1) Organizational strategy, i.e. strategy formalization, implementation, and employee involvement, with an emphasis on innovation and continuous improvement; 2) Knowledge absorption capabilities, i.e., organizational ability to acquire, assimilate, transform, and apply new technological and strategic knowledge; 3) Organizational culture, i.e., values, social climate, and preferred employee profiles; 4) Managerial practices, i.e., practices that promote discipline, support, trust, and goal-setting, about exploiting and exploring opportunities for innovation; 5) Ambidextrous strategies, i.e., perception of ambidexterity as an element of identity, and its integration into organizational practices; and 6) Customer relations and innovation, i.e., customer relations management, the balance between financial stability and risk-taking, and customer acceptance of innovative practices. Additionally, field notes were taken during the interviews, providing direct observations.

Informants were selected using a snowball sampling procedure. We interviewed top and division managers. The interviewees were significant as they influenced the cross-boundary collaboration process due to their roles, status, power, and experience. In total, thirteen in-depth interviews (six at Noventum and seven at XRM Vision) were conducted on-site with top and business unit managers, lasting between 45 and 90 min.

The coding process started by creating a provisional "start list" of categories based on the extant literature. All the transcripts were coded using the preliminary set of codes. The outcomes of this analysis constituted the logical chains of evidence.

3.2   Data Analysis

Our analysis was done at two levels. We analyzed the exploration and exploitation practices and mechanisms embedded within each organization to discover how different partnerships created ambidexterity and how various processes triggered firm-level ambidexterity. Next, we conducted an organization-level analysis to determine how the companies managed the ambidexterity between multiple DPE-based partnerships. We analyzed the data in three steps.

First, we studied context-related information from each company's broader organizational perspective as a complementor. The aim was to create a basic understanding of the types of services the two companies provide and how they align with other complementors within the platform ecosystem. Second, we thoroughly analyzed the interview transcripts, verifying the data as needed through follow-up telephone/Zoom calls, as well as emails. We transcribed interviews with members of different organizations (CEO, business unit leaders) and subsequently coded them in several rounds according to their ostensive and performative patterns of ambidextrous routines.

The first author took the lead (based on the collaboratively developed interview guideline), and the others commented and supplemented. The focus was on the relationship between the complementor and its clients, which, however, was structured at a high level by the relationship between the platform owner and the client. Third, we conducted a cross-case analysis using Eisenhardt's [13] suggested methods. We compared the cases to identify similarities and differences between them.

4   Findings

4.1   XRM Vision and the Microsoft Power Platform Ecosystem

In 2019, the company partnered with Microsoft and started using the new Microsoft Power Platform (MPP) toolkit to develop and sell digital sourcing services. XRM Vision acts alongside Microsoft, which owns the platform, as a complementor in its ecosystem. Microsoft offers a group of products called MPP, which are used to develop and automate complex business solutions. XRM Vision utilizes Dynamics 365, a cloud-based suite of business applications built on MPP, to deliver integrated solutions to clients. This includes combining CRM components with productivity tools (*power apps*) and artificial intelligence tools. Microsoft's MPP (Microsoft Power Platform) offers a unified approach to building data-driven solutions. To further support this approach, Microsoft uses the concept of Industry Solution Accelerators.

These accelerators are industry-specific components that serve as a foundation for Microsoft partners, such as XRM Vision, to build solutions based on industry standards and best practices, while being supported by Microsoft. With the help of these accelerators, XRM Vision was able to extend the MPP and create customized solutions for specific industries, including local insurance brokers and the Canadian manufacturing sector. This enabled XRM Vision to deliver tailored solutions optimized for its clients' specific industry needs and requirements, while leveraging the power and flexibility of the MPP.

Intra-organizational Social Mechanisms. XRM Vision's top management has deployed several mechanisms to enable the intra-organizational flow of information, capitalize on the diversity of profiles, and generate new business opportunities and ideas. First, *Innovation islands* have been established to create synergies at the operational level at XRM Vision. To do this, temporary teams were formed with employees from the same trade (e.g., architects, analysts, developers, etc.). Management asked them to meet once a week to identify *"pain points" (Senior Architect 1, XRM Vision)*, i.e., problems or opportunities for improvement related to operations, such as delivery methods and training.

Second, *Internal hackathons* (Hack-in-a-day) were organized, and employees were invited to identify opportunities to improve the MPP tools. The objective was to develop power apps useful to XRM Vision and address real-life problems identified by its employees during project implementations with their clients. *"Hack-in-a-day is one way to expose yourself. We are creating a new way of doing things. This is our approach to corporate hackathon" (CEO, XRM Vision).* Third, Lunch-&-Learn & Tip-&-Tricks sessions have been held since 2019. All employees are invited to attend one-hour monthly presentations (Tip-&-Tricks) on a given topic related to XRM Vision's activities, which employees organize to provide an opportunity to share information, generate discussions, and stimulate creativity. The idea behind 'Tips-&-Tricks' was to share what an employee has recently learned in five minutes. *"These are 'wake-up calls,' so instead of spending an hour on a specific subject which may not be of interest to everyone, like in 'Lunch-&-Learn,' we have a one-hour meeting, where we address 12 subjects instead of one" (VP Operations, XRM Vision).*

Inter-organizational Social Mechanisms. In the context of a DPE, we found three categories of social mechanisms that enabled the exchange between ecosystem actors: a) platform-core relationships, b) ecosystem partner relationships, and c) platform-user relationships. By studying these three categories, we identified how XRM Vision explores new opportunities further to strengthen its capabilities and position in the DPE.

Platform-Core Relationships. We found evidence that XRM Vision established a profound relationship with the platform core owner, specifically with Microsoft. Based on the interview data, we found that Microsoft's Power Platform comprises a set of solutions regularly adapted from a technological perspective. To explore new opportunities, XRM Vision is closely aligned with Microsoft, using partner meetings in which they are informed about new functionalities (releases). In doing so, XRM Vision gains access to relevant technological opportunities. By attending partner meetings and information sessions, and studying state-of-the-art whitepapers released by Microsoft, XRM Vision can explore new ideas that may ultimately result in new products and/or services. *"When Microsoft's Power Platform arrived, we [XRM Vision] had to rethink our practices to foster innovation. To do so, business developers and architects attended several conferences organized by Microsoft on the Power Platform. By discussing the opportunities that the Power Platform offers, we were able to understand its possibilities and develop new solutions for our clients" (CEO, XRM Vision).*

The interviewees revealed that XRM Vision recognized the full potential of Microsoft's Power Platform in developing products and services for clients. To underpin their skills and expertise in the Power Platform XRM Vision context, they decided that one of their solution architects would obtain Microsoft's Most Valuable Professional (MVP) nomination. The idea behind XRM Vision's expert (solution architect) in Microsoft Power Platform technologies was to develop new practices on this technology platform and enhance organizational knowledge. It would also promote, both externally and internally, the expertise of XRM Vision and the affordances of the Power Platform. This appointment required time investments on Eric's part and financial assets on XRM Vision. The solution architect is now recognized as an expert within the Power Platform community and by clients and partners. This enables him to deliver presentations at external partner events and create promotional materials for XRM Vision products and services. *"The goal to have an MVP was to create a significant presence on social media, easier access to Microsoft knowledgebase, to specialized and private events, and privileged access to a vast network of partners, but also competitors" (VP Operations, XRM Vision).*

Platform Client Relationships. To strengthen the relationships with platform users, XRM Vision organized several events to train platform clients to independently build applications (*power apps*). XRM Vision labeled these events *'app-in-a-day'* to illustrate the opportunities and the convenience of using the Power Platform. XRM Vision's 'app-in-a-day' event allowed it to reach platform users and reveal its services and expertise. However, these initiatives were viewed both positively and negatively.

On the one hand, XRM Vision's operations managers consider such initiatives a waste of time and money. On the other hand, business development employees perceived them as a mechanism to raise awareness of the platform's possibilities and identify and give visibility to new practices and business opportunities. *"We organized about twenty events open to all platform users called 'app-in-a-day' in which we trained approximately 300–400 people on the Power Platform" (VP Operations, XRM Vision).*

Platform Generativity. The interviews reveal that XRM Vision established ecosystem partner relationships to achieve two primary objectives: developing new applications based on the MPP toolkit and assessing the degree of test user acceptance of these new applications. To accomplish both goals, XRM Vision organized global and customized hackathons. By organizing global hackathons, XRM Vision was able to develop new applications using innovative methods and approaches. During the hackathons, they had the opportunity to co-create new power apps and gain new insights and knowledge into how these applications can create value for both the ecosystem (complementors) and partners that are competitors in the DPE, as well as for the platform core owner (Microsoft). By organizing global hackathons, they also experienced that some ecosystem partners were competitors in other client relationships.

However, XRM Vision and its ecosystem competition noticed that co-creating new applications benefited all ecosystem partners as each party needed help to develop them. Coopetition, a portmanteau of cooperation and competition, is a strategy used by members of a digital platform ecosystem to compete and collaborate for their mutual benefit

[37]. In a coopetitive environment, ecosystem members recognize that they must work together to create value for the ecosystem while competing to capture a share of that value. *"We organized a global hackathon to showcase the expertise of MPP and XRM Vision. During this hackathon, some platform users were direct competitors and co-developed knowledge about the MPP within the digital platform ecosystem" (Director Customer Relationship, XRM Vision).*

The interview data revealed that organizing hackathons with ecosystem partners was crucial for XRM Vision in developing a robust ecosystem around the MPP and understanding the possibilities and opportunities offered by the technology. Based on the knowledge accumulated during these events, XRM Vision had the opportunity to start developing Industry Solutions Accelerators. Hence, XRM Vision can continually contribute to the MPP, creating complements to the platform core (Microsoft). Since most of the MPP solutions that XRM Vision uses have been migrated and integrated back into the MPP, they contribute to the platform's core ownership and, consequently, to the DPE.

4.2   Noventum and the SAP Platform

Noventum is a 'result-driven thought leader' IT Management Consulting company with 100 employees. They support DAX-listed (German stock index) clients in their IT challenges and efforts to establish a modern company culture. Noventum's Managing Partner emphasizes a *"culture of trust and performance"* as a prerequisite for sustainable success. The company has been providing digital sourcing services to its customers to optimize their business and logistical processes, mapping them into the SAP system since 1996. The company has established a reputation for its expertise and has become a preferred partner of SAP. Noventum has the latest know-how and expertise to design effective client processes at any time. As a result, Noventum is well-equipped to provide its clients with the most up-to-date solutions and services, helping them achieve their goals and stay ahead in their respective industries.

The SAP platform ecosystem comprises various technologies, applications, and services provided by SAP to help organizations manage their business processes more efficiently. It comprises a wide range of tools and technologies that are integrated and designed to work together seamlessly. Noventum provides two critical components of the SAP platform to its clients: 1. SAP ERP (S/4HANA) – represents the core enterprise resource planning system that integrates all the business processes of an organization and provides real-time data processing and analytics capabilities, enabling organizations to make faster and better-informed decisions; and 2. SAP Business Intelligence (BI) - a suite of tools and applications that allow organizations to analyze and visualize their data, providing insights into business performance and trends.

Intra-organizational Social Mechanisms. At Noventum, exploration is recognized as inevitable (due to continuous IT innovation in the sector) and a critical differentiator from the competition. Yet, it is recognized as challenging to establish an exploration mindset within an organization where billable hours are a crucial performance metric and daily pressure is exerted by demanding project work. *"Necessary exploration is at risk of being crowded out by exploitation" (Managing partner, Noventum).*

The company has established structures and related practices that distinguish innovation (and R&D) and highlight it as a distinctive feature. Noventum organizes a cross-divisional *Trending workshop* as part of its annual strategy meeting, which focuses on assessing market innovations and reflecting on their potential for business development and positioning of business units. To achieve this, the seven Division Directors (excluding the Managing Partner) meet once a year for a full week to identify the leading IT trends in their respective markets and explore how new technologies can help Noventum enhance its solutions or develop new ones. *"In September, we sit down, and everybody gives their idea of the business plan for the following year [...] So we challenge each other, and sometimes there are projects that are done jointly by several business units for the following financial year" (Division Director 1, Noventum).*

The leadership at Noventum has developed and aligned a repertoire of social mechanisms, characterized as having an "engaging management style" (managing partner, Noventum). In our interviews, we encountered enlightened and sensitive individuals (directors) who were aware of the challenges of ambidexterity. They claimed to strive for a balance between exploitation ('billable hours') and freedom, while also encouraging exploration, such as training and personal development. Noventum allows employees to take a half-day weekly to engage in individual research and idea generation.

Additionally, the Division Directors regularly organize team-building idea generation sessions (once a month). *"My developers are constantly looking for a challenge in terms of programming. I will ensure they have a room where no other departments can reach them and the team session is based on the perspective: don't blame the mistake, look for the solution, push, push, push to the solution, and don't dwell too long on mistakes" (Division Director 3, Noventum).*

Thus, we identified variations of an ambidextrous work design that effectively implements several social mechanisms to foster a culture of collaboration and knowledge sharing.

Inter-organizational Social Mechanisms. In the context of a DPE, we found three categories of social mechanisms that enabled the exchange between ecosystem actors: a) platform-core relationships, b) platform client relationships, and c) platform generativity.

Platform-Core Relationships. The privileged relationship between Noventum and SAP involves Noventum, as a partner, being granted certain benefits and advantages in exchange for its commitment to selling SAP's products and services. This requires access to exclusive training and support resources, preferential pricing on SAP products and services, early access to new product releases and updates, and the ability to participate in joint marketing and sales initiatives with SAP. Overall, both parties work together to drive sales and revenue growth while delivering high-quality products and services to customers.

Platform Client Relationships. Over the years, Noventum has found that one way to improve a project is by sharpening it, which can prevent future building obstacles and enable the incorporation of new technologies and methods. *"Our approach involves enhancing a project that is already 80% complete to deliver the best possible outcome for the customer. This provides an opportunity for our consultant to introduce new ideas and innovations. We are looking for ways to integrate this into our client projects and prioritize learning how to utilize it effectively" (Division Director 2, Noventum).*

A typical scenario is that Noventum's clients in the SAP platform ecosystem approach a Noventum consultant when they plan to purchase a new software or a new release, which typically requires some customization. Noventum organizes a *knowledge-sharing forum* comprising several meetings, where the client is provided with knowledge transfer and demonstrations to better understand the product before committing to the project. Sometimes, when the client enquires about Noventum's consultancy approach, it initiates a conversation about processes, data owners, stakeholders, and other key factors. This discussion helps the client better understand Noventum's method, process model, and distinctive contribution, which is both a) a more nuanced and specific understanding of the clients' problems and needs and b) a unique set of project management skills, e.g., in post-merger integration. *"The message we want to convey is that we prioritize understanding our client's needs and ensuring they are on board with our business practices" (Division Director 4, Noventum).*

Platform Generativity. One key benefit of coopetition within a digital platform ecosystem is that it enables members to leverage each other's strengths and capabilities to create new products and services that they could not develop independently [37]. One example of coopetition among complementors in the SAP platform ecosystem is the collaboration initiative between Noventum and MicroStrategy. MicroStrategy provides comprehensive reporting, analysis, and monitoring software, enabling top companies worldwide to make informed decisions.

This mutually beneficial partnership allows both complementors to expand their DPE customer base and provide more comprehensive solutions to their clients. As a complementor in the SAP DPE, Noventum offers SAP-based accelerators that enable organizations to connect their SAP systems to Microsoft-based data platforms easily. Noventum's added value lies in its precise data extraction from SAP connections utilizing SAP BI Content Data sources. Clients engage with predefined interfaces instead of basic tables, which deliver multiple critical benefits to the Microsoft and SAP platforms. Additionally, Noventum's accelerator simplifies exposing SAP ERP data to all areas of the organization, allowing for greater collaboration and improved efficiency.

5 Discussion

Even if exploitation and exploration are depicted as two opposing forces and can be conceptualized as the two ends of a continuum, they are paradoxically interrelated in a natural cycle. Indeed, innovations and opportunities generated through exploration can evolve into exploitation, while the income from the slack resources generated by exploitation can enable further exploration. Nevertheless, as these twin requirements compete for limited organizational resources, organizations must make decisions and take organizational actions to reconcile these conflicting pressures and balance these two forces.

Like most business consulting firms, Noventum and XRM Vision face essential management challenges that are sometimes conflicting. These include pursuing growth strategies while increasing process efficiency, as well as encouraging their employees to identify business opportunities and fostering the operational excellence expected by their clients within their respective DPEs. Our study is focused on a specific industry segment. Digital sourcing service providers, as consultants, typically emphasize the exploitation and successful delivery of projects. Yet, exploration is seen as key to service excellence and, thus, as a differentiator. Exploration manifests as specialization, the ability to identify and deliver customized services.

We found a culture of project-based learning practices in each company, embedded in close, trusting, and recurring customer relationships. Conceptually, we identified two modes of organizational ambidexterity (OA): 1. Exploration to (continuously) improve exploitation (*exploration-for-exploitation*) engaged via intra-organizational relationships, an orientation towards continually improving the quality of the service delivery, and 2. Exploration is integral to DPE-related project-based exploitation (*exploration-through-exploitation*), an approach engaged through relationships with clients and the DPE owner, characterized by project-driven learning.

The platform owner's innovations and product developments created downstream challenges for the client to keep the local installation (instance) aligned with the platform version(s). Alternatively, process adaptations by the client or other projects created adaptation needs, which were addressed by the complementor. The relationship with other complementors is primarily focused on strategic positioning, differentiation, and profiling. In this competitive landscape, the complementors highlighted their ambidextrous competencies – ongoing innovation and effective project execution—and successful client relationship management, resulting in over 90% repeat business.

Based on our data analysis, we found that it is vital for innovators in the digital sourcing services industry to create a minimum viable product, an essential product for learning purposes that helps organizations better understand their customers' needs by seeking their feedback on the product in question [34]. Our data analysis suggests that the two complementors established various social mechanisms that foster innovation. XRM Vision and Noventum engaged in multiple collaborative initiatives that strengthened their relationships with ecosystem partners and fostered trust in the development and sharing of knowledge. This relates to social interaction ties (ecosystem ties) used as channels for information and resource flows [41]. This is also consistent with Capaldo [6], who found that interpersonal relationships, trust, and reciprocity play a significant role in inter-organizational processes. Strengthening the ecosystem ties between complementors and the platform owner has a positive impact on innovation.

Our study shows that focusing on implementing structural mechanisms in a DPE, specifically (e.g., open access, microculture), contributes to increased innovation lead times for the complementor under study. Our findings on social mechanisms show that knowledge-intensive learning between a complementor and other DPE actors contributes to the development of innovative solutions. Table 1 provides a summary of the organizational ambidexterity-related social mechanisms.

Our data analysis suggests that the complementor's paradoxical mindset in managing OA led to the implementation of several social mechanisms. By applying social mechanisms related to the complementor, XRM Vision explored new ideas that effectively developed novel accelerators within short lead times. The social mechanisms fostered by XRM Vision and Noventum's innovation processes initiated internal patterns (e.g., events, actions) among ecosystem actors, leading to the development of complementary

Table1. Social Mechanisms for Organizational Ambidexterity

Social mechanisms		XRM Vision	Noventum
Intra-organizational relationships (OA Mode: *Exploration-for-exploitation*)	1. *Collaboration initiatives*	Innovation islands Lunch-&-Learn & Tip-&-Tricks sessions	Cross-division learning sessions (trending workshop)
	2. *Social connectivity*	Internal Hackathons	Team building idea generation sessions
Inter-organizational relationships (OA Mode: *Exploration-through-exploitation*)	1. *Motivation-based platform-core relationships*	Privileged relationship with Microsoft	Privileged relationship with SAP
	2. *Platform client relationships*	App-in-a-day events	Knowledge-sharing forums
	3. *Generativity*		
	3.1 Social dimension	Coopetition-motivated global hackathons	Partnerships (knowledge sharing and assimilation)
	3.2 Technical dimension	MPP-based Industry Solutions Accelerators	SAP-Content Data Sources Accelerators

products (accelerators). However, context matters. This implies that a complex phenomenon, such as OA, analyzed in the context of a DPE, is perceived as an emerging process through a sequence of temporal events and actions. The latter is consistent with Gross [21], who argues that social mechanisms explain intermediate events. To summarize, social mechanisms, as applied by a complementor, provide insights into innovation-driven processes. This provides a causal explanation identifying the processes underlying exploration and exploitation in the context of a DPE, which is consistent with Avgerou [3].

Beyond their consultant-client nature, inter-organizational relationships have evolved and are now deployed as partnerships and arenas for learning. In other words, engaging with vendors and clients in a learning mode and learning relationships is part of the ambidextrous skill set and competence development, which aligns with an integrated view of ambidexterity. *"Exploration can be when it's an innovative project in the area of the client, then we do a lot of knowledge development" (Division Director 1, Noventum); "Some of our clients use it as a kind of protected playground to try out new ideas." (Senior architect, XRM Vision).*

In his research on business partnerships, Lascaux [33] mentions the importance for organizations to maintain mutual trust and engage in repeated interactions with familiar partners, and this has been observed in both case companies: *"We have lots of long-term customers, with established trusted relationships. One client, the first sentence after the greeting was: ignore the contract, just look around and do something useful" (VP Operations, XRM Vision); "We are – to use a restaurant metaphor - the hired chef that brings in a cook, servants, pots, pans, food, but we're cooking with a team that's made up of the client that is already using the kitchen" (Division Director 2, Noventum).*

Both organizations' digital sourcing service philosophy highlights a holistic view of consultant-client relationships, which requires technically, methodically, and socially competent consultants. Project-driven learning serves both the client, as the service is refined, and the consultant, who achieves *organic ambidexterity*: learning and project execution are intricately linked. In this type of organization, any effective transfer of knowledge is contingent upon the environment (their respective DPEs), which gives employees psychological safety and allows them to share all relevant (unfiltered) information [2].

6   Conclusion, Contributions, and Future Research

We have empirically explored OA practices and developed a contextualized view of ambidextrous challenges and responses at both organizational and inter-organizational levels in two digital sourcing service providers operating in a distinctive, competitive, and innovative industry. Our research has aimed to study how complementors develop organizational ambidexterity in the context of a DPE. The identified social mechanisms have revealed how a complementor creates and discusses new ideas with other DPE actors to foster capability development (exploration) and transform these ideas into practice (exploitation). Our findings suggest that a complementor's support of a platform is associated with a greater commitment to the platform owner. This partially addresses a research proposition advanced by Cenamor [8], which states that the "bilateral dependency between a complementor and a platform owner becomes more significant as the platform ecosystem matures" [p. 338]. More specifically, this corresponds to the generativity practices by the complementors in our study.

This study highlights how complementors in DPEs enable organizational ambidexterity by engaging in structured value-creation mechanisms that support both exploration (innovation and capability development) and exploitation (quality, scalability, and efficiency). Our findings provide new insights into how complementors strategically balance these dual forces, thereby enhancing value across the platform.

6.1   Complementors as Orchestrators of Value-Driven Ambidexterity

Traditional OA research often assumes firms develop internal mechanisms to balance exploration and exploitation [35]. However, in a DPE context, complementors serve as orchestrators. They leverage their position within the platform ecosystem to facilitate incremental improvements (exploitation) and radical innovations (exploration) not only for themselves but also for the broader platform ecosystem [24]. Complementors introduce new services and technologies that enhance the platform's functionality beyond the original vision of the platform owner. Their capacity to create industry-specific accelerators (e.g., XRM Vision's Microsoft Power Platform solutions) represents a systematic approach to exploration.

These innovations act as value multipliers for the platform, increasing its appeal to new users and industries. Complementors refine existing services to improve efficiency, ensuring reliability and seamless integration within the platform. This was evident in

Noventum's efforts to optimize SAP-based solutions, where process refinement translated into improved interoperability and service delivery, reinforcing the platform's core value proposition.

6.2 Social Mechanisms as Enablers of Ambidextrous Value Creation

Our study found that complementors employ social mechanisms—both relational and structural—to facilitate ambidextrous engagement with platform stakeholders [6]. These mechanisms facilitate knowledge exchange, cooperation, and controlled competition, directly influencing value creation dynamics. Through cross-company hackathons, platform-driven training events, and ecosystem partnerships, complementors embed exploration within exploitative structures, reducing the risk of innovation failure while maintaining efficiency. This aligns with coopetition, where competitors innovate to generate shared benefits [37].

Our research directly contributes to the literature on digital sourcing by enhancing the understanding of digital sourcing as a fundamental practice in DPEs. We emphasize the relational and structural mechanisms that facilitate knowledge flows and co-creation within these ecosystems.

6.3 Redefining Complementors as Agents of Platform Evolution

Our work suggested that complementors are not merely followers of platform governance structures; they actively shape them. Unlike previous assumptions that platform owners dictate the rules [9], our findings suggest that complementors co-define governance through participation in value-generating activities:

1. By co-developing industry accelerators and influencing API integrations, complementors dictate how value is structured and distributed within the platform.
2. By acting as adaptive agents, ensuring the platform's long-term sustainability by filling gaps in service provision and evolving alongside technological advancements.

In our study, we have been examining the relationships between the individual, organizational, and inter-organizational layers. We have identified and evidenced two instances of contextual ambidexterity: intra-organizational *exploration-for-exploitation*, in other words, continuous improvement of service delivery, and inter-organizational *exploration-through-exploitation*, i.e., project-based or project-induced learning. Both have become refined, essential components of the ambidextrous practices in the two case companies.

Regarding the practitioners, our findings have direct managerial implications for business management consulting firms that act as complementors in a DPE. We recommend that senior management develop a cohesive social structure and adopt a balanced approach to overcome the challenges of joint exploitation and exploration. The closer you look, the more the distinction between perfection at delivery on one hand and continuous improvement, creativity, and innovation on the other hand becomes blurred (cross-over between exploration and exploitation).

We found a dominating commitment to outstanding consultancy services (exploitation) in a competitive environment, such as a digital platform. Recruiting, training, empowering, and thereby retaining competent teams of consultants on one side, and building and maintaining long-lasting, trusting relationships with clients and the platform owner on the other, provide the setting not only for excellence in exploitation but also for distinctive ways of exploration.

Our findings are highly contextualized and contingent upon the digital platform, positioning of the companies, and client organizations. They demonstrate successful differentiation as the *raison d'être* of these companies, trying to escape the commoditization of their digital sourcing services (clients have a choice). This includes diverse practices aimed at achieving ambidextrous capabilities. Our multi-case study identifies various avenues for further research.

Complementors are not merely independent actors; they are dynamic digital sourcing intermediaries that reshape traditional supply chain models by leveraging platform-driven sourcing opportunities. Future research should investigate how digital sourcing strategies vary across different platform types and governance models, as well as how complementors balance strategic autonomy with platform dependencies in digital sourcing arrangements. We also recommend more in-depth research about the social interaction ties between DPE actors. Insights may shed some light on the norm of reciprocity when actors focus on ecosystem innovations. Moreover, we suggest examining the shared vision and language between complementors in a DPE by applying a social capital lens. This may create insights about how members of different complementors share knowledge.

Acknowledgments. This research was supported by the Social Sciences and Humanities Research Council of Canada (SSHRC) (Grant #430–2018-0351).

References

1. Adner, R.: Match your innovation strategy to your innovation ecosystem. Harv. Bus. Rev. **84**(4), 98–107 (2006)
2. Albers, S., Wohlgezogen, F., Zajac, E.J.: Strategic alliance structures: an organization design perspective. J. Manag. **42**(3), 582–614 (2016)
3. Avgerou, C.: Social mechanisms for causal explanation in social theory-based IS research. J. Assoc. Inf. Syst. **14**(8), 420–451 (2013)
4. Baiyere, A., Grover, V., Lyytinen, K.J., Woerner, S., Gupta, A.: Digital "x" – charting a path for digital-themed research. Inf. Syst. Res. **34**(2), 463–486 (2023)
5. Boudreau, K.J., Hagiu, A.: Platform rules: multi-sided platforms as regulators. In: Gawer, A. (ed.) Platforms, Markets and Innovation, pp. 1–18. Edward Elgar, Cheltenham, UK (2009)
6. Capaldo, A.: Network governance: a cross-level study of social mechanisms, knowledge benefits, and strategic outcomes in joint-design alliances. Ind. Mark. Manage. **43**(4), 685–703 (2014)
7. Ceccagnoli, M., Forman, C., Huang, P., Wu, D.J.: Cocreation of value in a platform ecosystem! the case of enterprise software. MIS Q. **36**(1), 263–290 (2012)
8. Cenamor, J.: Complementor competitive advantage: a framework for strategic decisions. J. Bus. Res. **122**, 335–343 (2012)
9. Cennamo, C., Santaló, J.: Generativity tension and value creation in platform ecosystems. Organ. Sci. **30**(3), 617–641 (2019)

10. Chang, Y., Hughes, H., Hotho, S.: Internal and external antecedents of SMEs' innovation ambidexterity outcomes. Manag. Decis. **49**, 1658–1676 (2011)
11. Cusumano, M.A., Gawer, A.: The elements of platform leadership. Sloan Manag. Rev. **43**(3), 51–58 (2002)
12. Deilen, M., Wiesche, M.: The Role of Complementors in Platform Ecosystems. In: Innovation Through Information Systems: Volume III: A Collection of Latest Research on Management Issues, pp. 473–488. Springer (2021)
13. Eisenhardt, K.: Building theories from case study research. Acad. Manag. Rev. **14**(4), 532–550 (1989)
14. Eisenhardt, K., Graebner, M.E.: Theory building from cases: opportunities and challenges. Acad. Manag. J. **50**(1), 25–32 (2007)
15. Engert, M., Evers, J., Hein, A., Krcmar, H.: The engagement of complementors and the role of platform boundary resources in e-commerce platform ecosystems. Inf. Syst. Front. **24**(6), 2007–2025 (2022)
16. Fayezi, S., Ghaderi, H.: What are the mechanisms through which inter-organizational relationships contribute to supply chain resilience? Asia Pac. J. Mark. Logist. **34**(1), 159–174 (2022)
17. Gawer, A.: Platform dynamics and strategies: from products to services. Platforms Markets Innov. **45**, 57 (2009)
18. Gibson, C.B., Birkinshaw, J.: The antecedents, consequences, and mediating role of organizational ambidexterity. Acad. Manag. J. **47**(2), 209–226 (2004)
19. Ghazawneh, A., Henfridsson, O.: Balancing platform control and external contribution in third-party development: the boundary resources model. Inf. Syst. J. **23**(2), 173–192 (2013)
20. Goh, J.M., Gao, G., Agarwal, R.: Evolving work routines: adaptive routinization of information technology in healthcare. Inf. Syst. Res. **22**(3), 565–585 (2011)
21. Gross, N.: A pragmatist theory of social mechanisms. Am. Soc. Rev. **74**(3), 358–379 (2009)
22. Haghshenas, M., Østerlie, T.: Coordinating innovation in digital infrastructure: the case of transforming offshore project delivery. In: Agrifoglio, R. et al. (Eds.) Digital Business Transformation, pp. 251–266. Springer International Publishing (2020)
23. Hanseth, O., Lyytinen, K.: Design theory for dynamic complexity in information infrastructures: the case of building the internet. J. Inf. Technol. **25**(1), 1–19 (2019)
24. Hein, A., et al.: Digital platform ecosystems. Electron. Mark. **30**(1), 87–98 (2020)
25. Heracleous, L., Papachroni, A., Andriopoulos, C., Gotsi, M.: Structural ambidexterity and competency traps: insights from Xerox Parc. Technol. Forecast. Soc. Chang. **117**, 327–338 (2017)
26. Jansen, J.J., Tempelaar, M.P., Van den Bosch, F.A., Volberda, H.W.: Structural differentiation and ambidexterity: the mediating role of integration mechanisms. Organ. Sci. **20**(4), 797–811 (2009)
27. Kauppila, O.-P.: Creating ambidexterity by integrating and balancing structurally separate interorganizational partnerships. Strateg. Organ. **8**(4), 283–312 (2010)
28. Knoben, J., Oerlemans, L.A.G.: Proximity and inter-organizational collaboration: a literature review. Int. J. Manag. Rev. **8**(2), 71–89 (2006)
29. Krancher, O., Sabherwal, R., Oshri, I., Kotlarsky, J.: Digital sourcing: a discussion of agential, semiotic, infrastructural, combinatorial, and economic shifts. J. Inf. Technol. **39**(2), 262–269 (2024)
30. Li, D., Jia, F., Schoenherr, T., Liu, G.: How do platforms improve social capital within sharing economy-based service triads: an information processing perspective? Prod. Plann. Control **35**(5), 507–524 (2024)
31. Korpela, K., Hallikas, J., Dahlberg, T.: Digital supply chain transformation toward blockchain integration. In: Proceedings of the 50th Hawaii International Conference on System Sciences, Big Island, HI, pp. 4182–4191 (2017)

32. Langley, A., Smallman, C., Tsoukas, H., Van de Ven, A.H.: Process studies of change in organization and management: unveiling temporality, activity, and flow. Acad. Manag. J. **56**(1), 1–13 (2013)
33. Lascaux, A.: Absorptive capacity, research output sharing, and research output capture in university-industry partnerships. Scand. J. Manag. **35**(3), 101045 (2019)
34. Lorenzo, O., Kawalek, P., Wharton, L.: Entrepreneurship, Innovation and Technology: A Guide to Core Models and Tools, 2nd edn. Routledge, London (2023)
35. O'Reilly, C.A., III., Tushman, M.L.: Organizational ambidexterity: past, present, and future. Acad. Manag. Perspect. **27**(4), 324–338 (2013)
36. Panico, C., Cennamo, C.: User preferences and strategic interactions in platform ecosystems. Strateg. Manag. J. **43**(3), 507–529 (2022)
37. Ritala, P.: Coopetition strategy-when is it successful? Empirical evidence on innovation and market performance. Br. J. Manag. **23**(3), 307–324 (2012)
38. Senyo, P.K., Liu, K., Sun, L., Effah, J.: Evolution of norms in the emergence of digital business ecosystems. In: Socially Aware Organisations and Technologies. Impact and Challenges: 17th IFIP WG 8.1 International Conference on Informatics and Semiotics in Organisations, ICISO 2016, Campinas, Brazil, Proceedings 17, pp. 79–84, Springer International Publishing (2016)
39. Smith, C., Smith, J.B., Shaw, E.: Embracing digital networks: entrepreneurs' social capital online. J. Bus. Ventur. **32**(1), 18–34 (2017)
40. Tiwana, A.: Evolutionary competition in platform ecosystems. Inf. Syst. Res. **26**(2), 266–281 (2015)
41. Tsai, W., Ghoshal, S.: Social capital and value creation: an empirical study of intrafirm networks. Acad. Manag. J. **41**(4), 464–476 (1998)
42. Van Beers, C., Zand, F.: R&D cooperation, partner diversity, and innovation performance: an empirical analysis. J. Prod. Innov. Manag. **31**(2), 292–312 (2014)
43. Vieru, D., Plugge, A., Bourdeau, S.: Leveraging ambidexterity in a digital platform ecosystem: insights from a complementor's perspective. In: Proceedings of the 56th Annual Hawaii Conference on System Sciences, Maui, HI, pp. 6280–6289 (2023)
44. Vrontis, D., Thrassou, A., Santoro, G., Papa, A.: Ambidexterity, external knowledge and performance in knowledge-intensive firms. J. Technol. Transfer, **42**(2), 374–388 (2016)
45. Wuyts, S., Dutta, S.: Benefiting from alliance portfolio diversity: the role of past internal knowledge creation strategy. J. Manag. **40**(6), 1653–1674 (2014)
46. Yoo, Y., Boland, R.J., Jr., Lyytinen, K., Majchrzak, A.: Organizing for innovation in the digitized world. Organ. Sci. **23**(5), 1398–1408 (2012)
47. Yoo, D.K., Roh, J.J., Cho, S., Yang, M.: Coopetition in a platform ecosystem: from the complementors' perspective. Electron. Commer. Res. **24**(3), 1509–1532 (2024)
48. Yoon, C., Lee, B., Yoon, B., Toulan, O.: Typology and success factors of collaboration for sustainable growth in the IT service industry. Sustainability **9**, 1–20 (2017)
49. Zhu, F.: Friends or foes? Examining platform owners' entry into complementors' spaces. J. Econ. Manag. Strategy **28**(1), 23–28 (2019)

The Effect of Generative AI on Creating Software Complements for Digital Platforms

David Rochholz$^{(\boxtimes)}$ (iD) and Daniel Beimborn (iD)

Univeristy of Bamberg, An der Weberei 5, 96047 Bamberg, Germany
mail@davidrochholz.de, daniel.beimborn@uni-bamberg.de

Abstract. This study investigates the impact of Generative AI (GenAI) on the creation of software complements in digital platform ecosystems. Based on semi-structured interviews with software developers from both platform owner and complementor perspectives, we examine how GenAI is applied to platform boundary resources, to either support complement creation or boundary resource improvements. Using the inductive "Gioia approach", we develop a data structure showing that GenAI improves platform access and expands platform owner and complementor capabilities. The findings offer four implications: GenAI can accelerate complement creation across platforms; it acts as a new type of boundary resource, merging technical and knowledge resources into conversational and code generating capabilities; it shifts developer focus from coding to the value of the complement; and it highlights the growing importance of managing and governing complement creation.

Keywords: Digital Platforms · Complementors · GenAI · Co-Innovation

1 Introduction

Digital platforms have increasingly been in focus of researchers from Information Systems, but also from other disciplines. To enable value co-creation from complementors, platform owners externalize platform functionalities. These external complements broaden the platform's initial capabilities, thereby strengthening the platform ecosystem's position [1–3].

The recent surge in software development support and automation, driven by modern AI tools such as GenAI, often poses as support and potential threat to software engineers' jobs [4]. GenAI tools like ChatGPT or GitHub Copilot are characterized through ability to generate new content, including text, images, or segments of software code [5]. Insights from various fields of research highlight the promising productivity gains of GenAI. For example, software developers using GitHub Copilot have been reported to increase their implementation speed even though other productivity aspects, such as software quality, have not been measured, yet [6].

Yet, it is not clear how digital platform ecosystems are affected by this promising emergency of GenAI productivity increases on software code creation. These missing insights are reflected by the current state of IS research. The timeline depicted in Fig. 1

M. Schreieck et al. (Eds.): DSPE 2025, LNBIP 563, pp. 34–55, 2026.
https://doi.org/10.1007/978-3-032-04512-6_3

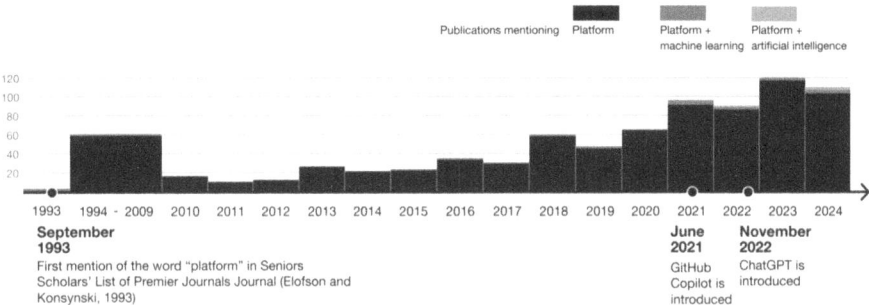

Fig. 1. Senior Scholars' List of Premier Journals publications mentioning "platform", "platform" and "machine learning", or "platform" and "artificial intelligence" over the years.

highlights a significant gap in the IS literature: only very few platform studies address machine learning or artificial intelligence in general. Furthermore, a search conducted in the Web of Science database found no publications from the Senior Scholars' List of Premier Journals that focused on the application of GenAI in the context of digital platforms. This gap signals a critical lack of insight into how GenAI influences platform ecosystems.

The absence of research on the impact of GenAI in these settings raises several important questions. Traditionally, IS research has imagined complementors as human entities. However, vibe coding[1] is reshaping this landscape by automating content and software development tasks, thereby boosting human productivity. Despite this potential, there remains a notable research gap: the implications of using GenAI to facilitate platform complement creation have not been at all explored. The prevailing understanding of network effects and their importance for the evolution of platform ecosystems is well established in the IS literature [3, 7, 8], yet the role of generative content and its impact on software platform remain largely unexamined. As tools like ChatGPT and GitHub Copilot continue to promise significant advancements in automating content creation and augmenting human capabilities [9], it is imperative to understand their effects on platform ecosystems.

In digital platform ecosystems, external software developers, or complementors, play an important role by building software complements to extend platform functionality. To enable this interaction, platform owners expose and explain functionalities through boundary resources, such as Application Programming Interfaces (APIs), or Software Development Kits (SDKs), including their documentation [10–12]. These interfaces serve as enablers for complement creation and therefore influence the overall platform ecosystem evolution. As such, investigating the application of GenAI at this intersection of platforms and complementors is particularly relevant.

Therefore, we ask: *How does GenAI impact the creation of complements for digital platform ecosystems?*

Our study investigates the experiences of software developers across various platform contexts. Through applying the Gioia method, we created a data structure that

---

highlights how GenAI positively affects platform access and improves the capacities of complement creation. The data structure suggests that GenAI influences the creation and consumption of boundary resources, which are critical for platform interactions and ecosystem evolution.

Our findings carry for a couple of implications: First, GenAI potentially affects indirect network effects as complementors might leverage it to accelerate complement creation across several platforms. Second, GenAI forms a new boundary resource by spanning across technical and knowledge boundary resources to offer conversational and code generating abilities. Third, platform owners and complementors benefit from new affordances in creating complements, that allows them to concentrate their efforts on the "what" rather than the "how". Finally, this potentially results in a shift from hands-on complement coding to governing and managing complement creation.

2 Background

2.1 GenAI

Generative Artificial Intelligence (GenAI) is a branch of Artificial Intelligence (AI) generating outputs such as text, audio, video, or other media that closely mimic or are often indistinguishable from content created by humans. The generation process is initiated through textual descriptions of the desired content, a technique known as prompting [13, 14].

Tools that utilize GenAI technology have been shown to enhance user productivity in content creation tasks. Noy and Zhang [9] found that writers using OpenAI's ChatGPT produced faster results with improved overall quality. These benefits were primarily achieved by the tool scaffolding text blocks, which users could refine after the initial generation. The authors suggest that the increased accessibility of prompting, as opposed to traditional programming, may result in a larger pool of programmers at a lower cost. Consequently, in the future, more attention may be given to questions regarding what content to create and why, rather than focusing on how to create it. Yet, applying GenAI to tasks traditional achieved by humans is not seen without risks as the exact same effect could lead to an increase in expert demand as only skilled software engineers would be able to judge GenAI outputs. Furthermore, especially less experienced developers have shown a potential "over-reliance" on tools like Copilot that led in spending more time on improving prompts than fixing suggested code [15].

Although the full impact of GenAI on organizations remains unclear—given that academic discussions about its benefits are still in their early stages (Santos Gabriel, 2024) and the technology may have limitations due to its reliance on training data for content quality and variety (Susarla et al., 2023)—it is worthwhile to investigate whether GenAI's text scaffolding capabilities are transferable to other content creation skills, such as developing software code for digital platforms.

2.2 GenAI and Software Development

Software developers use GenAI in multiple ways. Applying it directly inside the integrated development environments (IDE), does not force them to switch their problem-solving context by opening other programs, such as browsers, for researching their task.

However, also prompting the user interface of any GenAI platform, such as OpenAI's ChatGPT or Claude's Sonnet is a common way of discussing code or related challenges.

A prominent tool using GenAI for code creation is GitHub Copilot. Original research on Copilot discovered a 55.8% speed advantage for software developers using Copilot on a narrowly scoped task compared to developers not using it [6].

While the initial study focused on experienced software engineers, subsequent research provided GitHub Copilot to novice programmers at the beginning of their computer science studies. The results indicate that GenAI tools can bridge existing knowledge gaps and serve as learning aids but also risk leading students to produce code they do not understand [15]. Understanding the level of programming skill required to effectively use GenAI tools is critical for assessing their potential to increase productivity and expand resources for software creation. If expert programmers are needed to evaluate the outputs of large language models, programmer capacity may become even scarcer in the future. Conversely, if only testing outcomes and adjusting prompts are required, access to programming capacity could increase [9].

2.3 Digital Platforms and GenAI Software Development

Digital platforms deliver value to their users through the interactions they facilitate among their participants, a phenomenon known as the network effect. A platform creates a direct network effect if its users perceive value from direct interactions with each other, as seen in social networks. For example, platforms like WhatsApp or TikTok are becoming more valuable to its users with any user added. When the value of a platform is perceived through the size of its different user groups—such as software developers and software consumers—the network effects are indirect [3, 7, 16] or cross-side, since the effect involves different sides of the platform [8]. Thus, for innovation platforms, this effect hinges on the number, variety, and quality of the complements that users can consume or interact with. Mobile platforms such as Apple iOS and Google Android become more valuable with the amount and quality of apps (complements) available to its users. Attracting developers to create these complements is therefore critical for growing and sustaining an ecosystem. Once set to create software for a platform, the ability of developers to create complements depends on the external resources, also called boundary resources, that platform owners provide, such as raw data, SDKs, or APIs [10]. Access to knowledge about how to use these resources, can offer a significant advantage in attracting developers to an ecosystem. Classifications such as Foerderer et al.'s [12] approaches to knowledge boundary resources provide three distinct groups: Broadcasting resources, are standardized and available to every complementor, such as documentation, sample code or information portals. Brokering resources, such as helpdesks or dedicated account managers, introduce human interaction and are therefore available to a subset of complementors. Lastly, bridging resources are personalized and focus on the individual complementor level. These resources focus on one-to-one assistance or coaching.

It remains mostly unclear how GenAI affects platform ecosystems by aiding in the creation of complements, either by offering direct information on how complements are created or by scaffolding or completely creating them.

In recent years, the role of artificial intelligence (AI) in platforms has attracted increasing attention from researchers. For example, some studies have focused on how AI affects data network effects, this is the increased value delivered when a platform learns more about its users by collecting data about them [16, 17]. Other research examines whether the AI maturity of organizations, such as banks, impacts their platform strategy [18]. However, the content-creating perspective that GenAI offers in affecting indirect network effects remains understudied.

In summary, we argue that the understanding of GenAI in the context of complement creation for digital innovation ecosystems is limited or even non-existent. While GenAI has demonstrated benefits in content creation that extend into software development by enhancing developer productivity, this hints at untapped potential for both theoretical and practical advancements. To address this gap, we explore how developers are using GenAI to interact with the boundaries of platforms.

3 Methodology

To understand the real-world application of new technologies, conducting interviews with informants who have firsthand exposure to these technologies is a valid approach for gaining insights into their practical use [19]. We conducted semi-structured interviews to investigate how developers utilize GenAI for platform complement creation. This approach aims to provide a comprehensive understanding of how coding support systems are perceived and utilized by software engineers, as well as the potential benefits that arise from their application.

3.1 Data Collection

To gain insights into the use of GenAI for complement creation we interviewed twelve software developers who engage daily with third-party systems across various companies. Our data was collected via semi-structured interviews that allowed for a flexible, topic-oriented process. Specific questions were designed to explore scenarios where the developers had to interact with third-party systems, for instance, through APIs or software libraries, and where they designed their own boundary resources to open their systems. Our data was collected from a diverse group of software engineers, including machine learning experts, consultants, and developers working within corporate structures. The questions were refined iteratively as we conducted each interview, incorporating new insights to deepen our understanding of the subject.

We encouraged participants to share their experience on their use of GenAI, aiming to capture both the realized and unrealized potentials of these technologies. This method provided a nuanced understanding of developers' openness to and experiences with AI-assisted coding tools.

The participating developers worked in diverse industry contexts, ranging from machine learning experts in advisory roles, software engineers in retail-focused scale-up companies, to internal AI consultants in large multinational corporations. Details of the informants can be found in Table 1.

Interviews were conducted in either German or English, depending on the interviewee's preference. All interviews were subsequently transcribed, and German transcripts were translated into English. A total of twelve interviews were completed, with an average duration of 40:41 min per interview.

Table 1. Summary of interviews.

Pseudonym	Affiliation	GenAI used	Duration (hh:min:sec)	Language
Internal AI Consultant 1	• Multinational conglomerate	Self-hosted ChatGPT	00:42:15	German
Machine Learning Expert 1	• Consulting experience in Silicon Valley and Germany	GenAI in general	00:40:32	German
Tech Lead 1	• Multinational manufacturer of luxury vehicles 1	GitHub Copilot	00:38:49	English
Tech Lead 2	• Retail company of self-manufactured products	GitHub Copilot	00:52:30	English
Tech Lead 3	• Multinational retail and e-commerce company	GitHub Copilot	00:49:41	German
Software Engineer 1	• Multinational retailer	ChatGPT, Self-hosted ChatGPT	00:27:15	English
Software Engineer 2	• Multinational consulting company	ChatGPT, GitHub Copilot	00:35:19	German
Platform Engineer 1	• Energy company	ChatGPT, GitHub Copilot, Proprietary GenAI of platform owner	00:36:57	English
Platform Engineer 2	• Multinational fashion retailer 1	ChatGPT, GitHub Copilot, Self-hosted ChatGPT	00:45:58	English

(*continued*)

Table 1. (*continued*)

Pseudonym	Affiliation	GenAI used	Duration (hh:min:sec)	Language
Platform Engineer 3	• Multinational • consulting company • Retail company of self-manufactured products • Decentralized energy solution provider	ChatGPT, GitHub Copilot, Self-hosted ChatGPT	00:46:25	English
App Developer 1	• Multinational manufacturer of luxury • vehicles 2 • Premium global chauffeur service • Multinational retail and e-commerce company	ChatGPT, Self-hosted ChatGPT	00:42:34	English
Machine Learning Engineer 1	• Multinational fashion retailer 2	ChaGPT, Github Copilot	00:29:54	English
12			08:08:09	

3.2 Data Analysis

To extract patterns, concepts, and interconnected themes from our interview data, we employed the inductive methodology from [20]. This approach facilitated a systematic and rigorous analysis, ensuring that the emerging concepts were grounded in the participants' narratives.

We read the interviews and marked interesting segments. After the first round of reading and marking segments was concluded, a second round of re-reading was conducted to refine our selections and capture insights that may not have been fully developed or recognized during the initial reading. This iterative process allowed for a richer and more nuanced understanding of the data. All identified segments were then organized into preliminary conceptual groups, representing drafts of second-order concepts. Within each conceptual group, we developed first-order concepts by arranging similar appearing interview segments next to each other and naming the concept in an in vivo manner, using the interviewees' own language to maintain the authenticity of their voices. Strong and illustrative quotes were highlighted to be used as direct quotes in the findings section.

The first-order codes were then re-arranged inside the second-order clusters to ensure a logical and meaningful organization of the data. The clustering refinement step was

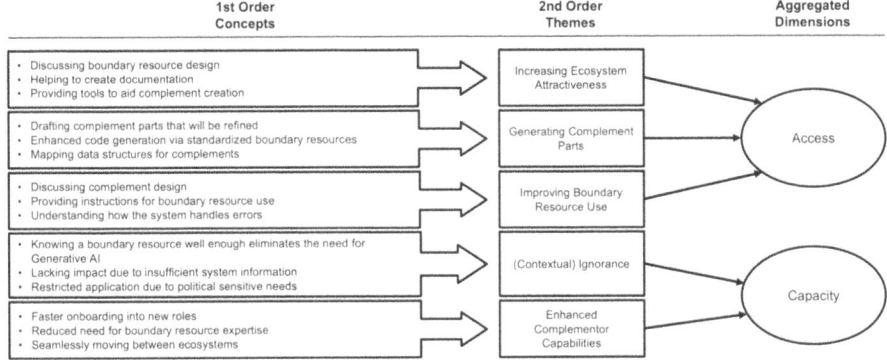

Fig. 2. Data structure.

followed by reformulating the second-order codes for an improved representation of the underlying first order concepts. The resulting data structure is shown in Fig. 2.

4   Findings

We identified 15 first-order concepts that we aggregated into five second-order themes. These were further summarized into two aggregated dimensions.

At an abstract level, developers use GenAI in platform ecosystems in two ways. First, it improves the access to platforms. From the complementor perspective, where GenAI is applied to generate parts of complements or to improve the interaction with boundary resources. Developers who are in the role of the platform owner use GenAI for increasing the ecosystem attractiveness by improving the access to their platform. Second, developers' active decision to use GenAI is use case dependent and based on the subjective judgement on whether results are helpful in the applied setting. GenAI in platform complement development therefore leads to potentially increased capacities that can but do not have to be activated.

4.1   Increasing Ecosystem Attractiveness

Software practitioners described various ways in which GenAI enhanced platform ecosystems through improved boundary resources and development tools. For instance, interviewees reported that they use GenAI to optimize API design. They found it valuable to feed API specifications to the AI and engage in discussions about design choices. As one software engineer explained,

> "[…] it is super comfortable to just like feed the API definition, the API spec to ChatGPT and use ChatGPT to, well, discuss the API design." (Software Engineer 1).

Software practitioners felt that through prompting, GenAI could provide helpful feedback on API endpoint design and implementation approaches, ultimately leading to more optimized API designs. The capability of GenAI to make sense of textual feedback provided by API users could be leveraged to automate the creation of suggestions for API improvements based on actual user feedback.

Further, GenAI was widely used to automate the creation of knowledge boundary resources such as documentation. One app developer described their approach:

> "[…] I give him an example, 'Hey, this is how we write our doc here. Please write it for this function.'" (App Developer 1).

Interviewees considered documentation a repetitive task that GenAI could efficiently support. They reported increased documentation speed, as the AI could often produce better readable English than the software engineers themselves. Practitioners also utilized GenAI for creating comprehensive documentation based on existing documentation and code samples. Some described a workflow where they would sketch out documentation structures using text blocks and bullet points, then have the AI expand these into complete documentation.

Also, software engineers encountered various AI support systems integrated into the platforms they used regularly. For example, AWS offered Log Insights with AI capabilities to improve queries, while Vercel introduced v0, a GenAI tool for creating Next.js components or even entire applications. However, not all AI support provided value from the developers' perspective. For instance, one developer found AWS Log Insights unhelpful for complex queries, while noting that AI assistance wasn't necessary for simpler queries. A machine learning expert suggested that platforms could enhance their accessibility through GenAI without developing entirely new models from scratch:

> "In my experience, at least if you have access to the proprietary systems and perhaps choose something like a retrieval augmented generation access, perhaps even hierarchically structured, so that you can somehow pull in code snippets as they are needed, I think you can gain a lot of ground." (Machine Learning Expert 1).

4.2 Generating Complement Parts

Software practitioners described how they used GenAI to create parts of platform complements. They reported drafting complement parts that would later be refined. Prompts to the GenAI that carried standardized properties led to functional complement skeletons, also called software scaffolds, in Android app development. These parts were not fully functional and had to be enhanced. The standardized prompts did not necessarily have to be in the language or standard the GenAI should create the complement in. For example, one app developer fed the GenAI an old XML standard for the creation of Android user interfaces, from which the GenAI generated code in the newer Jetpack Compose format.

Complement developers described how they benefitted from existing code, written by their team colleagues, that helped their orientation. The code base provided examples and best practices to them. For example, one developer described having trouble interacting with Firebase, a platform from Google that provides a set of ready-made functionalities for app developers. New projects did not offer the possibilities for developers to look at other parts of the code to learn how an API or an SDK works. The developer described productivity increases due to being able to ask ChatGPT for prototyping these functionalities in an empty project. However, some interview candidates emphasized the need to be specific in prompting. The less prompts were described, the higher the possibility for prompts to generate nonsense. The interviews furthermore showed clear indications that standardization could increase the output quality.

The interviews revealed enhanced code generation via standardized boundary resources. One platform engineer explained:

> "[…] given this OpenAPI YAML file, ChatGPT is able to tell you, hey, those are the methods that you need to implement. And then after we have finished implementing one method, which suggests to you, this is the next method you can put in the file, right? So it's able already to generate code on its own based on a specification." (Platform Engineer 3).

As seen in the app developer example with XML and Jetpack Compose, further interview data showed a quality increase when boundary resources were standardized. Complementors also used API specifications, such as Swagger (OpenAPI), for prompting ChatGPT to find out about the capabilities of an API. Obviously, these files could also be consumed by any complementor without using an AI. However, the GenAI now allowed any developer to ask targeted questions, so they arrived earlier at the results.

Next to specification files, complementors also used API responses in JSON format as GenAI input. Based on the standardized specifications or output formats, GenAI helped providing information about the functionalities that needed to be implemented to talk with an API and use its outputs. Based on the first implementation by the complementor, the AI then was able to prototype further implementations. In scenarios where two systems should be integrated so they could communicate with each other, standardization became even more crucial:

> "[…] two systems, where it is mainly about data mapping, that you have suitable data structures, wonderful task for [applying an LLM], because input and output are known and not much needs to be done in between." (Software Engineer 2).

One developer remembered an old case about converting an API from the gRPC protocol to REST where the application of ChatGPT would have been the perfect use case due to its text transformer nature. However, it was crucial that both data structures operated on similar underlying technical possibilities. An app developer described a case where a component was updated from an old into a new standard. However, the new standard did not support certain functionalities, therefore breaking the whole possibility of automating the update.

4.3 Improving Boundary Resource Use

GenAI emerged as a powerful companion for complement developers seeking to better understand and interact with boundary resources. Beyond merely generating code, GenAI served as an interactive guide through the complexities of platforms, APIs, and development frameworks.

When approaching new technologies, developers turned to GenAI to discuss complement design options. The earlier mentioned app development case leveraged ChatGPT to transition from familiar XML-based UI components to the newer Jetpack Compose framework. As they explained:

> "You can even try to copy a cool XML file, like the old way to build this UI and say, hey, I want this in Compose. How would you do that? And that works to a certain degree, I would say, but we have a lot of edge cases and they're quite complex things." (App Developer 1).

This conversational approach helped the developer navigate unfamiliar territory, though it was not perfect for handling every scenario, such as edge cases. Notably, the app developer did not only use GenAI to generate code but to first learn about the new way of creating user interfaces. A pattern seen in many interviews.

Developers frequently sought GenAI assistance when traditional documentation fell short. A Tech Lead described switching to GenAI when API documentation was missing, prompting discussions about implementation approaches in Golang. Similarly, another practitioner working with the AWS cloud development kit (CDK) found value in contextualizing their queries within the AWS environment. When asking about AWS SQS, the GenAI not only explained the service but suggested implementation strategies specific to CDK.

The fragmentation of documentation across multiple versions created particular frustrations that GenAI helped resolve. As one Tech Lead shared:

> "[…] you know, you ended up accidentally on your documentation for an older version and it doesn't make any sense or so on. And then I feel like Copilot is usually… Sometimes not far from always, but pretty good at explaining to me how I need to do things." (Tech Lead 1).

In these scenarios, GenAI essentially functioned as a knowledge boundary resource layered on top of technical boundary resources, synthesizing scattered information into coherent guidance.

Interestingly, not all developers aspired to master the boundary resources they used. Some viewed them merely as means to an end, with no desire to become experts. As one Machine Learning Engineer candidly admitted:

> "[…] I get a much faster understanding of how to use the new query language. And I don't really need to learn it. I just need to be able to put the pieces together without actually knowing it." (Machine Learning Engineer 1).

For these practitioners, GenAI provided just enough understanding to accomplish their goals without requiring deep domain expertise.

Error messages, often cryptic and frustrating, represented another area where GenAI proved invaluable. Tools like GitHub Copilot, with their awareness of the programming context through open files in the IDE, helped developers decipher complex error states. Those without integrated tools found themselves copying error messages into standalone GenAI interfaces to gain insights into their problems.

Despite these benefits, developers remained cautious about relying on GenAI for closed systems with poor documentation. The models' potential gaps in knowledge about proprietary systems created legitimate concerns about their reliability in these contexts, an issue that we will focus on as a key limitation in the "Contextual Ignorance" theme of the findings.

4.4   (Contextual) Ignorance

The effectiveness of GenAI in complementor development demonstrated clear limitations that manifested through what can be termed "Contextual Ignorance." This phenomenon appeared in three distinct findings across the interview data, each representing different scenarios where GenAI's utility diminished significantly.

The first finding emerged when developers possessed deep expertise with particular boundary resources, rendering GenAI assistance superfluous. A senior tech lead explicitly mentioned forgoing systems like GitHub Copilot when working with the GitHub API due to their extensive familiarity with it. This approach, while efficient in the short term, potentially limits future adaptability, particularly when APIs evolve or receive updates that might introduce unfamiliar elements that GenAI could help navigate.

The second finding revealed GenAI's limitations in politically sensitive organizational contexts. One interview participant deliberately avoided using GenAI for documentation that needed to address delicate inter-team dynamics, particularly where performance issues of another team required tactful articulation. The tech lead expressed skepticism about the AI's capacity for such nuanced communication:

> "I would have to prompt it so much with all the context that it would be quicker to just write it." (Tech Lead 1).

This highlights an important boundary where human judgment about organizational politics and interpersonal sensitivities supersedes the efficiency gains of automated content generation.

The third finding, perhaps the most technologically significant, concerned GenAI's limited effectiveness when dealing with proprietary or poorly documented systems. Developers reported substantially diminished utility when working with less popular programming frameworks or platforms with insufficient public documentation. Specific platforms like CommerceTools or Microsoft's GraphAPI represented particularly challenging domains where GenAI offered little practical assistance. As one platform engineer observed:

> "[…] one thing like I have also been complaining a bit about is that ChatGPT does not have good answers for the GraphAPI. And the thing is, the GraphAPI is badly documented. So, I am assuming the GPT does not also know so much about the GraphAPI. And that's why it's not answering my question." (Platform Engineer 3).

This observation illuminates a fundamental constraint of current GenAI systems: their capabilities remain bounded by the information available in their training data. When platforms operate in closed ecosystems with minimal public documentation and few open-source complements, the AI lacks the foundational knowledge necessary to provide meaningful assistance. This limitation creates an interesting question for proprietary platforms in scenarios where developer assistance might be most valuable.

4.5 Enhanced Complementor Capabilities

Adding GenAI into the development environment for complementors introduced new affordances to platform ecosystem development. First, complementors needed less expertise with boundary resources in order to build applications that leveraged platform functionalities. Second, this reflected in faster onboardings into new roles. Third, needing less expertise with boundary resources and having faster onboardings into platform ecosystems resulted in the ability to switch seamlessly between ecosystems.

The interviews revealed a reduced need for boundary resource expertise among complementors using GenAI. Similar to the previously mentioned example of the machine learning engineer who did not want to learn a boundary resource but just wanted to use its output, other interview candidates addressed their reduced need for learning boundary resources to get their work done. In the case of interacting with programming languages, a tech lead described the necessity of switching between multiple programming languages daily to interact with their teams:

> "It's not strange that I'm in three, four different languages in the same day. So just helping with a lot of those things that otherwise, maybe if you sit in a pretty small tech stack, you know, you have a lot of autopilot. I don't have that because our stack is so big and so different. I let kind of Copilot be that autopilot for me when it comes to those things.' (Tech Lead 1).

Other candidates showed similar patterns in the ecosystems they faced in their daily work, such as reduced need for learning Terraform to orchestrate cloud platform or on-premises resources.

The data also demonstrated faster onboarding into new roles when using GenAI. One platform engineer described the struggle of keeping up with colleagues who were advancing with complex solutions. Discussing these solutions with GenAI helped maintain pace with developments. Similarly, a seasoned Android app developer discussed their limited experience in iOS and the resulting ability to manage a complete mobile team building applications for both platforms because of GenAI:

> "[…] I have very limited iOS knowledge. But with the help of LLMs, I could solve almost any task, I would say." (App Developer 1).

These capabilities culminated in the affordance of operating and creating complements in several ecosystems simultaneously. One platform engineer described their experience asking GenAI about differences between two cloud platform services:

> "[…] the concept in AWS, you want a S3 Bucket, you want to do something with that, and some basic functionality. Then it's only actually a command, for example, to get all the data, which is in this S3 Bucket, and then you use the same functionality of Google [GCP], but you don't know the syntax, and you know

what you want to do, you can tell that, and then you can easily switch." (Platform Engineer 1).

This behavior was reflected by other interview candidates across different specializations. One candidate explained that using GenAI for tasks outside their own expertise felt like extending their overall abilities to a level that might not reflect the depth of their core expertise but allowed them to accomplish tasks that were previously beyond reach.

5 Discussion

This study set out to understand how generative AI influences the creation of software complements in digital platform ecosystems. In summary, our findings suggest that GenAI fundamentally reshapes complement creation by enhancing platform access and unlocking new capacity for both platform owners and complementors. In direct answer to our research question, GenAI lowers knowledge barriers and increases development efficiency in complement creation, while also introducing strategic considerations regarding platform openness and the design of boundary resources.

5.1 GenAI's Dual Impact on Platform Owners and Complementors

The use of GenAI is evident on both, the platform owner and complementor sides of the platform ecosystem, albeit in different ways. The interviewed developers on the platform owner side leverage GenAI to improve the usability and design of their boundary resources, thereby aiming at increasing the platform's attractiveness to other developers. For example, interviewees described using GenAI to refine API designs by feeding specifications to an AI and iterating on its feedback. This practice effectively turns GenAI into a collaborator in boundary resource design, enabling platform teams to get instantaneous suggestions for improvements that traditionally might emerge only from lengthy internal discussions or developer feedback cycles. As one software engineer noted, "it is super comfortable to just feed the API spec to ChatGPT and use it to discuss the API design," highlighting how GenAI serves as a knowledge partner in technical design decisions. In turn, this can accelerate the delivery of well-designed boundary resources and improve developers' access to platform functionality. Platform owners also reported semi-automating the creation of knowledge boundary resources like documentation through GenAI. Given that developers often find writing documentation onerous, do not have enough time to focus on it or do not possess the required expertise [21], delegating first drafts to GenAI can lead to faster documentation production and, in some cases, more polished language than the engineers might have achieved on their own. This points to GenAI's role as a scaffolding tool. It generates initial content that developers can then refine, echoing the productivity gains observed in other domains [9]. By semi-automating documentation and potentially other knowledge boundary resources, platform owners can streamline complementor onboarding, helping newcomers understand how to build on the platform more quickly. No participants indicated having formal review processes for AI-generated documentation, so its effectiveness still ultimately depends on expert validation and user feedback. Without careful curation, even an AI-generated guide may fail to fulfill its purpose, unless future GenAI systems learn what constitutes "good" documentation on their own.

Complementors, on the other hand, primarily use GenAI as an on-demand development assistant to more efficiently access and utilize platform resources. They described employing GenAI to generate snippets of code or suggest how to work with unfamiliar APIs or data objects. In essence, GenAI functions as a dynamic extension of the platform's knowledge resources, bridging gaps in a developer's expertise. Notably, complementors reported that GenAI allowed them to produce working code for platforms and programming language environments in which they had limited prior experience. This indicates a profound shift in required expertise: a developer can prompt the AI to "translate" their intent into platform-specific implementation, relying less on longer manual study of documentation. The result is faster problem-solving and a lower barrier to entry for creating viable complements. These findings align with early evidence that GenAI-based coding assistants improve development speed without necessarily harming quality [6, 9, 22, 23]. Importantly, our study adds that developers do not always use GenAI to learn new systems, but rather to get things done quickly. This observation echoes Prather et al. [15] or Krancher et al. [23], who note that GenAI can help engineers to work in an unfamiliar environment and learn systems faster; our interviewees likewise often treated GenAI as a means to an end, bypassing deep learning in favor of immediate productivity. Consequently, a complementor with only basic knowledge of one platform can potentially leverage GenAI to jumpstart work on another platform, effectively reducing the need for extensive boundary resource expertise.

5.2 New Affordances and Changing Dynamics

The introduction of GenAI in complement development has created qualitatively new affordances in the platform ecosystem. One key affordance is content scaffolding for software code. GenAI can generate functional code segments which developers then integrate and tweak. This is analogous to the text-block scaffolding that improved writers' productivity [9], now manifesting in software engineering. The decision support nature of GenAI means that developers can offload routine or boilerplate coding tasks to the AI and focus more on higher-level design and problem-solving. Overlapping with this is GenAI's potential role as a knowledge boundary resource in itself. Our findings suggest that GenAI effectively wraps around existing technical and knowledge resources to make them more accessible. In other words, GenAI serves as a conversational layer over APIs, SDKs, documentation, and further boundary resources, a layer that can interpret natural-language questions and produce relevant guidance or code using those underlying resources. This poses a shift in knowledge boundary resources, potentially merging broadcasting, brokering, and bridging resources [12] as the GenAI becomes sample code assistant, helpdesk, and coach in one. GenAI aggregates and contextualizes platform knowledge that might otherwise be too fragmented or complex for complementors to quickly digest. By acting as a universal translator and tutor, GenAI reduces the cognitive distance between a developer's intent and the specific implementations required on a given platform. An implication is that complementors may no longer need to master every detail of a platform's toolkit, they can rely on AI to fill in the details on demand. This affordance lowers entry barriers for less experienced developers or those moving between ecosystems, potentially expanding the pool of complementors. It also means that highly specialized knowledge of one platform becomes less of an advantage if GenAI can intermediate. As a result, we observed signs of faster onboarding: interviewees recounted how they could begin building on a new platform much more rapidly than in the past, since GenAI would handle the translation of concepts from platforms they knew to the one they were learning. For instance, a mobile app developer skilled in Android could ask GenAI how to implement a similar feature for iOS and receive usable starter code or pointers, an undertaking that previously might require hours of studying Apple's documentation. This ease of cross-platform translation indicates a broadening of complementor capabilities and hints at a workforce shift where developers are more deployable across platforms than before.

A related conclusion is that multihoming becomes more feasible. Multihoming refers to complementors creating and maintaining offerings on multiple platform ecosystems in parallel [24, 25]. Our findings suggest that GenAI can soften the barriers by serving as a consistent supporter across different environments. Indeed, several participants had experience using GenAI-assisted workflows for more than one cloud provider or moving their applications between frameworks, describing the process as more seamless compared to traditional manual re-learning. By reducing the need for platform-specific expertise, GenAI lowers switching costs and encourages complementors to navigate multiple ecosystems simultaneously. This could intensify competition between platform owners over developer attention and loyalty. If many platform services converge in features, a phenomenon sometimes driven by "platform pacing," where platforms imitate each other's features to retain developers [26], GenAI may further homogenize the development experience by abstracting away differences. An open question is whether the quality of complements will remain high in such GenAI-enabled multihoming scenarios. Platform owners may need to monitor the quality and perhaps invest in tools or guidelines to ensure that AI-assisted multihoming developers still produce high-quality, secure, and innovative complements on their platform.

GenAI's effectiveness, however, is not uniform across all contexts, and this is where open vs. proprietary ecosystem differences may become important. Interviewees suggested that GenAI tools like ChatGPT or Copilot were most helpful when ample public knowledge about a platform was available (e.g. well-documented APIs or widely discussed development frameworks). In such cases, the AI model likely had been trained on those public resources or could be supplied with them, acting almost like an encyclopedic "telephone book" of platform information, meaning the GenAI was able to provide information about several platforms at once. In contrast, for more closed platforms or proprietary APIs, the AI sometimes struggled, providing either generic advice or incorrect code, most probably due to gaps in its training data. This underscores a strategic consideration: platform owners with closed ecosystems face a trade-off. They could develop proprietary AI support systems fine-tuned on their internal knowledge to assist complementors, as seen in the attempts like AWS's AI log support or Vercel's platform-specific GenAI tools but doing so might require significant investment and may still fall short of the breadth of knowledge a general AI, such as ChatGPT or Claude, can draw on. Alternatively, they could embrace openness by making more of their documentation, code examples, and usage knowledge public, so that general-purpose GenAI models will naturally become more effective assistants for their platform. This implies GenAI may indirectly pressure platform owners toward greater openness of knowledge boundary resources, since being absent from widely used AI training data could become a disadvantage. If a proprietary platform's intricacies are invisible to GenAI, developers may perceive building on that platform as harder, tilting their preferences toward more AI-friendly ecosystems. In summary, GenAI currently acts as an amplifier of what is available: it excels when fed rich data about a platform, but its utility diminishes behind walled gardens. This dynamic could influence future platform strategies regarding ecosystem openness, documentation practices, and investment in AI toolkits.

5.3 Implications for Theory and Practice

Our findings carry several implications for information systems theory on platforms, boundary resources, and complementor innovation. First, we contribute to platform ecosystem literature by illuminating how GenAI can affect indirect network effects and ecosystem evolution. Classic platform theory holds that more and qualitative stronger complements strengthen a platform's value for its users [1, 3]. GenAI promises to accelerate complement creation by lowering development effort and expertise requirements for complementors, potentially leading to an increase in the quantity and diversity of complements available, if supported right. In other words, the positive indirect network effects, where more complements attract more users and vice versa, could be magnified as GenAI empowers a larger pool of developers, including those who might not have participated before. At the same time, our study provides potential concern that if GenAI is not managed properly, the distribution of complement quality and novelty might shift. If GenAI helps every developer solve common problems in similar ways, complements across platforms could become more homogeneous, challenging platforms to find new ways to differentiate their ecosystem's offerings. This raises interesting questions aligned with platform competition research [25, 26]: when multihoming becomes easy and complements converge, platform owners may need to devise new control points or incentives to retain exclusive complements. Our evidence of AI-enabled multihoming thus adds a new layer to theories of platform envelopment and competitive dynamics.

Second, our work extends the concept of boundary resources [10–12] by highlighting GenAI as a novel intermediary in the platform-complementor interface. Boundary resources are the tools and regulations through which platform owners facilitate and control third-party innovation, including APIs, SDKs, and documentation. The advent of GenAI suggests that a new type of boundary resource is emerging: AI-based knowledge services that help translate between the platform's formal offerings and the complementor goals. Notably, these AI services can be provided by the platform, as an intentional resource, or leveraged independently by developers, as an informal aid drawing on existing resources. Our findings indicate that when developers use general GenAI tools to interpret or generate code for a platform, those tools are effectively functioning as an extension of the platform's knowledge resources. Extending the insights of Foerderer et al.[12], one can view GenAI as a new boundary resource itself lying on top of other resources that creates a "wrapper" that synthesizes APIs, SDKs, or technical documentation, into a conversational and code generating form.

Third, our study contributes to understanding complementor capabilities and the innovation process on digital platforms. The affordances introduced by GenAI (fast prototyping, code translation, automated documentation) allow complementors to focus more on what to create rather than how to implement it technically. Our participants still cared about how to create a complement, but the "how" was, in some cases, rapidly simplified by AI serving as a decision-support and execution aid. In practical terms, platform owners should anticipate a more diverse complementor base and consider how to support it. For example, if more novice developers enter their ecosystem via GenAI help, platforms may need to adjust their developer support strategies: perhaps providing integrated AI assistants, tailoring sandbox environments for testing AI-generated code, or implementing stricter app review processes to catch AI-introduced errors. This could also mean lowering the entry barriers further to enable programmers with little or no programming experience through low-code or no-code solutions. Conversely, experienced developers might leverage GenAI to exponentially increase their output (e.g., a small team producing as many features as a large team could before), which could raise the competitive bar for complements in certain markets. For practitioners, our study highlights both the affordances and the challenges introduced by GenAI in platform ecosystems. Platform owners can harness GenAI to lower entry barriers, hoping to attract more complementors and stimulate innovation. For instance, investing in AI-enhanced documentation, code examples, or even in an official platform-specific AI assistant could significantly improve the developer experience. Some have already begun this, as noted with early platform-provided AI tools in our interviews, but ensuring that these actually deliver value is key. For complementors, the practical implication is to see GenAI as a powerful new tool in the development arsenal. Those who learn to effectively incorporate AI into their development workflow can potentially reduce development time and expand into new platforms. However, complementors must also remain cautious about the outputs of GenAI. As our interviews revealed, AI-generated code is not guaranteed to be optimal or even correct, especially in edge-case scenarios or with proprietary technology. Thus, complementors should treat GenAI as an assistant but still apply their own expertise to review and refine the results. Organizations may respond by adopting private GenAI instances or fine-tuned models to get the best of AI-powered development with proprietary knowledge included, but without exposing that knowledge publicly.

Finally, we observe a distinct implication: if generative AI's influence rises further, it could shift the primary role of complementors from hands-on coding to the governance and management of codebases. Conceptually, developers devote less effort to writing code line-by-line and more to orchestrating, curating, and supervising AI-generated outputs, ensuring that software aligns with design standards and business objectives. In practice, platform owners may need to revisit their governance strategies and provide new resources to help complementors manage AI-generated components, so that complement quality and compliance with platform standards are maintained. This shift also demands that AI tool designers integrate features facilitating effective oversight, such as robust error-checking, version control, and explainable code suggestions, to help developers efficiently govern AI-generated code moving forward.

5.4 Limitations and Future Research

While this study provides early insights into GenAI's impact on complement creation, it has several limitations that also suggest directions for future research. First, our qualitative evidence is based on a limited set of interviews, which, although rich in detail, cannot capture the full diversity of platform types and development scenarios. The participants spanned various roles, but future work should include a stronger theoretical sampling, possibly including developers from different industry domains and platform backgrounds. Other platform types, such as gaming platforms, Internet-of-Things ecosystems, or enterprise software marketplaces, were not explicitly covered. GenAI's utility may vary across these contexts; for example, building a hardware-integrated IoT solution might present different challenges for GenAI than building a pure software app. We encourage research that examines GenAI-assisted development in specific platform contexts to identify any domain-specific insights. Comparative studies could reveal if certain platform characteristics, such as proprietary or open platforms, impact the GenAI supported complement creation.

Second, the rapidly evolving nature of GenAI means our study captures a moving target. The capabilities of models available at the time of research, such as GPT-4o and contemporary coding assistants, will likely be surpassed by future iterations. Future research should continuously update these findings as technology progresses. What holds true today might change with more advanced models or specialized training. For instance, our interviewees unanimously treated GenAI as a tool for partial tasks rather than end-to-end development. None reported letting the AI entirely build a deployable complement from scratch. This could be a limitation of current GenAI in handling the complexity and context integration required for full software products. However, as GenAI models improve or as more platform-specific training data becomes available, the prospect of fully automated complement generation may inch closer. Recent work by Mayer et al. [27] already hints at near-automation of content-based complements in auto-generating content for a publishing platform. Testing whether and when similar possibilities become feasible for the creation of software complements, and in what types of platforms, is a compelling future research avenue.

Another limitation relates to GenAI's knowledge boundaries. Interview candidates addressed that GenAI's help was less effective for some platforms, probably because of their proprietary nature, less available documentation or limited amount of open-source complements. Our study did not deeply examine any single proprietary platform in isolation. It remains to be seen how GenAI can be leveraged in closed contexts. Will platform firms invest in their own fine-tuned AI agents, and will developers adopt them? One future research direction is to study cases where a platform provider introduces a custom AI assistant trained on its private documentation and code and compare developer uptake and performance with those using general-purpose AI on open platforms. This could inform whether platform-specific AI agents can compete with or outperform the broad knowledge of public models. Similarly, the question of GenAI's training data completeness is crucial. Keeping AI models up to date with the latest APIs and best practices could become a challenge.

Finally, our findings on multihoming warrant further investigation. We provide initial evidence that GenAI lowers the effort to participate in multiple ecosystems, which could upset the balance of power in platform markets. Yet, our study did not quantitatively measure switching costs or multihoming frequency; it only captured developers' perceptions and anecdotes. Future studies could use surveys or experiments to measure how much faster or easier developers can accomplish a task on a new platform with GenAI assistance versus without it. Such research would offer more concrete evidence of the reduction in onboarding time or required expertise. Moreover, the long-term strategic behavior of complementors in response to GenAI – for example, will more companies decide to multihome their complements across platforms because AI makes it feasible – and how will platform owners respond – is an open question.

We encourage other researchers to build on these initial findings with targeted studies that can test the generalizability and impact of GenAI across various platform settings.

5.5 Conclusion

In conclusion, generative AI is emerging as a transformative force in digital platform ecosystems, reshaping how software complements are created and who can create them. It enhances platform development by reducing knowledge barriers and providing intelligent assistance in coding and design, thereby empowering complementors to innovate faster and with less required expertise. Platform owners can leverage GenAI to improve the accessibility and attractiveness of their ecosystems, but they must also navigate new challenges around openness, quality control, and competitive differentiation. Our study offers an early, in-depth look at these dynamics, demonstrating that GenAI brings new affordances, such as cross-platform development or automated knowledge support, that both complement and extend existing platform theories. At the same time, it raises important questions about expertise, governance, and strategy that call for further inquiry. Ultimately, understanding GenAI's role in complement creation is crucial for both scholars and practitioners, as it will shape the future of innovation and competition in platform-based environments. By illuminating these initial patterns and implications, we hope to lay the groundwork for more research and informed practice at the intersection of generative AI and digital platforms.

References

1. Gawer, A.: Digital platforms' boundaries: The interplay of firm scope, platform sides, and digital interfaces. Long Range Plan. **54**, 102045 (2021). https://doi.org/10.1016/j.lrp.2020. 102045
2. Mini, T., Widjaja, T.: Tensions in digital platform business models: a literature review. In: Fortieth International Conference on Information Systems. Munich (2019)
3. de Reuver, M., Sørensen, C., Basole, R.C.: The digital platform: a research agenda. J. Inf. Technol. **33**, 124–135 (2018). https://doi.org/10.1057/s41265-016-0033-3
4. Laurent, L.: Coders and analysts Feel AI's breath on their necks (2024). https://www. bloomberg.com/opinion/articles/2024-02-08/layoffs-is-ai-coming-for-white-collar-jobs-cod ers-and-analysts-should-worry
5. Brynjolfsson, E., Li, D., Raymond, L.R.: Generative AI at work (2023). https://www.nber. org/papers/w31161. https://doi.org/10.3386/w31161
6. Peng, S., Kalliamvakou, E., Cihon, P., Demirer, M.: The impact of AI on developer productivity: evidence from GitHub Copilot. arXiv:2302.06590v1 (2023)

7. Bonina, C., Koskinen, K., Eaton, B., Gawer, A.: Digital platforms for development: foundations and research agenda. Inf. Syst. J. **31**, 869–902 (2021). https://doi.org/10.1111/isj.12326

8. Karhu, K., Heiskala, M., Ritala, P., Thomas, L.D.W.: Positive, negative, and amplified network externalities in platform markets. AMP. **38**, amp.2023.0119 (2024). https://doi.org/10.5465/amp.2023.0119

9. Noy, S., Zhang, W.: Experimental evidence on the productivity effects of generative artificial intelligence. Science **381**, 187–192 (2023). https://doi.org/10.1126/science.adh2586

10. Ghazawneh, A., Henfridsson, O.: Balancing platform control and external contribution in third-party development: the boundary resources model: control and contribution in third-party development. Inf. Syst. J. **23**, 173–192 (2013). https://doi.org/10.1111/j.1365-2575.2012.00406.x

11. Bianco, V.D., Myllärniemi, V., Komssi, M., Raatikainen, M.: The role of platform boundary resources in software ecosystems: a case study. In: 2014 IEEE/IFIP Conference on Software Architecture, pp. 11–20. Sydney (2014). https://doi.org/10.1109/WICSA.2014.41

12. Foerderer, J., Kude, T., Schuetz, S.W., Heinzl, A.: Knowledge boundaries in enterprise software platform development: antecedents and consequences for platform governance. Inf. Syst. J. **29**, 119–144 (2019). https://doi.org/10.1111/isj.12186

13. Santos Gabriel, V.: Generative AI: A literature review on business value. In: Thirtieth Americas Conference on Information Systems. Salt Lake City (2024)

14. Susarla, A., Gopal, R., Thatcher, J.B., Sarker, S.: The Janus effect of generative AI: charting the path for responsible conduct of scholarly activities in information systems. Inf. Syst. Res. **34**, 399–408 (2023). https://doi.org/10.1287/isre.2023.ed.v34.n2

15. Prather, J., et al.: "It's weird that it knows what i want": usability and interactions with copilot for novice programmers. ACM Trans. Comput. Hum. Interact. **31**, 4:1–4:31 (2023). https://doi.org/10.1145/3617367

16. Gregory, R.W., Henfridsson, O., Kaganer, E., Kyriakou, H.: The role of artificial intelligence and data network effects for creating user value. AMR. **46**, 534–551 (2021). https://doi.org/10.5465/amr.2019.0178

17. Clough, D.R., Wu, A.: Artificial intelligence, data-driven learning, and the decentralized structure of platform ecosystems. AMR. **47**, 184–189 (2022). https://doi.org/10.5465/amr.2020.0222

18. Schreieck, M., Huang, Y., Kupfer, A., Krcmar, H.: The effect of digital platform strategies on firm value in the banking industry. J. Manag. Inf. Syst. **41**, 394–421 (2024). https://doi.org/10.1080/07421222.2024.2340825

19. O'Leary, D.E.: Gartner's hype cycle and information system research issues. Int. J. Account. Inf. Syst. **9**, 240–252 (2008). https://doi.org/10.1016/j.accinf.2008.09.001

20. Gioia, D.A., Corley, K.G., Hamilton, A.L.: Seeking qualitative rigor in inductive research: notes on the Gioia methodology. Organ. Res. Methods **16**, 15–31 (2013). https://doi.org/10.1177/1094428112452151

21. Uddin, G., Robillard, M.P.: How API Documentation Fails. IEEE Softw. **32**, 68–75 (2015). https://doi.org/10.1109/ms.2014.80

22. Ernst, N.A., Bavota, G.: AI-driven development is here: should you worry? IEEE Softw. **39**, 106–110 (2022). https://doi.org/10.1109/MS.2021.3133805

23. Krancher, O., Sabherwal, R., Oshri, I., Kotlarsky, J.: Digital sourcing: a discussion of agential, semiotic, infrastructural, combinatorial, and economic shifts. J. Inf. Technol. **39**, 262–269 (2024). https://doi.org/10.1177/02683962241260841

24. Koh, T.K., Fichman, M.: Multihoming users' preferences for two-sided exchange networks. MIS Q. **38**, 977–996 (2014)

25. Cennamo, C., Ozalp, H., Kretschmer, T.: Platform architecture and quality trade-offs of multihoming complements. Inf. Syst. Res. **29**, 461–478 (2018). https://doi.org/10.1287/isre.2018.0779

26. Karhu, K., Ritala, P.: Slicing the cake without baking it: opportunistic platform entry strategies in digital markets. Long Range Plan. **54**, 101988 (2021). https://doi.org/10.1016/j.lrp.2020.101988

27. Mayer, A.S., Kostis, A., Strich, F., Holmström, J.: Shifting dynamics: how generative AI as a boundary resource reshapes digital platform governance. J. Manage. Inf. Syst. (2025). https://doi.org/10.1080/07421222.2025.2487312

Challenges in Adoption and Scaling of AI: A Case Study at a High-Tech Firm and Research Roadmap

Damian Tamburri[1], Marco Tonnarelli[1], and Jos van Hillegersberg[1,2(✉)]

[1] JADS.nl, TU/Eindhoven and Tilburg University, Den Bosch, The Netherlands
d.a.tamburri@tue.nl, j.vanhillegersberg@jads.nl
[2] University of Twente, Enschede, The Netherlands
http://www.jads.nl

Abstract. The rapid evolution of AI has created a wealth of possibilities for businesses, e.g. to enhance their operations, improve their innovativeness and advance customer interaction. Technology departments are under pressure to adopt AI in their enterprise architecture. The immense power and readily available services offered by big tech platforms seems make design, implementation and operation of AI applications, including machine learning and deep learning, seamless. The paradigm of Machine Learning Operations (MLOps) emerged to develop ML products and rapidly bring them into production at industrial scale. It has been found that DevOps teams can contribute to firm competitive advantage by building both business and technology-related capabilities which enable them to sense market opportunities, make fast and targeted decisions and transform their assets in case of changing circumstances. While increasingly popular, MLOps has shown to be difficult. Many ML initiatives fail to provide value, while many ML models never reach production. This study surveys challenges of AI adoption and discusses a framework based approach to facilitate the adoption and scaling of AI in a tech firm. The paper concludes that while a framework based approach does eliviate some adoption challenges, much research remains to be done. Such research challenges are presented and discussed.

Keywords: AI adoption · MLOps · Scalable AI

1 Introduction

The rapid advancement of Artificial Intelligence (AI) has profoundly transformed how businesses operate, innovate, and engage with customers [39]. However, as AI systems, particularly Machine Learning (ML) models, become increasingly integrated into enterprise architectures, organizations face mounting challenges in operationalizing these technologies at scale. The emergence of Machine Learning Operations (MLOps) has offered a structured paradigm for building, deploying, and maintaining ML models within production environments. While MLOps draws inspiration from Development and Operations (DevOps) [31], extending its principles to data-driven applications, the

M. Schreieck et al. (Eds.): DSPE 2025, LNBIP 563, pp. 56–77, 2026.
https://doi.org/10.1007/978-3-032-04512-6_4

complexity of managing AI systems introduces unique technical, organizational, and ethical challenges. For example, even simply staffing such pipelines with quality-aware experts capable of creating synergy between the business function and the MLOps role is hard at best [27].

On the one hand, the promise of MLOps lies in its ability to bring business stakeholders, data scientists, and engineers together to create scalable, efficient solutions that address complex business problems [15]. However, despite its popularity, the adoption of MLOps has proven difficult: over 90% of machine learning models fail to reach production, and many initiatives struggle to deliver tangible value. This high failure rate is largely due to a range of organizational, technical, operational, and business challenges, such as skill gaps, resistance to change, and slow processes create friction, while technical challenges related to data infrastructure, tooling, and standards further complicate implementation. In addition, from a more technical perspective, operational challenges include pipeline inefficiencies and trade-offs in implementation, limiting the scalability and sustainability of MLOps efforts [40].

Beyond these practical barriers, deeper concerns arise around the social, ethical, and technical sustainability of AI-driven software. As AI becomes more pervasive, the need for transparency, fairness, and accountability grows more urgent. For example, businesses must not only ensure that their AI models perform well but also that they align with societal norms, regulatory frameworks, and ethical standards. MLOps systems must provide explainability by design, ensuring that decisions made by AI models are traceable, interpretable, and justifiable and/or legally grounded [40]. Equally important is ensuring fairness, with ML models being free of biases that could lead to discriminatory outcomes, as well as accountability, where responsibility for AI behavior and decisions is properly assigned across the software supply chain.

In this paper, we propose a vision for addressing these multifaceted challenges in MLOps adoption. We outline a research agenda that explores (a) new methods for embedding explainability, fairness, and accountability into MLOps pipelines, (b) reducing technical debt in ML operations, and (c) enhancing human-centric collaboration. Furthermore, we advocate for more sustainable MLOps practices, which not only optimize performance but also minimize environmental impact, ensure long-term scalability, and support responsible AI development.

To support this vision, we present a case study study that demonstrates the use of the RADON tool-chain [9] to address specific MLOps challenges. The case study highlights how RADON enables the automation of data pipelines, improves efficiency, and ensures consistency in scalable machine learning workflows. This practical example serves to validate the feasibility of the proposed methods, offering a tangible pathway for overcoming barriers in MLOps adoption.

The general research approach we address harnesses comparative case studies and user-study research, through which we seek to uncover best practices for overcoming MLOps adoption challenges and accelerating the industrialization of AI stemming from realistic cases and the people and practitioners around them. By addressing these issues, the discipline shall aim to foster more reliable, ethical, and sustainable AI systems that can meet the needs of businesses and society alike.

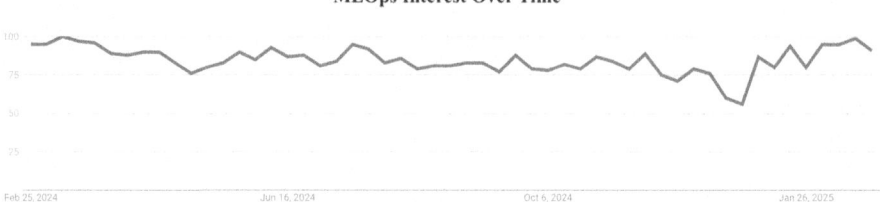

Fig. 1. Google Trends for'MLOps' in the past 12 months.

The rest of this paper is structured as follows. Section 2 addresses related work. Section 3.1 outlines and details a conceptual model of the research context and the challenges we identify therein. Section 4 includes a case study using the RADON toolchain to address these challenges, demonstrating its application and potential impact. In Sect. 5 we present our results by proposing a research road-map and by analyzing the outcome of the case study. In Sect. 6 we discuss our results, and in Sect. 7 we conclude.

2   Related Work

In this section, we provide an overview of research related to this study. In literature, several studies describe MLOps frameworks and challenges, spanning from organizational to technical factors. However, practices and tools to overcome this issues remain fragmented. MLOps remains a relevant topic, as depicted by Fig 1, which highlights the search for MLOps in the past year with Google Trends[1].

MLOps Frameworks and Adoption Challenges.   Several studies have sought to define MLOps as a set of practices for integrating ML models into production environments. Kreuzberger et al. [22] provide a comprehensive overview of MLOps, emphasizing its technical elements, including data management, model training pipelines, and service orchestration. However, these frameworks often fall short when addressing the organizational and human-centric challenges that arise in industrial settings. Research by Kolar Narayanappa et al. [29] reveals that up to 90% of ML models never reach production, citing critical barriers such as skill gaps, organizational resistance, and inefficient processes as major inhibitors of MLOps adoption.

Human and Organizational Factors in MLOps.   Organizational issues such as the lack of skilled human resources and resistance to change have been high-lighted by several works. Mishra et al. [24] emphasize that DevOps teams can provide firms with competitive advantages by aligning business and technological capabilities, but note that similar alignment in MLOps environments is still underdeveloped. The integration of business stakeholders with data scientists and engineers remains a significant hurdle. Numerous studies, including those by Testi et al. [41], underscore the importance of collaboration across teams, recommending new tools and frameworks to foster better communication and coordination. Yet, the human-centric dimension of MLOps remains underexplored,

---

[1] https://trends.google.com/trends/.

leaving room for research into how organizational culture and workflows can evolve to accommodate the growing demands of AI.

Explainability, Fairness, and Accountability in AI. As AI becomes embedded in more aspects of business operations, concerns surrounding the ethical implications of AI have gained attention. Tamburri [40] outlines the risks of AI systems becoming unsustainable from a social and organizational perspective if issues of explainability, fairness, and accountability are not adequately addressed. Furthermore, Widder et al. [43] argue for a "located accountability" approach, recognizing that accountability must be shared across the entire AI supply chain—from model designers to business operators. Research on fairness in AI, such as the work of Barocas et al. [2], investigates the potential for bias in machine learning models and emphasizes the need for fairness by design in AI systems. However, operationalizing these ethical principles within MLOps frameworks remains a largely unexplored area of research.

Sustainability and Technical Debt in MLOps. Another critical aspect of MLOps is ensuring the sustainability of AI systems, both from a technical and environmental perspective. Technical debt, the accumulated cost of managing and evolving complex systems, poses a significant risk to long-term MLOps adoption. Shankar et al. [35] discuss the specific technical debt challenges associated with ML systems, such as pipeline complexity, dependency management, and continuous iteration. The environmental impact of AI has also been studied, with Strubell et al. [38] noting the significant energy consumption of large-scale ML models, calling for more sustainable practices in AI development. However, sustainable MLOps practices that address both technical debt and environmental concerns are still in their infancy.

Tooling. The 2019 study by Sandobalin et al [33] is strictly related to our work as, even if it does not tackle RADON or similar methodologies, it gave us a model to follow to conduct our experiments.

RADON is presented in [10]: the main objectives and early results are presented. Yussupov et al. [44, 45] extend TOSCA specifications to support the modeling and deployment of function orchestrators in a serverless environment, by using two tools that compose the RADON tool-chain, namely Eclipse Winery and xOpera, in combination with BPMN modeling language. In these study is presented the actual tool-chain and approach we tested in our study: it not the full RADON approach, but a subset of it. A similar approach is presented also in another paper [7] by Calcaterra et al. who worked with Yussupov et al. in other studies. BPMN and TOSCA modeling is also enhanced by the same authors in another study [12] where they introduce the Continuous Testing Tool, which is part of RADON IDE and it is based on their previous works.

A methodology and tool-chain similar to RADON is presented by Di Nitto et al. [30], where the SODALITE[2] environment is presented. SODALITE provides a set of tools to address issues related to complex task configuration, deployment and operations, enabling faster development of IaC.

We finally mention other two studies by Sokolowski et al. [36, 37] that, even if do not directly related to case studies around the RADON tool-chain, they investigate the automation of serverless deployments in MLOps teams.

---

[2] https://www.sodalite.eu.

Positioning of This Work. This paper builds on these foundational works, seeking to contribute new insights into the challenges of MLOps adoption, particularly in the areas of explainability, fairness, accountability, and sustainability. By conducting a detailed case study of a global high-tech firm, we aim to bridge the gap between theory and practice, providing actionable strategies for overcoming the complexities of MLOps in industrial environments.

3   Methodology

3.1   MLOps for BI: Theoretical Formulation and Conceptual Landscape

Figure 2 visualizes the complex landscape of MLOps adoption and the dynamic interactions between the different challenge areas. Each part offers potential research directions and practical implications. The framework for understanding the adoption of MLOps in industrial settings begins with the research context [16]. At its core, this context focuses on how enterprises can effectively operationalize machine learning models at scale, navigating through various interrelated challenges. For instance, large tech companies frequently encounter difficulties when managing the deployment of machine learning models across globally dispersed teams, highlighting the importance of overcoming these barriers, e.g., communication [42].

A critical component of this landscape is organizational challenges, which include issues such as the lack of skilled personnel, communication gaps, and resistance to change. These challenges slow down MLOps adoption, as demonstrated when an organization, despite its desire to implement MLOps, finds itself hampered by a shortage of employees skilled in cloud-based machine learning operations. Moreover, collaboration issues between different departments—such as IT and business teams—further complicate matters. For example, disagreements over strategy or implementation details can significantly delay deployment, making it evident that improved interdepartmental communication is crucial [18].

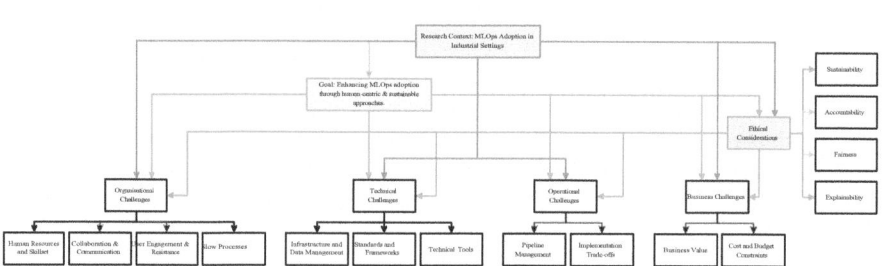

Fig. 2. MLOps challenges landscape.

Beyond organizational hurdles, technical challenges also play a significant role in MLOps adoption. These challenges often revolve around managing infrastructure and data, selecting the right tools, and ensuring compatibility with existing frameworks. For instance, a company might struggle to integrate machine learning models with its legacy IT systems, impeding smooth operations. The absence of unified standards across MLOps tools further exacerbates this issue, leaving teams to contend with compatibility challenges across different machine learning libraries like TensorFlow and PyTorch. Selecting the appropriate tools for managing and deploying machine learning models also becomes a significant hurdle, particularly when balancing proprietary and open-source solutions [40].

Moving from technical to operational challenges, companies often encounter issues related to pipeline management and implementation trade-offs. Efficiently managing the machine learning pipeline—from data collection and model training to deployment—is a significant task. For instance, frequent changes in data input can break existing machine learning pipelines, requiring constant manual intervention, which in turn delays production. Moreover, companies are often faced with trade-offs between model accuracy and deployment speed. A typical scenario might involve an organization opting for a less accurate model simply because it can be deployed faster, reflecting a common operational trade-off in MLOps environments [19].

On the business side, business challenges include demonstrating the value of MLOps investments and managing costs. Despite the promise of AI, many companies struggle to justify the high costs of maintaining and scaling MLOps infrastructure. For example, a business may invest heavily in cloud infrastructure to support model training, only to face budget cuts when the return on investment (ROI) isn't immediately clear. In such cases, proving the business value of AI initiatives becomes essential for securing continued investment in MLOps infrastructure.

A key element interwoven with all these challenges is ethical considerations, which encompass issues like explainability, fairness, accountability, and sustainability. These principles are increasingly crucial as AI systems become more pervasive in business operations. For instance, a healthcare AI system that makes decisions impacting patient care must be explainable, so doctors and patients can understand why certain decisions were made. Similarly, fairness is essential to prevent AI models from producing biased outcomes. This is especially important in high-stakes domains like criminal justice, where a biased AI system could unfairly target certain demographics.

Accountability is another ethical concern, as businesses need to clearly define who is responsible for AI-driven decisions, particularly when they lead to regulatory violations or adverse outcomes. Lastly, sustainability has become a major issue, as the continuous training of large AI models consumes significant energy. Businesses must balance the performance of their AI systems with their environmental impact, ensuring that their operations remain sustainable in the long term.

The relationships between these challenges and ethical considerations are dynamic. Ethical principles such as explainability, fairness, and accountability directly influence organizational practices, technical choices, operational processes, and business decisions. For example, ethical considerations may require the introduction of fairness checks into machine learning pipelines, complicating technical processes and adding complexity to operational management. Moreover, businesses may need to invest additional resources in compliance measures to ensure their AI systems are ethical and transparent, impacting both operational efficiency and cost.

The goal of the research context is to enhance MLOps adoption by addressing these intertwined challenges through human-centric and sustainable approaches. A successful strategy might involve creating more inclusive tools that empower non-technical business leaders to participate in AI model evaluation, ensuring that these leaders understand and trust the decisions made by AI systems. This human-centric approach, coupled with a focus on sustainable practices, can drive broader and more ethical adoption of MLOps, ultimately enabling businesses to harness the full potential of AI systems while minimizing risks and ensuring long-term sustainability.

By resolving organizational, technical, operational, and business challenges —while simultaneously embedding ethical considerations into MLOps practices— companies can significantly improve their ability to adopt and scale AI systems in production. This holistic approach promises to create a robust and trustworthy MLOps environment, leading to more efficient AI operations, greater business value, and stronger alignment with regulatory and societal expectations.

4   An Industrial Case Study: The RADON Methodology

In this section, we present a case study [13] conducted within a semiconductor company to evaluate the real-world impact of MLOps adoption.

The semiconductor industry, characterized by its heavy reliance on datadriven processes [3], has increasingly adopted MLOps practices to enhance operational efficiency and data utilization. In such environments, data pipelines are integral to predictive maintenance, process optimization, and real-time decision-making. However, these pipelines face challenges, including scalability, efficiency, and maintaining consistency across complex workflows.

By implementing the RADON methodology [9], we assess whether MLOps practices can effectively address the organizational, technical, operational, and business challenges previously identified. This study provides an empirical perspective on how MLOps influences workflow automation, deployment efficiency, and overall business value in a high-tech industrial setting. Through this case, we examine the practical benefits and limitations of MLOps, offering insights into its feasibility, scalability, and potential for broader adoption in complex enterprise environments. The case study was guided by the following research question:

What is the most effective and practical methodology for designing, deploying, and managing function orchestrators in an MLOps environment?

The case study investigates the comparative advantages and limitations of innovative approaches, such as the RADON tool-chain, against traditional methods, aiming to determine the optimal strategy for managing function orchestrators in real-world scenarios [7].

4.1 Challenges in Semiconductor MLOps Environments

In MLOps environments, data pipelines are essential for maintaining a continuous flow of high-quality data that supports machine learning models. These pipelines handle complex tasks, such as ingesting, transforming, and storing vast amounts of heterogeneous data in near real-time, while ensuring the data is clean and reliable for accurate predictions and decision-making. However, the semiconductor company faced significant challenges in this process [5, 6]. Much time and effort were required for scripting and configuring serverless functions due to a lack of standardized practices, leading to inefficiencies. Workflow management was hindered by inconsistencies across teams and tools, exacerbated by the dynamic demands of the MLOps environment. Scaling the pipelines to meet growing data volumes and complexity proved challenging, and the reliance on diverse, often incompatible tools further complicated the integration and smooth operation of workflows.

4.2 RADON

The RADON methodology was implemented to address critical challenges in the semiconductor company's MLOps environment by providing a robust framework that integrates standardization, automation, and scalability. Its foundation lies in the TOSCA (Topology and Orchestration Specification for Cloud Applications) [26] standard, which ensures consistent and reproducible workflow design and deployment. By leveraging TOSCA templates, RADON reduces errors and establishes a repeatable process for deploying serverless functions. Furthermore, the integration of BPMN (Business Process Model and Notation) enables intuitive, visual workflow modeling, improving collaboration among MLOps teams. RADON's automated tools streamline operations to enhance efficiency and reliability. Eclipse Winery, part of its tool-chain, supports the design of TOSCA-compliant cloud application topologies, while xOpera automates the deployment of predefined plans, seamlessly integrating with MLOps workflows. These tools reduce manual effort, improve precision, and ensure workflows are adaptable to evolving requirements. Additionally, RADON's capability for scalable function orchestration enables dynamic deployment, allowing data pipelines to handle increasing data volumes and complexity without loss of performance [44] (Fig. 3).

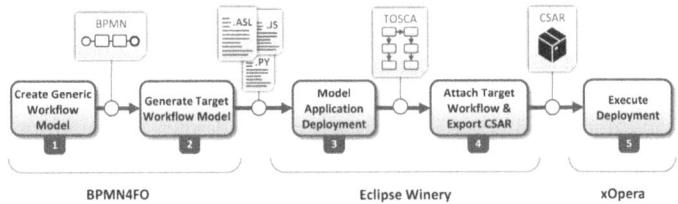

Fig. 3. Tool-chain for modeling and deployment of function orchestrations [45].

Figure 4 describes which challenges are covered by the whole RADON methodology. This table has been derived according to the official RADON documentation, which has

		Organisational Challenges				Technical Challenges			Operational Challenges		Business Challenges	
		Human Resources and Skillset	Collaboration & Communication	User Engagement & Resistance	Slow Processes	Infrastructure and Data Management	Standards and Frameworks	Technical Tools	Pipeline Management	Implementation Trade-offs	Business Value	Cost and Budget Constraints
RADON	Development Pipeline, Modelling, Templates		X		X	X	X	X	X			X
	Verification and Defect Prediction	X	X		X	X		X				X
	Continuous Testing Tool	X			X	X		X	X	X		X
	CI/CD Workflow		X	X	X		X		X	X		
	Deployment Tool (xOpera)				X		X		X	X		
	Decomposition Workflow	X	X	X			X				X	X
	Monitoring Tool			X		X			X		X	X

Fig. 4. MLOps challenges covered by the RADON tool-chain.

been mapped to the challenges described by the previous section. As we can observe, RADON tools cover most of the challenges, except for the ethical considerations, as they are out of the scope of this tool-chain.

4.3 Case Study: Methodology

The case study was designed to evaluate the capabilities of the RADON methodology within an MLOps environment, focusing on automating data ingestion pipelines critical to the training and monitoring of machine learning models.

By implementing RADON, the study aimed to assess its effectiveness in addressing common challenges such as inefficiency, lack of standardization, and scalability constraints. A key aspect of this evaluation involved comparing the RADON methodology to the company's existing baseline approach. The comparison sought to identify tangible improvements in workflow efficiency, reliability, and scalability, providing a clearer understanding of RADON's potential in enhancing MLOps practices. We split the main research question in four subquestions:

- *RQ1: Which is the most effective approach to design and deploy function orchestrators?* This question evaluates whether modern methodologies like RADON outperform traditional approaches in efficiency, scalability, and reliability, focusing on their ability to meet operational demands in MLOps.
- *RQ2: Which is the perceived easiest approach?* This question explores the perceived ease of use of RADON compared to traditional methods, considering user familiarity, documentation, and overall accessibility.
- *RQ3: Which approach is more useful?* This question examines the usefulness of RADON and traditional approaches in solving challenges like platform migration and infrastructure reuse in diverse scenarios.
- *RQ4: Which tool is intended to be used?* This question investigates the adoption intentions for RADON versus traditional approaches, considering onboarding ease, community support, and tool maturity.

The case study employed the Method Evaluation Model (MEM) [25], a theoretical framework derived from the Technology Acceptance Model (TAM) [11], to assess the effectiveness of the RADON methodology in comparison to the company's baseline app-roach. MEM provided a structured approach for evaluating both the practical adoption and actual efficacy of the methodology through six key constructs, depicted in Fig. 5:

1. *Actual Efficiency*: This dimension measured the effort required to apply the RADON methodology relative to the outcomes it achieved. By focusing on the reduction of manual tasks and error rates, the study assessed whether RADON streamlined workflows more effectively than the baseline.
2. *Actual Effectiveness*: The degree to which RADON met its intended objectives was evaluated. This included its impact on workflow automation, data quality, and pipeline scalability.
3. *Perceived Ease of Use*: To capture user experience, the study examined how intuitive and straightforward the RADON tools were for practitioners. Both novice and expe-rienced team members were surveyed to understand their level of comfort with the new methodology.
4. *Perceived Usefulness*: This construct assessed whether users believed RADON effec-tively addressed the challenges faced in the MLOps environment, such as inefficiency, scalability constraints, and lack of standardization.
5. *Intention to Use*: The likelihood of future adoption was measured by gauging participants' willingness to continue using RADON after the case study phase.
6. *Actual Usage*: Observations of how the RADON methodology was deployed and utilized in practice provided insights into its real-world application.

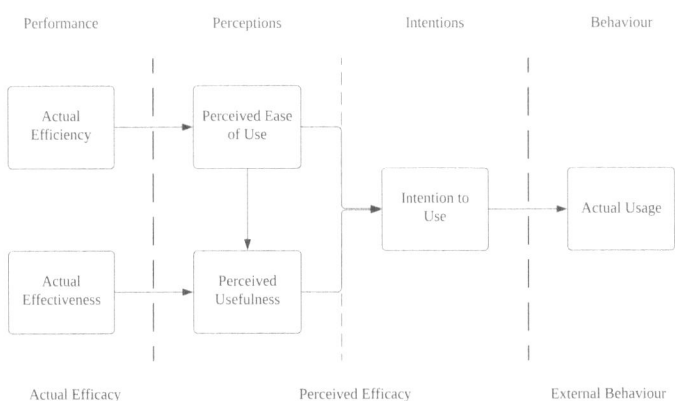

Fig. 5. Method Evaluation Model.

By combining these dimensions, MEM allowed the study to evaluate not only the technical performance of RADON but also its practical applicability and acceptance within the team. Data collection included both quantitative metrics, such as deployment times and error rates, and qualitative feedback from participants. This dual approach ensured a comprehensive understanding of RADON's impact on the company's MLOps processes. The MEM framework also facilitated a direct comparison with the baseline approach, highlighting RADON's advantages and areas for improvement.

Table 1. List of dependent variables.

Name	Measure	Scale
Effectiveness (EFCT)	Number of Requirements Satisfied Total Number of Requirements	Ratio
Efficiency (EFFC)	Effectiveness Time	Ratio
Perceived Ease of Use (PEOU)	5-point Likert Scale	Ordinal
Perceived Usefulness (PU)	5-point Likert Scale	Ordinal
Intention to Use (ITU)	5-point Likert Scale	Ordinal

Table 1 summaries the dependent variables used during our experiments, based on the MEM model, and the metrics employed to measure them.

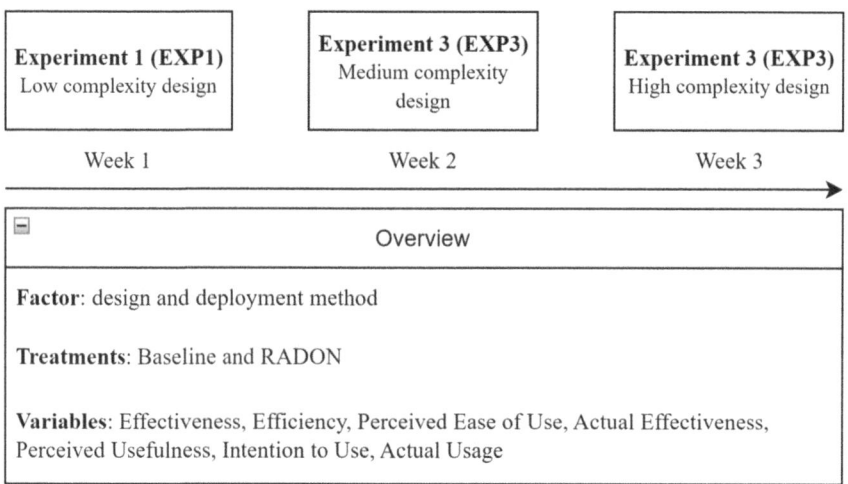

Fig. 6. Sequence of experiments with factor, treatments and variables involved.

Experimental Design. We followed the approach adopted by Santos et al. [34]. The experimental setup involved a detailed analysis of two distinct approaches to managing data ingestion pipelines: the existing baseline methodology and the RADON-based solution. The baseline approach relied heavily on manually scripted processes, which were prone to frequent errors and inefficiencies due to the absence of a standardized framework. This manual methodology not only required significant effort but also posed challenges in maintaining consistency across workflows. Figure 6 provides and overview of the experiments we conducted. In contrast, the RADON approach introduced the use of TOSCA-based templates and automated deployment plans. By leveraging these standardized tools, RADON sought to streamline the deployment process, reducing the need for manual intervention and minimizing the risk of errors. The experiments were structured to assess the impact of RADON across several critical dimensions. First, the focus was placed on workflow automation, where the goal was to eliminate unnecessary manual steps in data ingestion and transformation processes. Second, the integration of data pipelines with machine learning models was closely monitored to ensure the delivery of high-quality data that could effectively support downstream ML workflows. Lastly, the scalability of the system was tested to determine its capacity to handle increasing data volumes while requiring minimal configuration changes.

The experiments evaluated the RADON methodology across three levels of complexity—low, medium, and high—to test its scalability and adaptability under varying operational demands. These levels have been derived during iterative design session with experts within the organization's team. At the low complexity level, the focus was on basic ETL job execution with simple concurrency checks and error handling, assessing fundamental reliability. The medium complexity level added requirements such as IP space checks, a retry mechanism for snapshot jobs, and prioritization of tasks, introducing intermediate orchestration challenges. For high complexity, the system required dynamic scheduling, where the job orchestrator read real-time conditions from a schedule table, significantly increasing operational demands. The complexity was quantified by counting the steps and branches in each orchestration model, providing a robust comparison of how RADON and the baseline approach scaled with increasing requirements. The experiments have been conducted by the authors of this study, with the support of trained practitioners, i.e., the other eight team members, who have experience that spans from a minimum of two year to several decades in the field.

The participants where crucial to measure the variables we previously defined.

4.4 Null Hypotheses

For each of the three experiments, the same Null Hypotheses hold. The Null Hypotheses have been directly derived from the dependent variables. The Null Hypotheses of our experiments are:

- **$H1_0$**: EFCT (RADON) = EFCT (Baseline);
- **$H2_0$**: EFFC (RADON) = EFFC (Baseline);
- **$H3_0$**: PEOU (RADON) = PEOU (Baseline);
- **$H5_0$**: PU (RADON) = PU (Baseline);
- **$H6_0$**: ITU (RADON) = ITU (Baseline);
- **$H7_0$**: AU (RADON) = AU (Baseline);

4.5 Implementation

The implementation phase involved applying RADON to existing data pipelines that aggregated and processed diverse datasets required for machine learning model training and prediction tasks. The project began with the use of Eclipse Winery[3], a TOSCA-compliant tool, to design pipeline workflows as reusable templates. These templates provided a standardized structure that allowed for consistency and repeatability across multiple deployments. Once the workflows were designed, the deployment process was

---

[3] https://github.com/eclipse/winery.

automated using xOpera, a deployment engine capable of executing the predefined plans created in Eclipse Winery. This automation not only reduced the time required for deployment but also integrated seamlessly with the company's existing MLOps infrastructure. The implementation process ensured that the pipelines were capable of delivering high-quality data efficiently and could scale dynamically to meet increasing demands. By combining the capabilities of Eclipse Winery and xOpera[4], the case study demonstrated the practical benefits of RADON in overcoming traditional limitations and advancing the efficiency of MLOps pipelines.

5 Results

In the context of business intelligence (BI), MLOps holds immense potential for transforming how companies leverage data-driven insights to make strategic decisions. Business intelligence refers to the process of collecting, analyzing, and presenting data to help businesses make informed decisions. Traditionally, BI relies on structured data and dashboards to generate insights. However, with the advent of machine learning and AI, organizations are increasingly moving beyond static reports and toward predictive and prescriptive analytics that can offer dynamic, actionable insights.

The case study results demonstrate how MLOps methodologies, such as the RADON tool-chain, can address several of these challenges in BI. For example, RADON's ability to automate data ingestion, model training, and deployment processes showcased significant improvements in pipeline efficiency, scalability, and consistency—key requirements for BI systems handling large, diverse datasets. Additionally, the experiments highlighted the role of structured frameworks in ensuring data quality and enabling the reuse of infrastructure components, which are crucial for managing the massive and heterogeneous datasets typical in BI environments.

By automating complex processes and fostering collaboration, the conceptual model combined with the findings from the case study experiments creates an environment where machine learning can significantly enhance BI systems. These enhancements enable businesses to deliver predictive and prescriptive analytics that surpass traditional BI, driving clear ROI and supporting more agile, datadriven decision-making.

5.1 Results from the Theoretical Formulation and Conceptual Landscape

The conceptual model of MLOps adoption addresses many of the challenges that businesses encounter when integrating AI-driven business intelligence systems into their operations. The organizational challenges—such as skill gaps and collaboration issues— are particularly significant in the BI space. Business intelligence teams, data scientists, and IT departments must work together to build models that provide value. For example, teams often struggle to interpret machine learning outputs and translate them into business insights, exacerbating the skillset issue. Organizational resistance to AI also plays a role, as some departments may prefer traditional BI methods over AI-driven insights.

From a technical perspective, integrating MLOps with BI systems requires seamless infrastructure and data management. The RADON case study revealed how dynamic

---

[4] https://github.com/xlab-si/xopera-opera.

orchestration of serverless functions can adapt to changing data sources and workloads, ensuring up-to-date insights and quick responses to market conditions. This capability directly supports BI's need for real-time insights to avoid missed opportunities or outdated recommendations. Additionally, explainability becomes critical in BI, as business leaders need to trust and understand the outputs of machine learning models, which directly influence decision-making. Ensuring fairness and avoiding bias in models that drive key decisions is essential, especially in areas such as customer analytics and sales forecasting, where biased data could lead to unfair business strategies.

Table 2. Experiments results. Values represent the average over the experiments; values are dimensionless, except for duration which unit is hours, and values are derived by the data collected during our experiments, with the variables described in 1

Variable	RADON	BASELINE
Effectiveness	1	1
Efficiency	0.077	0.69
Duration	15.33h	14.66h
Perceived Ease of Use	2.66	3.66
Perceived Usefulness	4.33	4
Intention to Use	2.67	4.33

In terms of operational challenges, MLOps adoption in BI systems needs to focus on automating data ingestion, model training, and deployment processes to ensure the pipeline can respond quickly to changing market conditions. Business intelligence depends on up-to-date insights, and delays in deploying models or retraining them can lead to missed opportunities or outdated recommendations. Finally, the business challenges in MLOps for BI revolve around proving the value of machine learning investments. It is essential to demonstrate that AI models offer predictive and prescriptive analytics that go beyond traditional BI, delivering clear ROI.

5.2   Results from the Case Study

The results of the case study evaluation, summarised in Table 2, provided a clear comparison between the RADON methodology and the baseline approach. While both methods demonstrated similar effectiveness in meeting the defined requirements, RADON showed a notable improvement in efficiency, with significantly reduced manual effort and errors during deployment. However, the perceived ease of use was slightly lower for RADON due to the learning curve associated with adopting new tools and methodologies. Despite this, participants rated RADON higher in perceived usefulness, reflecting its ability to address key challenges in workflow automation and scalability. Intention to use RADON was moderate, indicating that while its benefits were recognized, further refinement and integration support would be needed for broader adoption. These findings highlight RADON's potential as a transformative solution in MLOps environments, albeit with some areas for improvement.

Considering our initial Hypotheses, we found that:

- $\mathbf{H1_1}$: EFCT (RADON) = EFCT (Baseline);
- $\mathbf{H2_1}$: EFFC (RADON) > EFFC (Baseline);
- $\mathbf{H3_1}$: PEOU (RADON) < PEOU (Baseline);
- $\mathbf{H4_1}$: PU (RADON) > PU (Baseline);
- $\mathbf{H5_1}$: ITU (RADON) < ITU (Baseline);

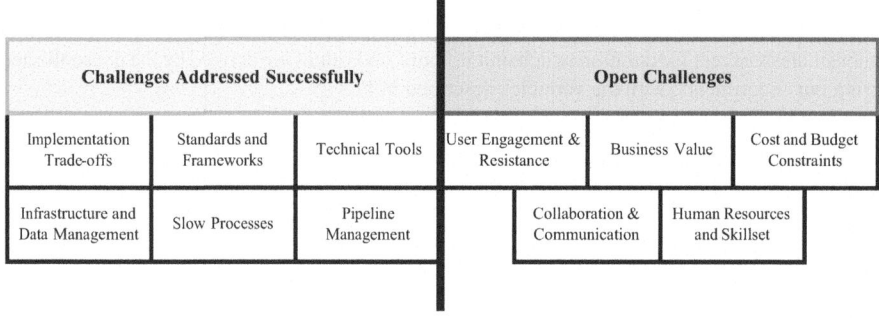

Fig. 7. Summary of the challenges addressed by our study, and the challenges still open.

In particular, for the Effectiveness variable we can say that, although reached in different ways, all the objectives and requirements were satisfied in both cases. For what concerns the Efficiency, which is measured as effectiveness over time, given the same level of Effectiveness reached in both methods, time was higher for the Baseline approach and the two-step process necessary to deploy the IaC, while RADON provides a seamless tool-chain which improves the delivery times. However, this does not mean that the Perceived Ease of Use is lower for RADON but, as opposite, it is lower for the Baseline approach. The Perceived Usefulness is higher for RADON since the benefits have been recognized to be important. Nonetheless, the Intention to Use is still lower for RADON since it is unclear how it will be improved in the future and to what extent will be supported by the community.

Figure 7 highlights which challenges has been addressed by our study. Considering Fig. 4, where we describe the challenges claimed to be addressed by the RADON tool-chain, Fig. 7 is built considering our experimental results. This shows how, even if, in theory, the tools should address many aspects of MLOps implementation, in practice the resistance from practitioners and the limited adoption of such methodology does not allow to state that the whole set of challenges has been solved, leaving open questions for research.

We can now provide an answer to each research question.

RQ1: Which is the most effective approach to design and deploy function orchestrators? The RADON tool-chain proved to be the most effective approach for designing and deploying function orchestrators. It enhanced efficiency, reduced dependency on specific services, and improved communication of complex projects, even for non-technical stakeholders.

RQ2: Which is the perceived easiest approach? The baseline approach was perceived as easier to use due to its familiarity and comprehensive documentation from cloud platform vendors. In contrast, RADON faced challenges with low maturity, limited documentation, and minimal community support, making it less intuitive for users.

RQ3: Which approach is more useful? RADON was considered more useful in environments requiring frequent platform migration or infrastructure reuse. Its structured design stages and blueprint reuse capabilities offered significant advantages in these contexts, surpassing the utility of traditional approaches.

RQ4: Which tool is intended to be used? Despite its benefits, the intention to use RADON was low. Challenges such as insufficient documentation, lack of debugging interfaces, and high initial adoption effort deterred participants from choosing RADON over the baseline approach for immediate implementation.

6   Discussion

The exploration of MLOps for business intelligence (BI) uncovers critical research directions that can significantly influence how machine learning systems are integrated into business decision-making processes. In this chapter we discuss our results, by first focusing on MLOps challenges and practices and then by proposing a research road-map.

6.1   On MLOps Challenges and Practices

MLOps adoption in Business Intelligence (BI) requires a balance between collaboration, scalability, and ethical responsibility. Effective implementation depends on strong alignment between data scientists, IT teams, and business stakeholders, ensuring smooth integration and reducing resistance to AI-based decision-making [28]. Research should focus on bridging communication gaps and embedding ethical principles—such as explainability, fairness, and accountability—directly into MLOps pipelines to foster trust and regulatory compliance. Scalability and sustainability are essential for maintaining efficient and cost-effective MLOps in dynamic BI environments. Optimizing pipelines, automating processes, and managing technical debt will be crucial as data volumes and operational complexity grow. Businesses that successfully integrate MLOps can achieve faster insights, improved decision-making, and a competitive edge while ensuring responsible AI use [32].

From an industrial perspective, organizations must break down silos to encourage collaboration, develop scalable yet sustainable infrastructures, and measure MLOps' impact on business value [8]. Demonstrating clear ROI—such as more accurate forecasts and better analytics—will be key to securing long-term adoption. The case study evaluation demonstrated the benefits of adopting MLOps principles, by significantly improving efficiency, reducing manual effort and deployment errors.

Detecting such smells, enables mitigation. Many studies already investigated such smells, proposing several methods to overcome them. However, methods are not sufficient. This is because, depending on how they are implemented, successful outcomes might differ. For this reason, we highlight the importance of developing tools since, without automation, it is not possible to manage properly [21]. For this reason tools such as RADON, even if they do not improve over all the challenges we highlighted, are a step forward towards a standardized way to approach and solve them [4, 20].

From a societal standpoint, fairness, transparency, and sustainability must be at the core of AI-driven BI. MLOps practices should mitigate bias, ensure explainability for non-expert users, and optimize resource usage to minimize environmental impact. Prioritizing these factors will build public trust in AI, support equitable outcomes, and drive long-term sustainability, benefiting businesses and society alike [1].

6.2 A Research Roadmap for MLOps in Business Intelligence

In this section, we present a Research Roadmap for MLOps in Business Intelligence, structured around five key research questions. The questions emerged as part of a Delphi—following a protocol similar to Eldridge et al. [14]—study in industry thus structured: (1) long-term strategic objectives drawn from the internal Issue-Tracking systems of two top-tier tech organizations were elicited manually and scrubbed for content; (b) the manual validation of the extracted text was subjected to the attention of two senior business intelligence analysts from the same companies, one per company; (c) a delphi-like focus-group session of 2+ hours was used to converge towards the questions reported in this section. The questions and challenges reported in this section emerged from the exercise recaped before. The resulting roadmap is designed to address most critical challenges and opportunities in integrating MLOps within BI systems [1, 23, 27], and it is derived by the previous results in their respective BI systems within the organizations target of this study. These research questions also align with the results of our case study, as the open challenges are strictly related to the human factors within the MLOps stages and to the business value driven development of such applications.

The proposed framework aims to guide future research and practical implementations in this domain.

Research Question 1: How can MLOps frameworks be adapted to address the unique organizational challenges in business intelligence? The objective of this research question is to explore how MLOps can be tailored to facilitate better collaboration between business intelligence teams, data scientists, and IT departments, focusing on overcoming organizational resistance and skill gaps. This can be done according to the following research methods:

– Qualitative Case Studies: Conduct in-depth case studies of organizations that have successfully integrated MLOps into their BI systems, focusing on their approaches to fostering collaboration and skill-building.
– Interviews and Surveys: Collect insights from business intelligence stakeholders, data scientists, and IT teams to identify pain points and successful strategies in organizational alignment.

Research Question 2: How can MLOps pipelines be optimized to ensure explainability, fairness, and accountability in AI-driven business intelligence systems? The idea is to develop methods for ensuring that machine learning models used in BI are explainable, free of bias, and accountable for decision-making processes. This can be achieve with the following research methods:

– Experimental Design: Set up controlled experiments comparing different model development frameworks to assess their effectiveness in promoting explainability and fairness within BI systems.
– Algorithmic Development: Create new techniques or frameworks for embedding explainability by design in MLOps pipelines, focusing on models that are used for decision support in business intelligence.

Research Question 3: What operational strategies can improve the scalability and sustainability of MLOps pipelines in dynamic business intelligence environments? We suggest to investigate ways to automate and scale MLOps pipelines to handle the real-time demands of business intelligence, while also ensuring sustainability in terms of technical debt and environmental impact. The recommended research methods are:

– Simulation Studies: Simulate different pipeline configurations to assess their scalability and sustainability, considering the impact of frequent data changes and real-time requirements in business intelligence.
– Action Research: Work closely with a business intelligence team to iteratively refine MLOps processes, observing how automated pipelines respond to evolving data and organizational demands.

Research Question 4: How can MLOps demonstrate clear business value in the context of business intelligence? The goal is to identify the metrics and frame-works that can help organizations evaluate the return on investment (ROI) of MLOps for business intelligence, by adopting the following research methods:

– Economic Analysis: Perform cost-benefit analyses to quantify the value added by MLOps in BI systems, looking at specific use cases such as customer segmentation, sales forecasting, and operational optimization.
– Comparative Studies: Compare traditional BI systems with AI-augmented BI systems to measure differences in performance, accuracy, and decision-making speed.

Research Question 5: How can MLOps promote ethical AI practices in business intelligence to mitigate bias and ensure sustainability? We recommend to explore the ethical dimensions of AI in business intelligence, focusing on how MLOps can ensure fairness, transparency, and sustainability in decision-making models. Suggested research methods:

– Ethical Audits: Conduct audits of existing BI models to identify bias and other ethical concerns, using these insights to propose improvements to the MLOps pipeline.
– Sustainability Modeling: Model the environmental impact of different MLOps strategies and propose energy-efficient approaches to maintaining AI-driven BI systems.

7 Conclusion

The research presented in this paper contributes to the growing field of MLOps in Business Intelligence by identifying key challenges and proposing structured solutions for improving AI-driven decision-making processes. Through the conceptual model and proof-of-concept evaluation, we demonstrated how MLOps frameworks, particularly the RADON methodology, can enhance the efficiency, scalability, and sustainability of machine learning operations in BI environments. The comparative analysis between RADON and a baseline approach highlighted RADON's advantages in reducing deployment effort and errors while maintaining effectiveness. However, challenges related to usability, documentation, and adoption barriers underscore the need for further refinement before such methodologies can achieve widespread industrial implementation.

Beyond the technical findings, this study emphasized the importance of organizational collaboration in successful MLOps adoption. Ensuring alignment between data scientists, IT teams, and business stakeholders is critical to overcoming resistance and operational inefficiencies. Additionally, ethical considerations such as explainability, fairness, and accountability must be embedded into MLOps pipelines to foster trust and compliance with evolving regulatory standards. These dimensions remain essential for businesses seeking to integrate machine learning into their BI workflows while maintaining transparency and ethical responsibility.

The insights from this research pave the way for future investigations into optimizing MLOps pipelines for large-scale business environments. Further work is needed to refine automation strategies, improve model interpretability, and establish industry-wide benchmarks for evaluating the business impact of MLOps adoption. Additionally, advancing methodologies to mitigate bias and ensure sustainability will be crucial for building responsible AI systems. By addressing these challenges, future research can support the broader goal of creating scalable, efficient, and ethical MLOps practices that empower organizations to make more data-driven and informed business decisions.

References

1. Bansal, A., Dasarathy, A.K., Gangadharan, S., Rajeshwari, R.R., Ismail, M.M., Halaf, N.K.A.: Ethical considerations of AI implementation in business planning: ensuring fairness and transparency. In: 2023 International Conference on Innovative Computing, Intelligent Communication and Smart Electrical Systems (ICSES), pp. 1–6 (2023). https://doi.org/10.1109/ICS ES60034.2023.10465461

2. Barocas, S., Hardt, M., Narayanan, A.: Fairness and Machine Learning: Limitations and Opportunities. MIT Press (2018)

3. Bauer, H., Burkacky, O., Kenevan, P., Mahindroo, A., Patel, M.: How the semiconductor industry can emerge stronger after the covid-19 crisis. McKinsey (2020). https://www.mckinsey.com/industries/industrials-and-electronics/our-insights/how-the-semiconductor-industry-can-emerge-stronger-after-the-covid-19-crisis. Accessed 26 Feb 2025

4. Brown, N., et al.: Managing technical debt in software-reliant systems. In: Proceedings of the FSE/SDP Workshop on Future of Software Engineering Research, pp. 47–52. FoSER 2010, Association for Computing Machinery, New York, NY, USA (2010). https://doi.org/10.1145/1882362.1882373

5. Burkacky, O., de Jong, M., Mittal, A., Verma, N.: Value creation: how can the semiconductor industry keep outperforming? McKinsey (2021). https://www.mckinsey.com/industries/sem iconductors/our-insights/value-creation-how-can-the-semiconductor-industry-keep-outper forming. Accessed 26 Feb 2025

6. Burkacky, O., Kingsbury, U., Pedroni, A., Poltronieri, G., Schrimper, M., Weddle, B.: How semiconductor makers can turn a talent challenge into a competitive advantage. McKinsey (2022). https://www.mckinsey.com/industries/semiconductors/our-insights/how-semiconductor-makers-can-turn-a-talent-challenge-into-a-competitive-advantage. Accessed 26 Feb 2025

7. Calcaterra, D., Tomarchio, O.: Policy-based holistic application management with BPMN and TOSCA. SN Comput. Sci. **4** (2023). https://doi.org/10.1007/s42979-022-01616-w

8. Cheng, Q., Long, G.: Federated learning operations (flops): challenges, lifecycle and approaches. In: 2022 International Conference on Technologies and Applications of Artificial Intelligence (TAAI), pp. 12–17 (2022). https://doi.org/10.1109/TAAI57707.2022.00012

9. Dalla Palma, S., Catolino, G., Di Nucci, D., Tamburri, D.A., van den Heuvel, W.J.: Go serverless with radon! A practical Devops experience report. IEEE Softw. **40**(2), 80–89 (2023). https://doi.org/10.1109/MS.2022.3170153

10. Dalla Palma, S., Garriga, M., Nucci, D., Tamburri, D., Heuvel, W.J.: DevOps and quality management in serverless computing: the RADON approach, pp. 155–160 (2021). https://doi.org/10.1007/978-3-030-71906-7_13

11. Davis, F.: A technology acceptance model for empirically testing new end-user information systems (1985)

12. Düllmann, T.F., van Hoorn, A., Yussupov, V., Jakovits, P., Adhikari, M.: CTT: load test automation for TOSCA-based cloud applications. In: Companion of the 2022 ACM/SPEC International Conference on Performance Engineering, pp. 89–96. ICPE 2022, Association for Computing Machinery, New York, NY, USA (2022). https://doi.org/10.1145/3491204.3527484

13. Eisenhardt, K.M.: Building theories from case study research. Acad. Manage. Rev. **14**(4), 532–550 (1989). http://www.jstor.org/stable/258557

14. Eldridge, S., et al.: Defining feasibility and pilot studies in preparation for randomised controlled trials: development of a conceptual framework. PloS one **11**, e0150205 (2016). https://doi.org/10.1371/journal.pone.0150205

15. Ellenrieder, S., Jourdan, N., Biegel, T., Bretones Cassoli, B., Metternich, J., Buxmann, P.: Toward the sustainable development of machine learning applications in industry 4.0 (2023). https://EconPapers.repec.org/RePEc:dar:wpaper:138521

16. Faubel, L., Schmid, K.: MLOPS: a multiple case study in industry 4.0. In: 2024 IEEE 29th International Conference on Emerging Technologies and Factory Automation (ETFA), pp. 01–08 (2024). https://doi.org/10.1109/ETFA61755.2024.10711136

17. Girimurugan, B., Parthiban, K., Saxena, M., Talasila, G., Vamsi, N.S., Sai, P.T.: Revolutionizing business intelligence: Harnessing AI and machine learning for strategic insights and competitive advantage. In: 2024 2nd International Conference on Disruptive Technologies (ICDT), pp. 190–193 (2024). https://doi.org/10.1109/ICDT61202.2024.10489687

18. Hegedűs, C., Varga, P.: Tailoring MLOPS techniques for industry 5.0 needs. In: 2023 19th International Conference on Network and Service Management (CNSM), pp. 1–7 (2023). https://doi.org/10.23919/CNSM59352.2023.10327814

19. John, M.M., Gillblad, D., Olsson, H.H., Bosch, J.: Advancing MLOPS from Ad Hoc to kaizen. In: 2023 49th Euromicro Conference on Software Engineering and Advanced Applications (SEAA), pp. 94–101 (2023). https://doi.org/10.1109/SEAA60479.2023.00023

20. Kazman, R., et al.: A case study in locating the architectural roots of technical debt. In: 2015 IEEE/ACM 37th IEEE International Conference on Software Engineering, vol. 2, pp. 179–188 (2015). https://doi.org/10.1109/ICSE.2015.146

21. Kazman, R., Carriere, J.: Playing detective: reconstructing software architecture from available evidence. Autom. Softw. Eng. **6**, 107–138 (1999). https://doi.org/10.1023/A:1008781513258

22. Kreuzberger, D., Kühl, N., Hirschl, S.: Machine learning operations (MLOPS): overview, definition, and architecture (2022). https://arxiv.org/abs/2205.02302

23. Liu, J., Liu, P.: Research on the application of artificial intelligence technology in traditional business intelligence systems. In: 2024 4th International Symposium on Computer Technology and Information Science (ISCTIS), pp. 186–190 (2024). https://doi.org/10.1109/ISCTIS 63324.2024.10698971

24. Mishra, S.: AWS SAGEMAKER MLOPS brief overview. Medium (2023). https://med ium.com/@sripada.mishra/aws-sagemaker-mlops-brief-overview-8d22dfa95415. Accessed 26 Feb 2025

25. Moody, D.L.: The method evaluation model: a theoretical model for validating information systems design methods. In: European Conference on Information Systems (2003). https://api.semanticscholar.org/CorpusID:11092142

26. Moser, S., Lipton, P., Spatzier, T., Palma, D.: Tosca topology and orchestration specification for cloud applications version 1.0 (2013)

27. Mucha, T., Ma, S., Abhari, K.: Beyond MLOPS: the lifecycle of machine learning- based solutions. In: American Conference for Information Systems 2022 (2022), aMCIS 2022; Conference date: 10-08-2022 Through 14-08-2022

28. Mulongo, N.Y.: Best practices of machine learning system operations (MLOPS) in the South African manufacturing industry. In: 2024 International Symposium on Networks, Computers and Communications (ISNCC), pp. 1–6 (2024). https://doi.org/10.1109/ISNCC62547.2024. 10759008

29. Narayanappa, A., Amrit, C.: An analysis of the barriers preventing the implementation of MLOPS, pp. 101–114 (2024). https://doi.org/10.1007/978-3-031-50188-3_10

30. Nitton, E.D.: PIACERE: programming trustworthy infrastructure as code in a secure framework. In Short Papers Proceedings of the First SWForum Workshop on Trustworthy Software and Open Source, vol. 2878, pp. 8–15 (2021). https://ceurws.org/Vol-2878/paper4.pdf

31. Plant, O.H., Aldea, A., van Hillegersberg, J.: Improving Devops team performance through context-capability coalignment: towards a profile for public sector organizations. Inf. Softw. Technol. **178**, 107585 (2025). https://doi.org/10.1016/j.infsof.2024.107585, https://www.sci encedirect.com/science/article/pii/S0950584924001903

32. Prasad, J., Jain, A., Zachariah, U.E.: Comparative evaluation of machine learning development lifecycle tools. In: 2022 International Conference on Recent Trends in Microelectronics, Automation, Computing and Communications Systems (IC- MACC), pp. 1–6 (2022). https://doi.org/10.1109/ICMACC54824.2022.10093671

33. Sandobalín, J., Insfran, E., Abrahão, S.: On the effectiveness of tools to support infrastructure as code: model-driven versus code-centric. IEEE Access **8**, 17734–17761 (2020). https://doi.org/10.1109/ACCESS.2020.2966597

34. Santos, A., Gómez, O.S., Juristo, N.: Analyzing families of experiments in SE: a systematic mapping study. IEEE Trans. Softw. Eng. (2018). https://doi.org/10.1109/TSE.2018.2864633

35. Shankar, S., Garcia, R., Hellerstein, J.M., Parameswaran, A.G.: We have no idea how models will behave in production until production: how engineers operationalize machine learning. In: Proceedings of the ACM on Human-Computer Interaction, vol. 8, no. CSCW1, pp. 1–34 (2024). https://doi.org/10.1145/3653697

36. Sokolowski, D.: Infrastructure as code for dynamic deployments. In: Proceedings of the 30th ACM Joint European Software Engineering Conference and Symposium on the Foundations of Software Engineering, pp. 1775–1779. ESEC/FSE 2022, Association for Computing Machinery, New York, NY, USA (2022). https://doi.org/10.1145/3540250.3558912

37. Sokolowski, D., Weisenburger, P., Salvaneschi, G.: Automating serverless deployments for devops organizations. In: Proceedings of the 29th ACM Joint Meeting on European Software

Engineering Conference and Symposium on the Foundations of Software Engineering, pp. 57–69. ESEC/FSE 2021, Association for Computing Machinery, New York, NY, USA (2021). https://doi.org/10.1145/3468264.3468575

38. Strubell, E., Ganesh, A., McCallum, A.: Energy and policy considerations for deep learning in NLP (2019). https://arxiv.org/abs/1906.02243
39. Symeonidis, G., Nerantzis, E., Kazakis, A., Papakostas, G.A.: MLOPS - definitions, tools and challenges. In: 2022 IEEE 12th Annual Computing and Communication Workshop and Conference (CCWC), pp. 0453–0460 (2022). https://doi.org/10.1109/CCWC54503.2022.9720902
40. Tamburri, D.A.: Sustainable MLOPS: trends and challenges. In: 2020 22nd International Symposium on Symbolic and Numeric Algorithms for Scientific Computing (SYNASC), pp. 17–23 (2020). https://doi.org/10.1109/SYNASC51798.2020.00015
41. Testi, M., et al.: MLOPS: a taxonomy and a methodology. IEEE Access **10**, 63606–63618 (2022). https://doi.org/10.1109/ACCESS.2022.3181730
42. Warnett, S.J., Zdun, U.: On the understandability of MLOPS system architectures. IEEE Trans. Software Eng. **50**(5), 1015–1039 (2024). https://doi.org/10.1109/TSE.2024.3367488
43. Widder, D.G., Nafus, D.: Dislocated accountabilities in the "AI supply chain": modularity and developers' notions of responsibility. Big Data Soc. **10**(1) (2023). https://doi.org/10.1177/20539517231177620
44. Wurster, M., Breitenbücher, U., Képes, K., Leymann, F., Yussupov, V.: Modeling and automated deployment of serverless applications using TOSCA. In: 2018 IEEE 11th Conference on Service-Oriented Computing and Applications (SOCA), pp. 73–80 (2018). https://doi.org/10.1109/SOCA.2018.00017
45. Yussupov, V., Soldani, J., Breitenbücher, U., Leymann, F.: Standards-based modeling and deployment of serverless function orchestrations using BPMN and TOSCA. Software: Pract. Exp. **52** (2022). https://doi.org/10.1002/spe.3073

Common European Data Spaces in Health Care: A Privacy-Preserving Ecosystem for Cancer Research

Simon Dalmolen[1,3] (ID), Jos van Hillegersberg[1(✉)] (ID), Hans Moonen[1,2] (ID),
Erik Cornelisse[3] (ID), Jildau Bouwman[3] (ID), and Andre Boorsma[3] (ID)

[1] Industrial Engineering and Business Information Systems, University of Twente,
Drienerlolaan 5, 7522 NB Enschede, Netherlands
j.v.hillegersberg@jads.nl
[2] CGI, George Hintzenweg 89, 3068 AX Rotterdam, Netherlands
[3] TNO, Anna Van Buerenplein 1 2595 DA, Den Haag, Netherlands

Abstract. The Dutch healthcare system faces significant challenges, including rising costs, administrative inefficiencies, and increasing pressure on the workforce. The European Health Data Space (EHDS) offers a promising solution to support data sharing for research and innovation while preserving data privacy and sovereignty. This paper outlines a technical and organizational framework for implementing privacy-preserving data sharing in cancer research. The proposed infrastructure leverages a combination of federated learning, multi-party computation, and FAIR Data Points to enable decentralized analysis of real-world health data. Key challenges, such as balancing data utility and privacy, are addressed through governance structures, including data permit management, certification processes, and rigorous identity management. The approach also considers the difficulties in sharing high-dimensional data while maintaining both privacy and usability. By integrating standardization efforts, privacy-enhancing technologies, and robust governance models, the framework aligns with the EHDS vision for a secure, interoperable, and patient-centric data ecosystem. This paper thus contributes to advancing cancer research through responsible secondary use of health data, fostering trust among stakeholders, and enabling the development of innovative healthcare solutions while ensuring compliance with GDPR and other relevant regulations.

Keywords: European Health Data Space · EHDS · Privacy-Preserving Technologies · FAIR Data Points · Data Sovereignty · Data Governance

1 Introduction

The healthcare landscape in the Netherlands, constituting roughly 11% of the Gross Domestic Product (GDP) and providing employment to 16% of the national workforce, is grappling with a multifaceted set of challenges. These challenges encompass administrative inefficiencies, concerns regarding staff retention, disparities in health outcomes,

M. Schreieck et al. (Eds.): DSPE 2025, LNBIP 563, pp. 78–98, 2026.
https://doi.org/10.1007/978-3-032-04512-6_5

and the inadequate exchange of electronic data. Particularly noteworthy is the "Integraal Zorgakkoord" (IZA) or in English, "Integral Care Agreement"[1] of 2022, which underscores these challenges and warns of a potential scenario by 2040 where an alarming 25% of the workforce could be absorbed by the healthcare sector, especially driven by the aging population —a situation that could strain both the labor market and healthcare affordability. Additionally, the IZA raises concerns about the possibility of healthcare costs skyrocketing threefold by 2060 without appropriate intervention.

Artificial Intelligence (AI), while not a universal remedy, offers promising avenues for addressing these challenges by aligning with the core principles of the IZA. It has the potential to revolutionize healthcare delivery by focusing on patient-centric care, optimizing resource allocation, fostering patient engagement in treatment plans, facilitating timely interventions, prioritizing preventative healthcare measures, and simplifying administrative burdens for healthcare professionals.

However, the effective utilization of AI in healthcare hinges on efficient access to and utilization of patient data. A significant hurdle lies in the sensitivity surrounding patient data and the reluctance to share it for broader research and development initiatives. Urgent action is required to develop innovative solutions that strike a balance between safeguarding patient privacy and leveraging the potential benefits of collaborative healthcare data usage. This strategic shift is in line with the overarching goals outlined in the IZA.

This paper describes a vision and the technical innovation being realised within several privacy preserving projects and the role of service providers and how to source specific services in this complex business environment. In aiming and creating a secure and privacy-preserving environment for the exchange and sharing of health data across organization borders in the Netherlands and EU-wide. To facilitate the sharing of health data.

1.1   Common European Data Space(S)

Common European Data Spaces create secure and interoperable environments for data sharing, ensuring data sovereignty and promoting innovation. This includes domains such as Health and Industry 4.0, operationally represented by data spaces like Catena-X (https://catena-x.net/en/1), the Smart Connected Supplier Network (https://smart-connected.nl/en) and the European Health Data Space(https://health.ec.europa.eu/ehealth-digital-health-and-care/european-health-data-space_en).

The question is how well these data spaces' governance structures and technical architectures scale to create a single market for data?

Obligations in rulebooks fail to solve the complexities of managing permissions for each potential use case—some of which have not yet been imagined. Effective data governance, AI-driven data translation, and automated compliance can contribute to solving this scaling challenge, which needs to be empirically investigated. The European Health Data Space is particularly interesting for doing fundamental scientific research on FAIR (https://www.go-fair.org) [2, 3] data and governance.

In Europe, generating, sharing, and re-using data will contribute to an expanding and sovereign data economy. With 175 Zettabytes of data produced in 2025 alone, automated approaches for secure and trusted trading, sharing and using such data (whether by people or organisations) is increasingly important. Without automation, overcoming technical, legal, trust, ethical, and organisational barriers will be difficult. Initiatives like Data Spaces and Open Data Portals have emerged to overcome these barriers, producing innovative data-sharing technologies, regulatory frameworks, and new data value chains that cut across boundaries. In addition, the rise of symbolic, machine learning, and generative AI could automate data governance throughout the data lifecycle (harvesting or data generation, enrichment, processing, analysis, and knowledge extraction).

As this constantly evolving data and AI ecosystem in Europe is rising and developing, legislation has been introduced to provide legal clarity on a variety of aspects, including Acts such as the General Data Protection Regulation (GDPR)[1], Data Governance Act[2], Data Act[3], the Digital Services Act[4], the Digital Markets Act[5], and the Artificial Intelligence Act[6] that passed the European Parliament recently in March 2024. These regulations have / will have a significant impact on the data-driven activities needed for successful business, public administration and civil society in the data economy.

2 Background

2.1 State of the Art on Data Spaces (Scientific and Practitioner View)

Federated ecosystems are increasingly foundational for modern data spaces, allowing entities to collaborate while controlling their data. However, managing and scaling these ecosystems presents governance challenges related to data access, consent management, and regulatory compliance [4, 5].

AI-infused data translation is critical in federated data environments where semantic heterogeneity hampers seamless data integration. Current approaches often lack adaptability and context-awareness, limiting their effectiveness. Developing AI-enhanced connectors and vocabulary hubs can mitigate these issues by dynamically translating data across formats and standards.

The digital infrastructure supporting data spaces must incorporate (automated) governance mechanisms to ensure continuous compliance. Existing frameworks often rely on manual processes that are prone to error and delay, highlighting the need for more advanced, automated solutions that can enforce policies and adapt to regulatory changes in real-time [6].

2.2 European Health Data Space

The European Health Data Space is a health-specific ecosystem that aims to provide a consistent, trustworthy, and efficient setup for the use of health data for research, innovation, policy-making, and regulatory activities. It is a framework that establishes clear

---

[1] https://eur-lex.europa.eu/eli/reg/2016/679/oj.

[2] https://digital-strategy.ec.europa.eu/en/policies/data-governance-act.

[3] https://digital-strategy.ec.europa.eu/en/policies/data-act.

[4] https://digital-strategy.ec.europa.eu/en/policies/digital-services-act-package.

[5] https://commission.europa.eu/strategy-and-policy/priorities-2019-2024/europe-fit-digital-age/digital-markets-act-ensuring-fair-and-open-digital-markets_en.

[6] https://digital-strategy.ec.europa.eu/en/policies/regulatory-framework-ai.

rules, common standards and practices, infrastructures, and a governance framework to enable the EU to make full use of the potential offered by a safe and secure exchange, use, and reuse of health data. The European Commission launched the European Health Data Space as part of the Commission's proposed wider "Data Strategy" to leverage quality data for use by public authorities and businesses across certain sectors and areas of public interest. The European Health Data Space is the first common EU data space in a specific area to emerge from the European Union [7].

The European Health Data Space aims to empower individuals through increased digital access to and control of their electronic personal health data, at national level and EU-wide. It also aims to foster a single market for electronic health record systems, relevant medical devices, and high-risk AI systems. Sharing health data between European countries will allow individuals to receive more personalized and comprehensive care, and doctors will have a clearer understanding of their patients' medical history [7].

The European Health Data Space sets out a common EU framework allowing for the use of health data for research, innovation, public health, policymaking, regulatory activities, and personalized medicine. It will draw on the wealth of health data across Europe to turn it into knowledge at the service of citizens, and to better prevent, diagnose, and treat diseases. The proposal provides a uniform basis for secondary research and clarifies uncertainty over the use of health data for research purposes.

The European Health Data Space, while promising, also presents several challenges and concerns. These include based on the regulation text:

- *Interoperability*: One of the key challenges is establishing an interoperability framework that ensures the appropriate use of health data across different systems and countries. This involves addressing technical, legal, and ethical issues to enable seamless data sharing and integration.
- *Data privacy and security*: The European Health Data Space aims to empower individuals by giving them increased digital access and control over their personal health data[3]. However, ensuring the privacy and security of this data is crucial. Striking the right balance between data accessibility and protection is a challenge that needs to be addressed.
- *Legal and regulatory framework*: The success of the European Health Data Space depends on having the right legislation and policy decisions in place. Harmonizing data protection laws and regulations across EU member states is essential to facilitate cross-border data sharing while maintaining data privacy and security.
- *Data governance and consent*: Establishing a governance framework that governs the collection, storage, and use of health data is critical. Ensuring that individuals give informed consent for the use of their data and having clear guidelines on data ownership, access, and usage rights are important considerations.
- *Technical infrastructure*: Building a robust and scalable technical infrastructure to support the exchange, use, and reuse of health data is a significant challenge. This includes addressing issues related to data standardization, data quality, data integration, and data storage.
- *Stakeholder engagement and trust*: Engaging various stakeholders, including healthcare providers, researchers, policymakers, and the public, is crucial for the success of the European Health Data Space. Building trust among these stakeholders

and addressing concerns related to data misuse, discrimination, and commercial exploitation is essential.

Addressing these challenges and concerns will require collaboration among EU member states, policymakers, healthcare professionals, researchers, and technology experts. It will involve developing clear guidelines, implementing robust security measures, ensuring transparency, and fostering public awareness and trust in the use of health data for research and innovation.

In the context of secondary use of data, the EHDS is designed to allow health data to be used for purposes beyond direct patient care ("primary use"), such as research, policymaking, and innovation in health technologies. This includes using data for developing AI-driven health solutions, conducting large-scale health studies, and improving public health strategies.

2.3 Privacy Enhancing Technology, Anonymisation and Flexibility on Using Rare Cancer Data

Secondary use of data in research on rare types of cancer requires data sharing in any form. Generally, there is simply too little data available per healthcare centre to conduct thorough research, compute statistics and ultimately collect solid evidence to impact patient care. *Is it like searching for a needle in a haystack regarding the necessary analysis, or do we need the whole haystack?*

In recent years, a lot of research has been conducted on privacy-preserving technology to ensure privacy protection. The privacy-enhancing movement is seen as a kind of "holy grail" [8]. The only "way out" to open data/read access in any way, for example for research purposes, while also protecting individuals' privacy [8]. Privacy Enhancing Technologies (PETs), which have advanced rapidly over the past few years, such as Multi-Party Computation (MPC), Federated Learning, allowing analysts to gain insights without access to sensitive, person-identifiable data or the centralisation of data.

In this way, the researcher has the opportunity to harness the full potential of multiple datasets while the data holder remains in control. However, current PETs do not address the most relevant practical issue: how to share high-quality individual data in a way that ensures privacy is maintained, but the full potential of a dataset can be utilised. This is particularly crucial to foster innovation in the field of rare types of cancer.

What is often seen in the preparation of many datasets is "cleaning" the data to ensure anonymity/pseudonymity. For example, removing certain fields so that the identity can no longer be traced. In the Netherlands, it is in general not possible to use the BSN number for secondary use. Non-government organisations may only use the BSN if this is required by law. Besides MPC and Federated Learning, synthetic data has recently gained quite a bit of momentum. With again golden promises, but in practice faces the same challenges. The data most vulnerable to privacy attacks under anonymisation techniques, statistical outliers that often belong to minority subpopulations, can only be protected from privacy breaches if the published synthetic data does not retain the full promised value of the original dataset (Stadler and Troncoso 2022).

A lot of research has shown that sharing high-dimensional datasets in a way that preserves both privacy and high usability is nearly impossible. Recent scientific research has highlighted the significant challenges in sharing high-dimensional datasets while preserving both privacy and usability. The following key findings from recent papers substantiate that claim:

- The fundamental tension between privacy protection and data utility is particularly pronounced for high-dimensional datasets. As the number of attributes increases, it becomes increasingly difficult to maintain both strong privacy guarantees and high data utility [9, 10].
- Traditional de-identification techniques like k-anonymity and l-diversity have been shown to be inadequate for high-dimensional data. These methods often result in excessive information loss or fail to provide meaningful privacy protection when applied to datasets with many attributes [10].
- The "curse of dimensionality" poses a major challenge for privacy-preserving data publishing. As the number of dimensions increases, data points become more sparse and unique, making it easier to re-identify individuals even from seemingly anonymized data [9, 11].

While progress is being made, the fundamental tension between privacy and utility in high-dimensional data sharing persists. Current research suggests that achieving both strong privacy guarantees and high usability for such datasets remains an open challenge in the field of privacy-preserving data publishing.

We therefore conclude that the pursuit of a data release mechanism that simultaneously achieves full flexibility, high usability, and strong privacy guarantees approaches an inherently unattainable objective, given the fundamental trade-offs involved. As difficult as it may be, both researchers and practitioners should finally accept the inherent trade-off between high flexibility in data usage and strong privacy guarantees, even if this means reducing the scope of data-driven applications. Depending on the data used, the goals of data sharing, and their privacy requirements, data holders will need to make explicit choices about the data-sharing methods most suitable for their use case [8].

We conclude that privacy researchers and policymakers need to reconsider their current approach to supporting data holders in their goal of sharing data in a privacy-preserving way. As a first step, both groups should give up the futile search for a panacea for all-purpose-utility high-privacy sharing of detailed data. Instead, we argue that data holders must accept that the set of use cases that can be addressed under strict privacy guarantees may be limited, and so too are the data-driven business models linked to them. Privacy researchers should therefore reorient their efforts toward developing tools that help data holders identify those use cases that can be addressed simultaneously under good privacy and good usability conditions. Finally, we recommend that policymakers, together with technical experts, develop guidelines to help data holders navigate the complex landscape of Privacy Enhancing Technologies (PETs). These guidelines should not only focus on matching use cases with their appropriate sharing technologies but also include recommendations for empirical evaluation methods that can assure the public that any loss of privacy is balanced against the promised societal benefits.

It thus remains a kind of constant balancing act, in making trade-offs. The governance & process of how to handle (meta) data with the data holder as well as the data processor is crucial. After which technology (partly) contributes to protecting/safeguarding privacy, but it remains a balance on a thin line.

There are a few approaches in this regard, namely anonymity (pseudonymising and/or anonymising individual data) and separately perhaps obtaining prior patient consent.

For example, the choice can be made to work with anonymous data per research centre. This is to avoid a substantial legal burden. As described above, both paths are valid, but ensuring anonymity is not straightforward.

Example: Three healthcare centres conduct a federated learning/analysis. Where anonymity is established based on several criteria (aside from what these are), but the data sets are, of course, not very large due to the rare types of cancer. If a researcher conducts this analysis at time A and then conducts another analysis at time B with a different result, it could mathematically be deduced who this new individual is. Of course, this involves complex calculations, but the risk cannot be completely ruled out.

Given the challenges described above, having clear and explicit agreements is crucial. Such an agreement framework or rulebook helps reduce risks or at least be aware of them. Governance is crucial, this has been thought through by making several preliminary agreements. A steering board/committee issues several conditions beforehand, such as when data is considered anonymous, algorithms and study protocols must be pre-approved, after which the researcher can use these approved building blocks. By integrating process and technology from the start, one can speak of privacy-by-design. As mentioned earlier, ruling everything out is impossible, and such risks cannot be excluded; otherwise, it becomes unworkable.

Making data available to a researcher is crucial depending on the respective goal/purpose, with the data minimisation principle[7] applied. In addition, the other requirements of the GDPR must be met.

- adequate – sufficient to properly fulfil your stated purpose;
- relevant – has a rational link to that purpose;
- and limited to what is necessary – you do not hold more than you need for that purpose.

(ICO definition - Principle (c): Data minimisation I ICO).

Whereby it is not always clear what is adequate, relevant and limited. This remains partly a grey area per member state within the EU. Everything obviously depends on the purpose limitation.

A lung cancer screening and risk prediction study for example illustrates the challenges in determining what data is adequate, relevant, and limited. Here's an elaboration on why these distinctions ares not always clear-cut. Determining what constitutes adequate data for lung cancer research can be complex considering the smoking history. While pack-years of smoking is crucial, it may not capture the full picture. For instance, the intensity of smoking (cigarettes per day) and duration might have different impacts on risks [12]. Assessing relevance can be challenging in case of Ethnicity. Its inclusion is relevant due to varying risk factors among different groups, but it's not always clear how to categorize mixed ethnicities or how much detail is necessary [12]. Limiting data collection while ensuring comprehensive risk assessment can be tricky in case of a partial postcode for example. While limited to protect privacy, it might not provide sufficient granularity for accurate air pollution exposure assessment.

---

[7] Principle (c): Data minimisation I ICO.

In general it is not always clear because of:

- Evolving research: New studies constantly reveal new risk factors or refine our understanding of known ones. For example, recent research has highlighted the importance of considering younger populations for lung cancer risk [12];
- Individual variations: What's adequate or relevant for one person might not be for another. For instance, occupational exposure might be highly relevant for some individuals but not others;
- Technological advancements: As diagnostic technologies improve, the definition of "adequate" data may change. For example, more sophisticated CT scans might provide more detailed information, blurring the line between adequate and excessive data;
- Balancing privacy and research needs: While limiting data collection protects privacy, it might hinder the development of more accurate prediction models. For instance, more detailed geographical data could improve risk assessment related to environmental factors but could also compromise anonymity;
- Intersectionality of risk factors: The relevance of certain data points might depend on their interaction with others. For example, the relevance of Body-Mass Index (BMI) might vary depending on smoking history or ethnicity;
- Future research potential: Data that seems irrelevant now might become crucial in future studies, making it difficult to determine what's truly limited to the current purpose.

In conclusion, the dynamic nature of medical research, individual variability in risk factors, and the need to balance comprehensive risk assessment with data protection make it challenging to definitively categorize data as adequate, relevant, or limited in lung cancer research. This complexity underscores the importance of regular reassessment of data collection practices in light of new research findings and evolving ethical standards[8], [13].

Everything revolves around risk management, which is why a table with possible measures to reduce risks concerning personal data, while maintaining some workability for secondary use, is essential. After all, collecting all data in one place, in a bunker, with guards checking whether the researcher's identity is correct, the purpose limitation, and then on a computer without an external connection, does not help to promote innovation.

3 Approach and Method – Open Infrastructure

We work together to develop a secure and privacy preserving open infrastructure for federated analysis of Real World Data (RWD). This creates an abundance of new insights that serve both public and private benefits. The open infrastructure is complemented with carefully formulated agreements between different actors within the ecosystem for a trustworthy and transparent environment.

New ways of evidence generation Real World Evidence (RWE) for novel health interventions and as support for Value Based Health Care is needed. Today access to RWE is

---

[8] https://ico.org.uk/for-organisations/uk-gdpr-guidance-and-resources/data-protection-princi ples/a-guide-to-the-data-protection-principles/the-principles/data-minimisation/.

hampered by highly siloed and unstructured health data in combination with fear of non-compliance to current (GDPR) and future (EHDS) regulation for health data exchange. Currently, the speed of acceleration medical research needs to be increased, improve patient care, and contribute to the development of innovative healthcare solutions.

Offering an open infra structure to create a network of secure and trustworthy data sharing spaces across partner organization(s), based on common standards and interoperability frameworks. This initiative will support the development of improving access to healthcare, promoting innovation, and empowering patients while also ensuring the protection of personal data and the respect of data protection rules (Fig. 1).

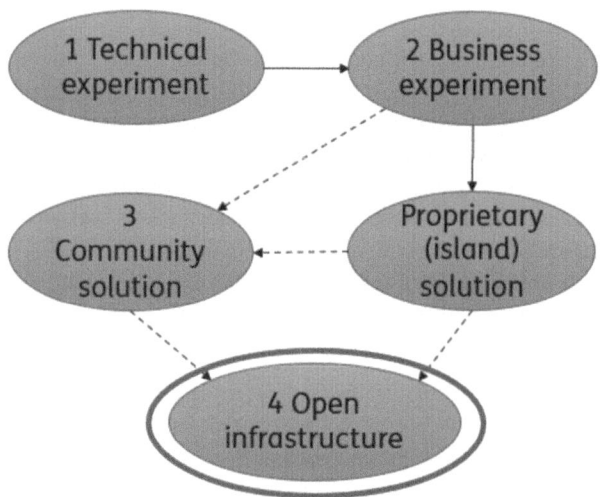

Fig. 1. The road *towards to an open infrastructure following business and technology.*

Basically the open infrastructure exists of various nodes, also referred to as FAIR (Findable Accessible Interoperable and Reusable) data stations. These are connected and accessed via International Data Spaces (IDS) [5]. The analysis of data cross different organisations is enabled via Privacy Enhancing Techniques (PET). Ensuring that these technologies are developed and used in a way that benefits everyone in Europe.

A technology stack defining the standardisation (open standards e.g. Observational Medical Outcomes Partnership (OMOP) Common Data Model (CDM)), the technical requirements for data access (International Data Spaces) and privacy-by-design data exchange (Open standards for PETs) will be defined. Once in place the ecosystem will be tested according to the schema below:

To create new insights (RWE) in peoples' health journeys by combining real world data from different organisations and sources. And a unified approach that can utilise the power of artificial intelligence for improving diagnostic, optimise care processes, improve interaction within the value chain of health. Currently two types of cancer are being analysed, namely lung cancer and ovarium carcinoma.

The challenge is to address the compartmentalized nature of healthcare systems while protecting privacy to create knowledge on people's complete health journey. This problem can be resolved with a sustainable future-proof decentralised infrastructure to analyse and access health data from multiple sources in a privacy-by-design way.

3.1 Data Space Protocol

The Data Space Protocol (DSP) is a framework designed to facilitate secure and efficient data sharing within decentralized ecosystems. It establishes standardized mechanisms for data exchange, ensuring interoperability, trust, and data sovereignty among participants. By leveraging principles such as data minimization, access control, and encryption, the DSP enables organizations to collaborate while maintaining compliance with data protection regulations. It is particularly relevant in industries like healthcare, finance, and smart cities, where sensitive data must be shared without compromising privacy or ownership. The DSP is currently adopted in a Eclipse Working Group - https://projects.eclipse.org/proposals/eclipse-dataspace-protocol.

"It provides a set of specifications designed to facilitate interoperable data sharing between entities governed by usage control and based on Web technologies. These specifications define the schemas and protocols required for entities to publish data, negotiate usage agreements, and access data as part of a federation of technical systems termed a dataspace.

Sharing data between autonomous entities requires the provision of metadata to facilitate the transfer of assets by making use of a data transfer (or application layer) protocol. The Eclipse Dataspace Protocol defines how this metadata is provisioned:

- How data assets are deployed as DCAT Catalogs and usage control is expressed as ODRL Policies.
- How contract agreements that govern data usage are syntactically expressed and electronically negotiated.
- How data assets are accessed using data transfer protocols.
- The specifications are organized into the following documents:
- Dataspace Model and Dataspace Terminology documents that define key terms.
- Catalog Protocol and Catalog HTTPS Binding documents that define how DCAT Catalogs are published and accessed as HTTPS endpoints respectively.
- Contract Negotiation Protocol and Contract Negotiation HTTPS Binding documents that define how contract negotiations are conducted and requested via HTTPS endpoints.
- Transfer Process Protocol and Transfer Process HTTPS Binding documents that define how transfer processes using a given data transfer protocol are governed via HTTPS endpoints.

This specification does not cover the data transfer process as such." [14].

4 Artifact: The Data Space Architecture

4.1 Design Objectives and Starting Points

One of the main objectives of is: *"to design and develop a generic health data space infrastructure, coupling International Data Spaces (IDS) standards with privacy-enhancing technologies (PETs) supporting the Personal Health Train set of agreements"*.

Multiple types of data sharing methodologies to train AI models will be made possible in the data space infrastructure. The approach A2D (Algorithm to Data) in which the data stays at the source, and the algorithm 'travels' to the data will be made in two distinctions:

- Federated learning (FL). Using this approach, machine learning models are trained locally, and only aggregated model parameters are shared. While it is primarily suitable for a 'horizontally partitioned' data setting (different organizations having the same type of data over different groups of patients), some first FL algorithms have appeared that can be used on a 'vertically partitioned' data setting: There are different data attributes at different organizations over the same group of patients.
- Multi-Party Computation (MPC), cryptographic techniques to jointly train AI-algorithms on encrypted data without sharing any underlying sensitive data, suitable for 'vertically partitioned' data. MPC is more secure than FL, but requiring more computation time. It has been applied in medical settings for vertically partitioned data before.

In all cases it is crucial that the algorithm is trusted by everyone in the ecosystem and the infrastructure will facilitate the strengthening of trust between the various stakeholders by making it explicit what data is used when, for what, by whom.

The main focus is to enable A2D (MPC/FL) in the vertical and horizontal setting in the Health Data Space. By working with different technologies and implementations, we ensure interoperability of infrastructures and create an open environment.

In particular, FAIR-principles for the description of available data are supported by IDS, in order for 'Machine2Machine' communication to be possible. Datasets and services should be Findable, Accessible, Interoperable and Reusable. Next to the FAIR principles the reference architecture of IDS is applied to specify per organization, user, algorithm which data can be used and for which reason.

The dataspace shall also be able to support data to the algorithm (D2A) so that the value chain can benefit from data integration e.g. clinical, radiological, lab, genetic pathological data.

4.2 System Context

The architecture describes the *infrastructure* which is a federations of *certified software services* using the *Dataspace* to exchange data in a secure and controlled way. Figure 2 describes the context of the *infrastructure* and the *types of actors* it interacts with.

To preserve privacy of the medical data, only certified software service are allowed core functionality is the Dataspace (blue central circle in Fig. 2) which provides secure exchange of data between trusted participants. This requires the identity and authentication of users such as researchers by a trusted Identity provider. For the infrastructure verifiable credentials is used based on YIVI. Not only to verify the correct inner working of the system as a whole based on a certification process, but also to monitor that the infrastructure works according to the commonly agreed terms and conditions of the dataspace. The governance board has the responsibility to manage and monitor the operations of the infrastructure but will be checked by periodic independent audits.

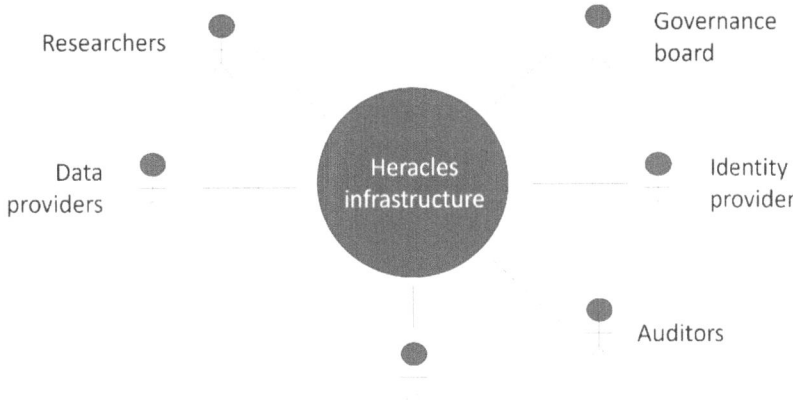

Fig. 2. Infrastructure context diagram.

4.3 Infrastructure Nodes

The infrastructure consists of an organisational and a supporting technical part. The technical part describes how the infrastructure is built of the separate nodes which contain the following main functional components, see figure below:

- A FAIR Data Point (FDP) enables discovery of available data at FAIR Data Stations to implement the "F" of findable in FAIR and to provide information about the data including the terms and conditions for using the data;
- A FAIR Data Station (FDS) (https://specs.fairdatapoint.org/fdp-specs-v1.2.html) enables controlled access to data to implement the "A" of accessible in FAIR where a copy of the data is being stored which is described in a FAIR Data Point. How the data is being processed can vary per research analysis and should be agreed and specified in advance as part of a Data Permit;
- Data Permit Management (DPM) supports a community driven approach to reach agreement about data usage. When all involved stakeholders agree on the research goal, approach and required means of resources and data in particular, the result will be a Data Permit. A Data Permit is an agreement for specific research goal, and describes the terms and conditions for using data at the FAIR Data Stations. A digital subset of the Data Permit will be used by the infrastructure to enforce the agreement and to control access accordingly.

Research applications are required for starting and handling the aggregated (anonymized) results collected at FAIR Data Stations. Research applications must implement the API's and must be known as part of the agreements to grant data usage but are not part of the infrastructure. Although the API's are based on European standards to connect with other Health dataspaces (Fig. 3).

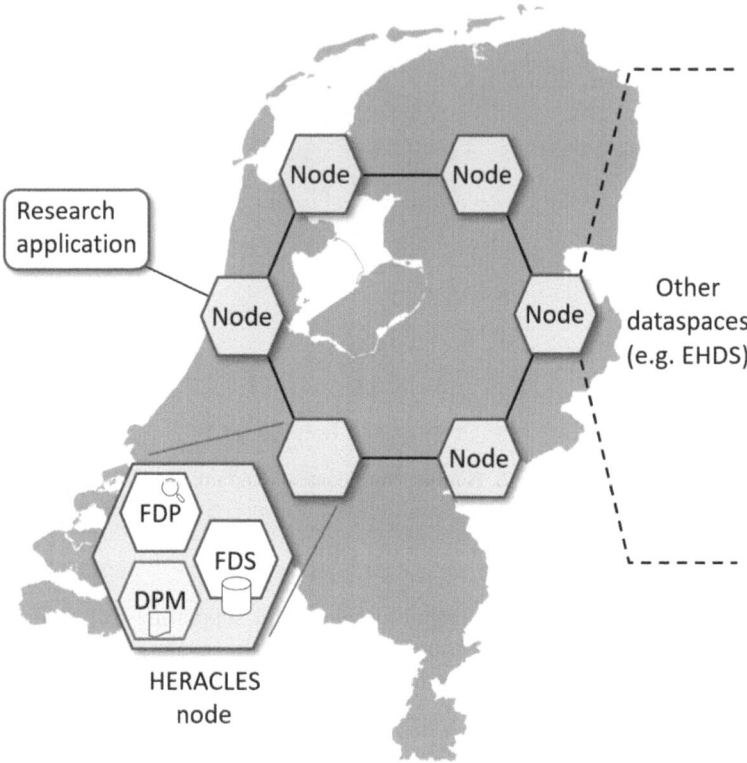

Fig. 3. Functional architecture of the infrastructure

4.4   Process View

The Process Layer specifies the interactions taking place between the different components of the infrastructure. It thereby provides a dynamic view of the architecture.

To be compatible with EHDS, the artifact user process flow should be compatible with the following revised user journey of EHDS (Fig. 4).

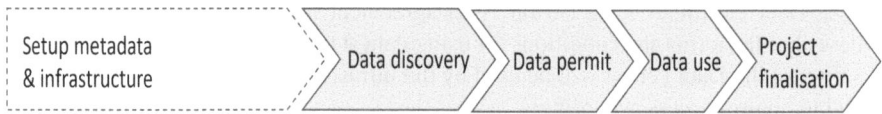

Fig. 4. EHDS user journey phases

The Setup metadata & infrastructure phase, is considered by EDHS not part of the user journey but is identified as a required and enabling step. In the proposed architecture there is a strong focus on establishing trust, identification management and certification which are part of this first step.

To explain more clearly the content of these processes and to reuse the dataspace processes defined in the IDSA Reference Architecture (IDS-RAM), the process names in the current infrastructure deviates slightly from the EHDS phase names, but their functionality is compatible with EHDS (Fig. 5).

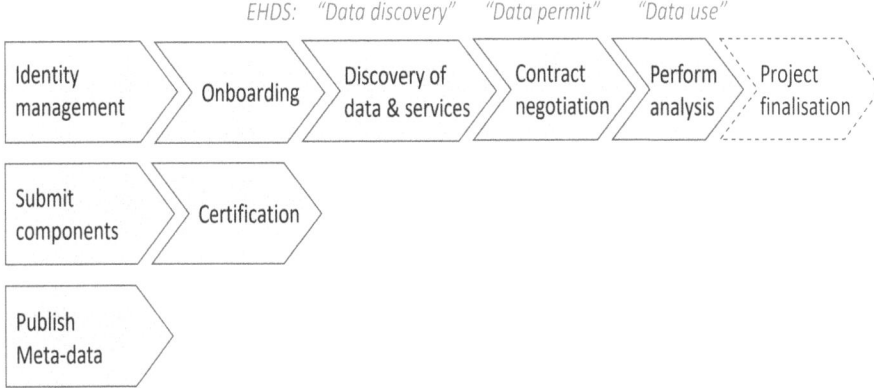

Fig. 5. Artifact user/research journey processes.

The first five processes on left in the user/research journey are considered to be generic processes and overlapping with the initial setup metadata & infrastructure step of EHDS. The infrastructure focuses first on creating the proper conditions to enable the use of data. Supporting the project finalisation process has a lower priority.

The processes Submit components, Certification, Publish meta-data are enabling the main user/research journey line therefore visualised beside the centre process flow. Identity management is in general the first step and applicable for all other processes because only participants who are successfully onboarded can be valid actors. Therefore, the identity management and onboarding processes are described first.

Identity Management

Identity management is a critical aspect of information security and online services, dealing with the identification, authentication, and management of individuals' digital identities. The following key-aspects are taken in account:

- Identification, the process of recognizing an actor or entity within a system. This involves a unique identifier to be stored in a register as a core functionality of the Dataspace;
- Authentication, the process of verifying that an individual or entity is who they claim to be. This is achieved through *verifiable credentials* based on Self Sovereign Identities which is a core functionality of the Dataspace;
- Verifiable Credentials are digital documents that are used to establish trust in the identity and attributes (claims) of an individual or entity. They are issued by a trusted authority and can be securely stored and presented by the individual when required.

Overall, identity management is essential for controlling access to resources in within the infrastructure, ensuring that users are accurately identified, authenticated, and granted appropriate access based on verifiable credentials.

Onboarding

After acquiring verifiable credentials, a user applies for registration via the onboarding process. The objective of this process is to admit only users with verified credentials and are compliant with the Governance model. The following steps are identified:

- User Registration, the user initiates the process by providing verifiable credentials as result of the previously described Identification management process. The self-sovereign identities contain the meta-information that the user wants to share;
- Verification of Verifiable Credentials, the provided verifiable credentials are verified by checking the digital signatures or cryptographic proofs against the issuing authority's public key to ensure authenticity and validity. Valid issuing authorities should be described in the Governance model. Verification of verifiable credentials is a core function of the Dataspace;
- Compliance with Terms and Conditions, the user is presented with the terms and conditions of the governance model of the system. This may include privacy policies, user responsibilities, and other regulatory compliances. The user must agree to these terms, often by checking a box or providing digital consent
- Assessment of Compliance, the system assesses if the user meets all the specified criteria and requirements as per the governance model. This may involve automated checks or manual review processes;
- Final Registration, if the user successfully verifies their credentials and agrees to the terms and conditions, the registration process will be completed and the user information will be stored securely, making them a recognized and authenticated entity within the system.

The result of a successful onboarding process is that the user's information is made findable within the system, subject to privacy settings and access controls. This means they can be identified and authenticated in future interactions, and they may be granted access to specific resources or services within the system. This process ensures that only verified and compliant users are onboarded, maintaining the integrity and security of the system.

Submit Components

The objective of this process is to identify software components and to make them findable. It starts with assigning a unique identification to a software component which will be registered in a so-called service catalogue, including meta data to describe the software component or service. This identification shall be linked to a verifiable signature of the software/service component.

Meta-data of software components including their identification and signature are stored in the service catalogue which is a core functionality of the Dataspace. The following three step approach is proposed:

- Collection and Preparation: This step starts with the software or service provider and involves gathering all the necessary meta-data including a description, categories, keywords for search optimization, a unique verifiable signature and privacy policies. The preparation phase involves organizing it in a structured format.
- Submission and Review: Once the software component or service and its meta-data are ready, the information is submitted to the service catalogue of the infrastructure. After submission, the Governance board is accountable for a review process to checks if the provided information is compliant with the terms and conditions as stated in the governance model regarding compliance with the guidelines, standards, technical requirements, and legal issues. After successful review the status of a software component or service changes to "candidate" and the certification process can start. Otherwise the submission will be rejected and the provider has to optimize the previous step.
- Post-submission Activities: After a successfully certification process, the post-submission activities include gathering user feedback, releasing updates to fix bugs, improve functionality, or add new features. All changes require a re-certification which practically means a submission of a new version and performing the preceding step of submission and review.

Overall, the submitted components (software or services) will only be visible to the infrastructure users after a successful certification process.

Certification

The objective of this process is to verify that a software component or service is compliant with the terms and conditions stated in the Governance model. The role of auditor and the procedure how to perform the verification has to be described in the Governance model as well.

The certification process is successfully applied if all participants of the infrastructure can trust a certified software component: that it preserves the privacy and security aspects and in general respect the *terms and conditions as defined in the Governance model*.

The result of a successful certification is a *verifiable certificate* linked to the identification and a verifiable signature of the software component or service. Practically it means that the certificate will be added to the service catalogue.

The certification of software components or services by an evaluation authority involves a detailed and methodical process. This process ensures that the software meets specific standards of quality, security, and compliance. The following steps are identified:

- Detailed Audit and Testing: The auditing party conducts a thorough examination of the software. This includes code reviews, security audits, performance testing, and compliance checks with relevant standards and regulations. The auditing process is comprehensive and aims to identify any vulnerabilities, defects, or non-compliance issues. The auditor may use a variety of tools and methodologies to assess the software. If issues are identified, the developer is typically given an opportunity to address them and resubmit the software for reassessment.
- Certification and Issuance of Certificate: Once the software passes the audit and meets all the required standards, the auditing party issues a certificate. This certificate is

linked to a unique identity and signature of the software, including details like the version number and release date. The certificate also features a verifiable signature from the auditing party, ensuring the authenticity and integrity of the certification. The software provider can then use this certification to demonstrate the reliability and compliance of their software to clients, users, or regulatory bodies.

- Publication Activities: After a successfully certification process the Governance board will publish the software component/service with a verifiable certificate in the service catalogue to become visible and findable within the infrastructure.
- Post-Certification: After receiving certification, the software provider must maintain the standards for which the certification was awarded. This may include regular updates, patches, and re-audits, especially if significant changes are made to the software or new regulations come into effect. The software provider should also monitor the software for any emerging threats or vulnerabilities and take prompt action to address them, ensuring continued compliance and security.

Overall, for the infrastructure, the certification process is an essential process to contribute to "trust" and mainly an organisational rather than a technical aspect.

Publish Meta-data

After successful onboarding, data providers can publish information (meta-data) via a FAIR Data Point about what kind of data they provide including the terms and conditions for usage for the meta-data itself as well for the data to be provided.

Publishing metadata involves several key steps to ensure that the information is accurate, accessible, and useful. The following steps are identified:

- Collection and Preparation: This step starts with the data provider and involves gathering all the necessary meta-data. The preparation phase involves cleaning the metadata, organizing it in a structured format, and ensuring it aligns with the standards or schema.
- Metadata Creation: In this step, the metadata is being uploaded to the Infrastructure in Data Fair Points. This includes adding the identity of the provider references to already defined / existing standards if applicable;
- Quality Assurance and Validation: Before publishing, it's crucial to ensure that the metadata is accurate, consistent, and adheres to the defined standards. This quality assurance might involve manual checks or automated validation processes. It's important to ensure that the metadata accurately represents the data it describes and is free from errors;
- Publication and Maintenance: The final step is to publish (release) the metadata so that it can be accessed by users or systems as part of the discovery process. After publication, regular maintenance is essential to keep the metadata up-to-date and relevant. This might involve updating records to reflect changes in the underlying data, adding new metadata as new data becomes available or correcting any errors that are discovered after publication.

Overall, the availability and the quality of meta-data are crucial for collaboration within the infrastructure and facilitates this via the concept of *FAIR Data Points*.

Discovery of Data & Services

This process is compliant with the EHDS Data Discovery phase of the EHDS users' journey to request access to health data for secondary use. In this phase/process, researchers should be able to search the data available and needed to perform their work. For the infrastructure this process is extended to finding supporting components (software/services) as well for specialized operations such as the use of Privacy Enhanced Technologies (PET).

This process depends fully on the previously described processes about Submitting Components & Services and Publishing meta-data. The following simplified steps are identified:

- Discovery of data: identifying and cataloguing various data sources, discovering the quality and availability of data resources. The outcome is a specification of data the researchers plan to use;
- Refine research objective and define approach: based on the available data (sources), the quality of data and the ability to join them, researchers can refine their plans. The research plan is required as justification to acquire permission to use the data but also specify how to use the data;
- Discovery of supporting components: helps researchers to identify tools, services, and resources that can aid in data analysis, visualization, and management. This can include tools for data cleaning, data mining, and data visualization.

The outcome is a plan that specifies which data from which data sources are needed, how this data will be used and which components will be used to obtain permission in the next phase.

Contract Negotiation (Request Data Permit)

This process is compliant the EHDS Data Permit phase, where researcher request data usage permission, and the governance board and all involved data providers verify compliancy with their usage policies. The following steps are identified:

- Request data permit application: a request contains a verified identity of the requester and a research plan which includes the research objective, a specification of the data that is needed and a description how the data is being processed;
- Request assessment: the Governance Board is accountable to verify compliancy of the request (c.q. the research plan) with legislation and the Governance model. This implies that the Governance model shall contain terms and conditions for data usage including applicable laws. The Governance Board is responsible to organise an operational process to perform the assessment in collaboration with the involved data providers. This operational process produces a compliancy list and a Data Protection Impact Assessment (DPIA);
- Contract negotiation: based on the compliancy list and the DPIA, omission, deviations and recommendations are return to the requester. In case the request is not compliant, a negotiation will be started to find out if the request can be altered or completed to become compliant with the law and the commonly agreed principles as stated in the Governance model;

- Grant permit or reject: in case a request is granted, the outcome is an agreed research plan, a DPIA and a technical permit in the form of an electronic contract. In case of a rejection, an explanation will be returned.

Overall, the Governance board is accountable for the contract negotiation process and therefore also for the permission. Involvement of the data providers in the assessment step is essential to enable data sovereignty and to ensure proper use of sensitive data.

The Data Permit phase c.q. this process of contract negotiation is currently a cumbersome and time-consuming procedure. Lead times of two years are not an exception but a huge obstacle to overcome for efficient and effect medical research. One of the objectives is to propose a procedure with a significant reduction in lead time.

5 Discussion

5.1 To Lower the Need for IT Expertise

Federated learning technologies, such as the Personal Health Train, have proven their value in research contexts, offering privacy-preserving ways to analyze distributed health data. However, despite their demonstrated potential, these technologies remain largely confined to research prototypes. Their practical deployment across institutions still requires ongoing support from developers and dedicated IT staff at each participating center. A scalable, production-ready Software as a Service (SaaS) model for federated learning is currently lacking. With the rise of European Health Data Space (EHDS), the EU is promoting standardization in technologies. This allows for technologies that enable data partners to apply for all their secondary data use applications (i.e. not exclusively for rare solid cancers in adults). Harmonized and interoperable technologies facilitate healthcare centers as they will simplify their IT strategy regarding data access and sharing.

The challenge is to use data within the federated registry which can be accessed and analyzed with minimal support from developers, such that researchers, healthcare professionals and other can utilize the data as-if they were in one place.

5.2 To Lower Technology Barriers

Hospitals IT may not be willing to adopt a data-sensitive technology dedicated only for one collaboration and one disease group, but seek scalable, proven applications that can be used for a wide range of users and disease domains. Working with proven technology, embraced by leading organizations creates trust with STARTER centers in both the technical solution as well as its sustainability.

The challenge is to create a federated registry that can easily implemented at participating centers.

6 Conclusion

The proposed artifact/infrastructure represents a significant advancement in the development and integration of a pan-European data infrastructure for rare adult solid cancers. This initiative not only enhances the quality of cancer research but also aligns closely with the broader objectives of the European Health Data Space (EHDS).

The proposed infrastructure is built on open standards. And is also one of the first infrastructures to adopt future European Standards e.g. CEN/CENELEC Trusted Data Transaction and the Data Space Protocol for secure transactions.

The EHDS aims to create a secure and standardized framework for the sharing of health data across the European Union, facilitating better healthcare delivery, research, and innovation. The proposed infrastructure efforts are a practical realization of these goals, particularly within the specialized field of (rare) cancers where secondary data is required. By leveraging a federated data infrastructure, the infrastructure ensures that sensitive patient data remains decentralized, thereby upholding the highest standards of data privacy and security while enabling comprehensive research.

6.1   Enhancing Data Privacy and Security Through Federated Learning

One of the core strengths of the proposed infrastructure is its adoption of federated learning and other Privacy-Enhancing Technologies (PETs). These technologies allow for the analysis of vast datasets without the need for data centralization, a method that directly addresses privacy concerns inherent in cross-border data sharing. By keeping data at the source within individual health centers, trying to minimizes the risks associated with data breaches and unauthorized access, a key requirement under GDPR and other European data protection regulations.

The implementation of tools such as FL demonstrates how the EHDS's objectives can be met while maintaining compliance with strict privacy standards. This approach not only ensures that patient data is protected but also enables researchers to draw meaningful insights from large, diverse datasets, which are crucial for advancing rare cancer research.

6.2   Bridging the Gap Between Local and Pan-European Data Initiatives

The current study offers an open-source blueprint for how local health centers and research institutions can contribute to and benefit from a pan-European data infrastructure. By maintaining autonomy over their data while participating in a larger federated system, these centers can contribute to a collective research effort without compromising their governance or data sovereignty. This model supports the EHDS's vision of a unified yet decentralized health data space, where data flows freely for the benefit of all, yet privacy and local control are preserved.

References

1. Ministry of Health, Welfare and Sport: Integraal Zorgakkoord: Samen werken aan gezonde zorg (2022)
2. Wilkinson, M.D., et al.: The FAIR Guiding Principles for scientific data management and stewardship. Sci. Data **3**, 1–9 (2016)
3. Mons, B., Schultes, E., Liu, F., Jacobsen, A.: The FAIR principles: first generation implementation choices and challenges. Data Intell. **2**, 1–9 (2020)

4. Bastiaansen, H., Kollenstart, M., Dalmolen, S., van Engers, T.M.: User-centric network-model for data control with interoperable legal data sharing artefacts: Improved data sovereignty, trust and security for enhanced adoption in inter organizational and supply chain is applications. Presented at the 24th Pacific Asia Conference on Information Systems: Information Systems (IS) for the Future, PACIS 2020 (2020)

5. Bastiaansen, H., Dalmolen, S., Kollenstart, M., Punter, M.: Infrastructural Sovereignty over Agreement and Transaction Data ('Metadata') in an Open Network-Model for Multilateral Sharing of Sensitive Data (2019)

6. Stolwijk, C., Punter, M., Timmers, P., Julian, R., Regeczi, D., Dalmolen, S.: Towards a sovereign digital future – the Netherlands in Europe. TNO (2024)

7. Hussein, R., et al.: Getting ready for the European Health Data Space (EHDS): IDERHA's plan to align with the latest EHDS requirements for the secondary use of health data. Open Res. Eur. **4**, 160 (2024)

8. Stadler, T., Troncoso, C.: Why the search for a privacy-preserving data sharing mechanism is failing. Nat. Comput. Sci. **2**, 208–210 (2022)

9. Shi, W., Zhang, X., Chen, H., Zhang, X.: High dimensional data differential privacy protection publishing method based on association analysis. Electronics **12**, 2779 (2023)

10. Gadotti, A., Rocher, L., Houssiau, F., Crețu, A.-M., de Montjoye, Y.-A.: Anonymization: the imperfect science of using data while preserving privacy. Sci. Adv. **10**, eadn7053 (2024)

11. Chu, Z., He, J., Zhang, X., Zhang, X., Zhu, N.: Differential privacy high-dimensional data publishing based on feature selection and clustering. Electronics **12**, 1959 (2023)

12. Callender, T., et al.: Assessing eligibility for lung cancer screening using parsimonious ensemble machine learning models: a development and validation study. PLoS Med. **20**, e1004287 (2023)

13. Chandran, U., Reps, J., Yang, R., Vachani, A., Maldonado, F., Kalsekar, I.: Machine learning and real-world data to predict lung cancer risk in routine care. Cancer Epidemiol. Biomarkers Prev. **32**, 337–343 (2023)

14. Data Space Protocol. https://projects.eclipse.org/proposals/eclipse-dataspace-protocol

Sharing Data in Ecosystems

Erik Beulen$^{(\boxtimes)}$![ORCID]

Alliance Manchester Business School, University of Manchester, Manchester, UK
`erik.beulen@manchester.ac.uk`

Abstract. Sharing data and insights in ecosystems is becoming more and more important in creating value in end-to-end value journeys. This sets a high bar for any organisation, as innovations are presenting themselves at an unprecedented pace, many ecosystems are very dynamic, and data volumes continue to grow significantly. On top of that, legislation related to data and artificial intelligence is growing, but always lagging behind the pace of change-organisations must often define their own boundaries and policies. There is a lot to take in for organisations.

The market research focuses on the implications of data sharing in ecosystems. This study is based on a survey including 59 responses of executives responsible and involved in digital transformations. The qualitative analysis of the survey provides practical insights and recommendations.

Operationalising cross-organisational governance turned out to be particularly difficult, as investing in tooling/platforms that facilitate the exchange of data is not straightforward and also challenging to integrate. Also, security concerns need to be addressed when sharing data.

Organisations need to adjust their operating models to be on the one hand more efficient and on the other hand to enable sharing data and insights in ecosystems creating intellectual property. Organisations also need to take a strategic orientation with a focus on understanding their market position, and market and regulatory developments – adjusting their business models.

Keywords: artificial intelligence · co-creation · data governance · data quality · data sharing · digital transformations · disruption

1 Introduction

Mant organisations are struggling with sharing data in ecosystems [1]. This is negatively impacting digital transformation success, as well as the performance of organisations [2].

Over decades organisations are involved in digital transformations [3–5]. Initially the focus of digital transformations was on digitisation followed by digitalisation [6]. In digitisation organisations automated processes and activities. This was not only more efficient but also improved the quality and decision-making [7]. In digitalisation organisations also enhance their business models [8].

In conjunction with digital transformations, also outsourcing got traction in many organisations, as they needed help from external service providers with their digitisation.

M. Schreieck et al. (Eds.): DSPE 2025, LNBIP 563, pp. 99–125, 2026.
https://doi.org/10.1007/978-3-032-04512-6_6

Additional and different caphabilities were needed. Initially this was a make-or-buy decision [9–11]. This also includes renewal decisions [12]. Over time a location element was added to outsourcing. The location element was initially cost driven only but later in time also capability driven [13–15]. In addition to outsourcing organisations were also setting up their own offshore centers – shared service centers [16]. Setting up the shared service centers has proven to be difficult due to high attrition and lack of scale [17], e.g. Bayer transformed their Indian shared service models, and in 2017 outsourced their IT operations to Capgemini (https://www.process-worldwide.com/capgemini-wins-it-con tract-from-bayer-a-371513/). Outsourcing and shared service centers are adjusting the operating model. Furthermore ecosystems require more flexible contracting facilitating agile and Dev(Sec)Ops ways of working [18].

Data sharing [19, 20] and ecosystems [21, 22] are more related to digitalisation. It is important that most organisations are involved in multiple ecosystems and that the composition and objectives of ecosystems change over time [23, 24]. This is complicating data sharing and requires a continuous monitoring of the ecosystems an organisation is involved in and of the market, as competitive relationships are in flux. With regards to data sharing organisations also must consider legislation and upcoming legislation, which is not limited to privacy [25] but also includes anti-trust [26, 27]. Anticipation is key to avoid non-compliance and weaken the competitive position. Data sharing and ecosystems create intellectual property and adjust the business models.

In conclusion, organisations need to focus on increasing their digital maturity to keep up the pace with digitalisation [28, 29].

2 Literature Review

Organisations need to collaborate to innovate [30], which might result in the development of intellectual property rights [31]. The collaboration can take place in external collabo-ration – ecosystems, which can be defined as "An innovation ecosystem is the evolving set of actors, activities, and artifacts, and the institutions and relations, including com-plementary and substitute relations, that are important for the innovative performance of an actor or a population of actors." [32, p.4] In innovation it is important always take the perspective of the final client, which is not limited to the B2C market but also applicable for the B2B market [33]. This perspective maximises end-to-end-value for all ecosystem partners. A complication in engaging in ecosystems is that ecosystems are dynamic, therefore anticipation is key [34].

In ecosystems partners share data, which starts with data quality [35]. It's more important that organisations are aware of the quality than have a high-quality data, as data quality issue can be shared and potentially jointly resolved [36]. Many organisations are improving their data quality by identifying business data owners and appointing data stewards to support the business data owners. In this context the concept of data mesh might be helpful [37–39].

Data sharing is also labelled as "linked data", which is quite a challenge in multiple networked organisations. This requires a trusted data sharing framework which is prefer-ably based on the 'need to know' principle [40]. The data sharing must be facilitated in the organisation [41]. This requires an organisational culture that supports sharing

[42], furthermore organisations must implement data classification as well as tooling. On top of the internal sharing, organisations also must facilitate external data sharing [43] which must have an innovation focus [44]. External data sharing is also addressed in BCG's 21 data maturity dimensions in "data ecosystems & partnership" [35].

In this context also data ecosystems are relevant, which can be defined as "socio-technical complex networks in which actors interact and collaborate with each other to find, archive, publish, consume, or reuse data as well as to foster innovation, create value, and support new businesses." [45, p. 589] In order to facilitate data ecosystems distributed data spaces are needed [46]. This increases the need for aligned identity and access management and combined cyber security effort [47].

Organisations need to consider the impact of artificial intelligence when sharing data in an ecosystem. By sharing data organisations need to take into account what insights they share in addition to sharing the data directly. In this context it is important to include the receiver's own data, the data that the receiver receives from other organisations and the data that the receiver has access to (e.g. open data, data marts). The additional data sources, in combination with artificial intelligence, can unlock unanticipated insights [36]. Furthermore, the artificial intelligence maturity of organisations needs to be high and the current and future artificial intelligence maturity has also to be taken into account in data sharing strategies. With regards to artificial intelligence maturity organisations can engage with external suppliers to mature their capabilities [48]. It can only be concluded that artificial intelligence has further complicated data sharing [49].

In the context of data sharing in ecosystems data governance has become more important. Janssen et al. [40, p. 2] define data governance as "organisations and their personnel defining, applying and monitoring the patterns of rules and authorities for directing the proper functioning of, and ensuring the accountability for, the entire life cycle of data and algorithms within and across organisations." In addition, security concerns need to be addressed when organisations are sharing data [50, 51]. For avoidance of doubt, these security concerns are different from concerns related to sharing cybersecurity data, which is basically sharing threat intelligence [52]. The security concerns also set a higher bar for information security awareness [53].

Data governance and data security are becoming increasingly important. This is not limited to the management level, also these topics are addressed in corporate governance. Organisations such as ASML, Proctor and Gamble, Santander and Walmart have a subcommittee for information technology. This can be labelled as IT & Innovation Committee and increases the focus for an increasingly more important topic such as technology innovation, in which data is playing an increasingly more important role [54].

In addition to privacy (e.g. European Union's GDPR, United States' California Consumer Privacy Act and China's Private Information Protection Law) and anti-trust legislation (e.g. Treaty on the Functioning of the European Union and Directive 2014/104/EU), also legislation for innovative technologies is on its way. This includes legislation related to Artificial Intelligence – the European Union AI act. The purpose of this act is facilitating responsible AI adoption. This includes a responsible set of enabling conditions for AI development and uptake in the EU, and focuses on making the EU the right place, and facilitating excellence from lab to market, as well as ensuring AI technologies work for people and build strategic leadership in the sectors. The act will set clear guiderails and will facilitate data sharing [55]. This act will be applicable in December 2025.

To ensure a stable foundation organisations must start with implementing enterprise architecture, followed by IT architecture and data architecture. This is no longer a sequential process. Organisations must take an integral approach to ensure value creation. In order to share data organisations transforming their vertical platforms into a super platform, which are industry agnostic, and shared infrastructure, both powered by Infrastructure as a Service solutions. Distributed data spaces are the next level [56]. In conjunction with the implementation of architectures organisations must implement tooling. Data management tooling can be currently qualified as 'best of breed' and not as 'best of suite' and despite the large number of acquisitions of tooling vendors (e.g. Collibra acquired amongst others Qldep in 2019, OwlDQ in 2021 and Husprey in 2023, and Informatica acquired amongst others GreenBay Technologies in 2020 and Privitar in 2023). 'Best of suite' will take at least a decade. Furthermore, tools are a prerequisite for advancing analytics capabilities [57], which is still the case in this day and age.

3   Research Topics

This research will include qualitative and explorative analysis focusing on 1. Disruption, 2. Data quality and data governance, 3. Artificial intelligence (AI) adoption and implementation, 4. Dealing with ecosystem dynamics and 5. Co-creation. In de context of digital transformations disruption is an integral element [58], where data quality and data governance are foundational [36]. AI is the most influential technology power digital transformation [59]. However, many organisations are still struggling in the adoption and the implementation of this technology [60, 61]. An additional complexity is the ecosystem dynamics [62] and co-creation, organisation are not in control and are dependent not only from the market and economic conditions but also from their partners.

To analyse and understand sharing data in ecosystems better the focus of this research is on the impact of data sharing on the operation model and the business model of in ecosystem participating organisations. The operating model is defined as the necessary level of business process integration and standardization for delivering goods and services to customers. [63, p.25]. A business model is defined as (a) an architecture for the product, service and information flows, including a description of the various business actors and their roles; and (b) a description of the potential benefits for the various business actors; and (c) a description of the sources of revenues [64, p. 4].

The round tables, subject matter interviews and the survey questions are centered around these areas. The analyses will be performed by external spend/type of spend, capabilities and market dynamics. The paper will also include best practices for sharing data in ecosystems.

4   Research Method

For this market research four round tables have been organised to explore the data sharing in ecosystems. +20 participants per round table have participated on 9 March, 11 May, 4 July 2023 and 16 January 2024. The round tables were on invitation only and the profile of the participants was c-level with responsibility for digital transformation. In addition, three subject matter interviews with digital executives have been conducted: Edgar van Zoelen - Global practice leader Performance - Analytics & Digital Transformation at Philips, Claudia de Andrade - Director Digital & Information Technology at Port of Rotterdam and Hessel Dikkers - Chief Information Officer at Dutch Railways. These three digital executives have personal experience in leading digital transformation and representing organisations that are currently involved in digital transformations in different sectors. Nevertheless, the data set is too limited to analyse and present sector-specific insights.

In addition, three executives from Wirpo and Boston Consulting Group (BCG) have participated in this market research including in the workshops: Paul Verkerk, Business Development Director at Wipro, Malay Srivastava, Head of Data, Analytics & Intelligence, BeNeLux and Johan Stockmann, Partner & Associate Director, BCG. They have also reviewed draft versions of this market research.

The primary data for this research is collected by a survey, roundtables and subject matter interviews, and a survey. The notes from the roundtable and the transcriptions of the subject matter interviews are analysed with a focus on the five research topics. The survey was submitted to ICT Media, a Dutch organisation that facilities IT decision makers in the Netherlands. The members of this community are Chief Information Officers and their direct reports. The members of this community are leading or involved in implementing digital transformations. The response rate was 2% (59 responses to 3,500 invitations).

The survey was conducted in English. The participants completed their response via a portal – Survey Monkey. The responses were collected from April to August 2023. The potential participants received one friendly reminder the first week the survey was introduced and reminders following the second and third workshops (May and July 2023).

The survey was an anonymous survey; therefore, it is not possible to conclude the representativeness of the sample. However, the spread over the different sectors and spread of the size of the organisations the respondents represent do not indicate that the respondents are not representative for the community, which was also confirmed by ICT Media.

5   Analysis

In the analyses there are five topics explored to address the three research questions: 1. Disruption, 2. Data quality and data governance, 3. Artificial intelligence adoption and implementation, 4. Dealing with ecosystem dynamics and 5. Co-creation.

Disruption

In the survey different levels of disruption are distinguished, ranging from 'no disruption' to 'existential changes'. This is detailed in Fig. 1, over 70% of the participating organisations face at a minimum 'major changes'. The two organisations that face 'no disruption' are both governmental organisations. Furthermore, the banking and financial services sector is predominantly facing at a minimum 'significant changes'. This might well be due to a combination of increasing legislation such as the Corporate Sustainability Reporting Directive (CSRD) and competition from FinTechs. An upcoming update of the Payment Services and Electronic Money Services Directive (PSD3) will result in additional disruptions in this sector. Remarkably none of the surveyed organisations in the Life Science and Healthcare sector reported a higher disruption level than 'major changes'. Given the speed of innovation and high legislation scrutinising this sector, one would expect more increased levels of disruption.

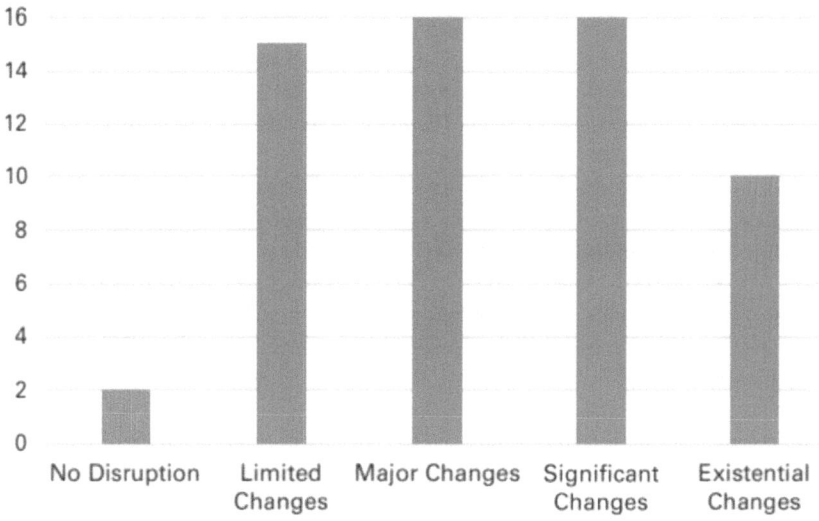

Fig. 1. Degree of Disruption (N = 59)

The overview of the importance of data sharing in end-to-end journeys is summarised in Fig. 2. Less than 10% of the surveyed organisations consider the importance of data sharing in end-to-end value journeys as 'limited'. It is remarkable that these organisations are all large international organisations with a revenue/budget over 1b Euro. Furthermore, over 60% of the organisations consider the importance of data sharing in end-to-end value journeys to a 'great extent', which includes 80% of the Dutch organisations. This indicates that data sharing in end-to-end value journeys is understandably more difficult for large international organisations.

Nearly 85% of the surveyed organisations share data in addition to transaction data with their ecosystem partners. However, it is remarkable that two-thirds of the nine organisations that only share transaction data indicate that the importance of data sharing in end-to-end journeys can be labeled as 'a great extent'. Apparently, these organisations don't see added value or are not able or allowed to share other types of data with their ecosystem partners. Nearly all organisations that also share other types of data, share data related to product and/or service innovations. The two exceptions are an organisation in the Hi-Tech and Professional Services sector and the other organisation in the Information Technology sector. The willingness to share data to support transacting in the ecosystem (current collaboration) is higher than sharing data related to exploring

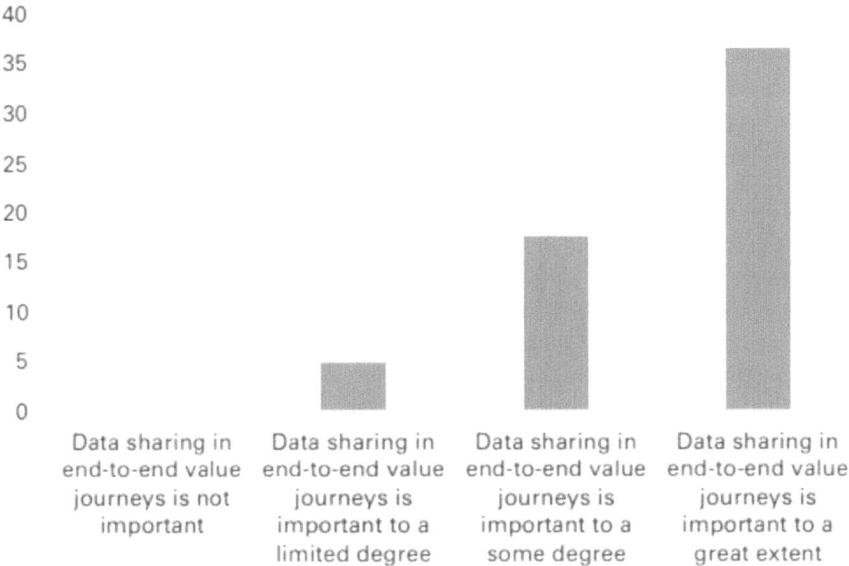

Fig. 2. The importance of data sharing in end-to-end value journeys (N = 59)

initiating innovation and/or future collaboration. The future collaboration is related to the demand as well as to analytics. Surprisingly, reference data for external collaboration is the least shared data type as it is generally not proprietary or competitive information and instrumental for data sharing. Just over 20% the surveyed organisations share this data. The organisations are predominantly Dutch organisations and also small organisations are overrepresented. Figure 3 provides an overview of the types of shared data in end-to-end value journeys.

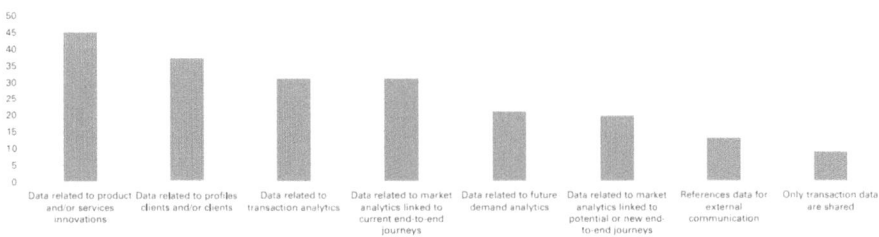

Fig. 3. Types of shared data in end-to-end value journeys (N = 59)

Data sharing can improve decision-making in many ways, ranging from better decisions, faster decisions and more efficient decision making. It might also enable the use of artificial intelligence and machine learning. This is all impacting operating models in organisations. Processes and roles and responsibilities are adjusted due to data sharing in ecosystems. The significance of these changes should not be underestimated. Similarly, data sharing can drive innovation and lead to the development of new business propositions, which will potentially result in adjusting business models of organisations in ecosystems. As the impact of both is significant, organisations need to take well-considered decisions related to data sharing.

Furthermore, addressing important matters such as data ownership, data policies and the allocation of the associated costs is important. In case for some of the ecosystem partners there is no benefit in sharing data, other ecosystem partners might consider offering compensation to these ecosystem partners for sharing their data. This will create value for all involved ecosystem partners and strengthen the entire ecosystem. Acknowledging this construct is complex, and it is pivotal to explore, as in any ecosystem there is no ecosystem partner equality. Valuing the contribution of each ecosystem partner is the start for strengthening partnerships in ecosystems.

The modus for both the impact of data sharing on the operating model and the business model is 'some degree of impact'. In over 75% of the organisations the impact of data sharing is 'some degree of impact' or beyond for both the operating model as well as the business model. This impact is not strongly related to size, sector or geography. However, business models are impacted to a larger extent than operating models. However, in conclusion, data sharing for sure will change both operating models and business models. The impact of disruption on data sharing is summarised in Fig. 4.

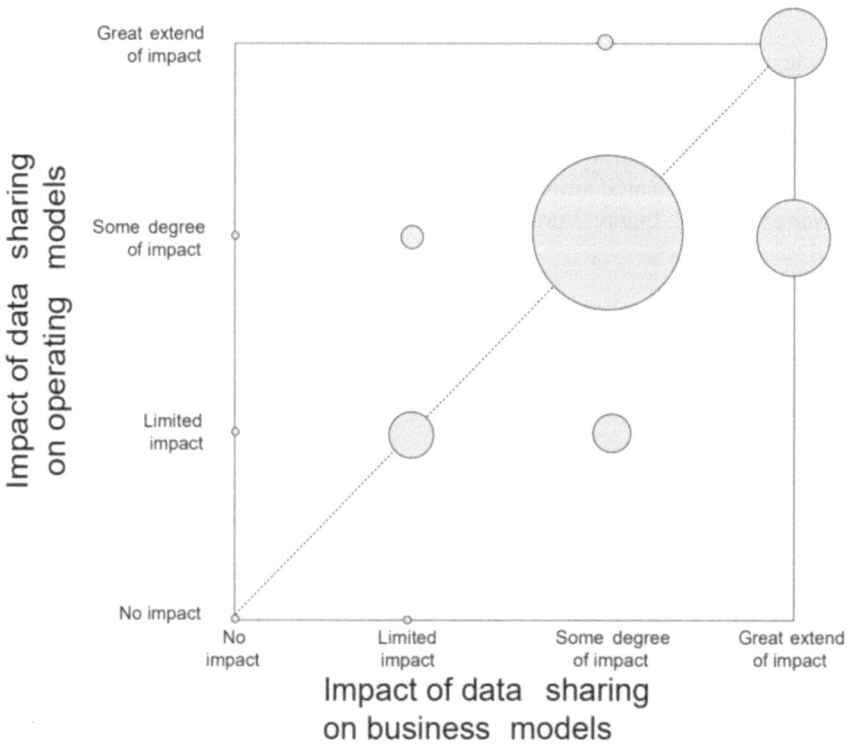

Fig. 4. The impact of data sharing on operating models and business models

Data Quality and Data Governance

The combination of data quality and data governance of shared data in ecosystems are foundational for creating value in end-to-end value journeys. The maturity of both data quality and data governance is still a challenge for many organisations.

Improving data quality starts with understanding the quality of the current data and understanding the future data requirements of an organisation. In improving the quality of the data, clear governance, policies and procedures, and tooling are essential. The policies and procedures include access rights, data classification, and data quality ratings, as well as specific measures to adhere to legislation, where data management tooling facilitates adherence to the policies and procedures and reduces errors by eliminating human interventions- including supporting data correction, cleansing, and consolidation. To be clear, data management tooling facilitates data processing and data access. This tooling is different from the tooling used in artificial intelligence. Also, for artificial intelligence, automated tooling is essential, but equally human oversight on algorithms is a must. The combination of tooling and human oversight further improves the data quality. Data quality in ecosystems is an even bigger topic, as sharing data of poor quality may lead to value destruction in the ecosystem and potentially jeopardising participation in the ecosystem. Also sharing data with partners in the ecosystem exposes organisations beyond using data internally. This is where data governance across the ecosystem plays an important role.

Many organisations are maturing their data governance. Their Chief Data Officers are still working hard on awareness and policies, where the focus in this day and age should be on enabling data owners and data stewards, implementing data management tooling and aligning closely with the data science, analytics, and technology executives and teams. Key to data governance in ecosystems is the alignment across organisations. This requires an additional governance layer with representatives of the ecosystem partners making decisions on what data will be shared. This includes frequency, aggregation level, masking and time lags to ensure commercial interests and compliance for all ecosystems partners are assured, as well as access rights and boundaries to what the shared data may or may not be used for. Dynamics in ecosystems jeopardize the effectiveness of data governance in ecosystems. Also setting up this governance representation must be considered, as for ecosystems with many partners, the workability of a representation of all ecosystems across the ecosystem governance body is low.

The surveyed organisations reported on a 1–7 Likert scale a higher data quality of shared data than their rating of data governance in ecosystems. This is detailed in Fig. 5. The combined maturity is remarkably high, over 40% of the surveyed organisations have a high maturity, where 34% of the organisations have a low maturity[1]. In previous HPDO studies the reported maturity was much lower. The large survey organisations, with a revenue/budget over 1b Euro, are more mature on both data quality and data governance. Although size is increasing the complexity, due to the size, investments in data quality and data governance are more affordable than for smaller organisations. Also, as expected,

---

[1] Both the data quality of shared data (DQ) and data governance in ecosystems (DG).maturity are scored on a 1–7 Likert scale. The maturity of the combination of DQ and.DG is classified as follows: Low maturity if either DQ or DG, or both have a score $=\ <3$. Moderate maturity if both DQ and DG are >3 and <6. High maturity is both DQ and DG $>\ =6$.

highly regulated sectors, such as banking and governmental organisations had higher maturity scores than organisations in other sectors.

The impact of data quality and data governance on both the operating models and the business models, in conjunction with the combination of the data quality of shared data and data governance in ecosystems, which is classified a low, moderate and high, is detailed in Fig. 6. No surveyed organisation indicated 'no impact' on both the operating model and the business model. Over 35% of the organisations reported that the impact on both the operating model and the business model was high. Across all surveyed organisations, the impact on the operating model is higher than the impact on the business model. This might be explained by the time it takes to truly innovate in an ecosystem, as the first step is to achieve efficiencies and improve decision-making. Data quality and data governance are intertwined, which explains the pared score. Seventy-five percent of the survey organisations report an equal impact on both the operating model and the business model.

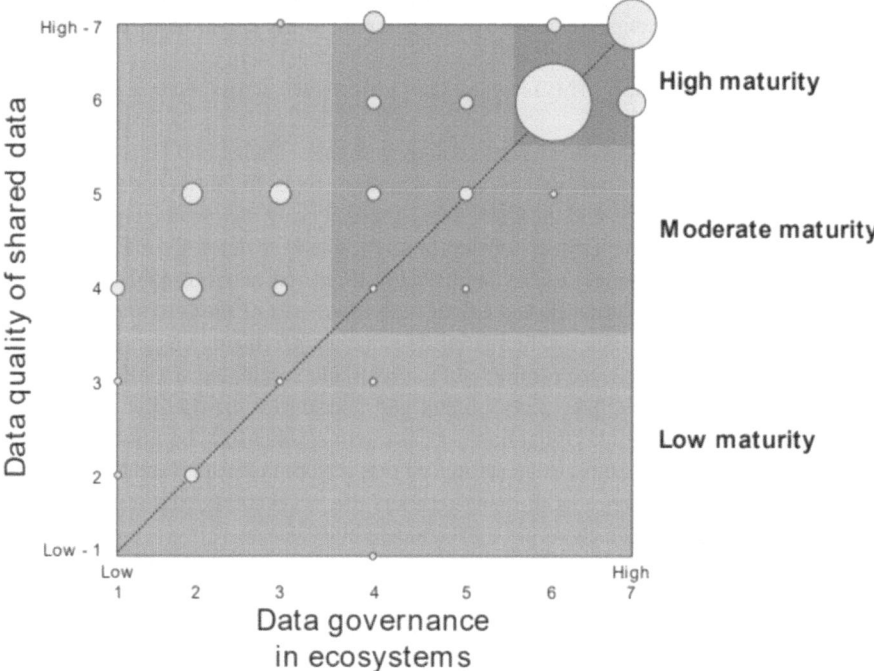

Fig. 5. The data quality of shared data and data governance in ecosystems – Likert scale 1–7 (N = 59)

Artificial Intelligence Adoption and Implementation
In the context of creating value in end-to-end value journeys, the purpose of artificial intelligence can be to achieve ecosystem efficiencies, create shared insights and stimulate innovation. This is not fundamentally different from the purpose of artificial intelligence

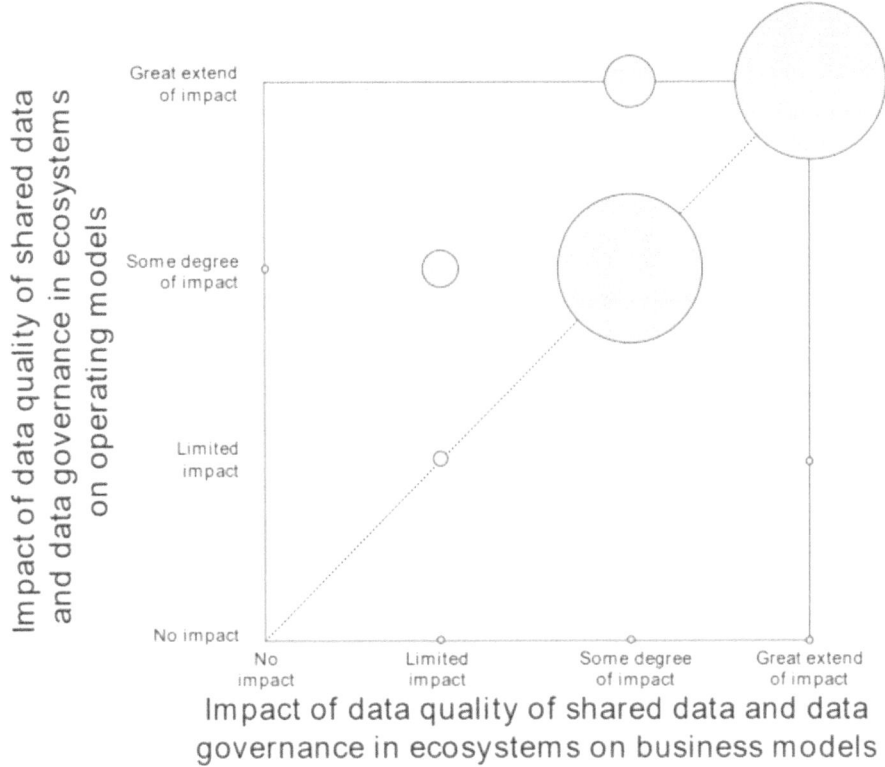

Impact of data quality of shared data and data governance in ecosystems on business models

Fig. 6. The impact of data quality of shared data and data governance in ecosystems on operating models and business models (N = 59)

for individual organisations, it is only more complex to implement across ecosystems. For implementation, understanding the requirements and objectives, as well as the technology and tooling stacks, of ecosystems partners is essential. Furthermore, sharing insights based on artificial intelligence has an increased risk level, from both competitive sensitivity as well as compliance perspective. This requires additional ecosystem data governance diligence. Furthermore, regulatory requirements both hinder the sharing of artificial intelligence insights, think anti-trust regulations, as well as drive the sharing of artificial intelligence insights. An example of the latter is European Union putting in place sustainability legislation related to product passports detailing the bill of material. The impact of this upcoming legislation is not yet fully clear.

Three purposes of artificial intelligence stood out. Nearly all surveyed organisations acknowledged process efficiency, insight generation and operational performance as a purpose of artificial intelligence in their organisation. There were no distinct differences for sectors, size and geography across the surveyed organisations. This might be related to the limited sample size. The overview of the purposes of artificial intelligence are detailed in Fig. 7. In addition, the surveyed organisations also use artificial intelligence for quality improvement, compliance monitoring, and internal and external behaviour analytics. The latter can be used for fraud detection and cyber resilience.

Many organisations still have large number of databases or multiple data lakes. Composing a fit for purpose data set for driving artificial intelligence insights requires a lot of effort in many organisations, let alone driving these insights in ecosystems. In addition to the implementation of policies, procedures and tooling, as well as data governance, automation in artificial intelligence is also important. Automation frees up time for data scientists and citizen data scientists to implement checks and balances – basically human oversight. This is, in the context of growing data volumes and the use of artificial intelligence in organisations, essential to avoid the generation of incorrect insights, and confidentiality and compliance breaches.

Introducing artificial intelligence in ecosystems sets the same type of governance requirements as in individual organisations. Being in control is however much more difficult, as the data originates in multiple ecosystem organisations, which hinders the verification of the quality of the data. Also reviewing algorithms is more difficult as there will be differences in the (ethical) values of the ecosystem partners. The latter sets additional requirements for selecting and, over time, evaluating ecosystem partners. This might result in adjustments in the collaborating group of ecosystem partners. Any organisation must focus on the highest possible maturity level of artificial intelligence as the impact of artificial intelligence is increasing due to the rise of data driven decision making. Therefore, the impact on the individual organisation and the ecosystem is significant. In addition to the effort of individual organisations, a collective ecosystem effort in implementing artificial intelligence governance is required.

Only two of the surveyed organisations have a higher 1–7 Likert score for the maturity of artificial intelligence governance than the artificial intelligence automation level. The differences are remarkable. Trusting that automation of artificial intelligence is not reducing the need for adequate artificial intelligence governance, it is providing a solid basis for the implementation of governance. The organisations reporting high levels of automation are the sectors with extended experience in artificial intelligence, such as the banking, and life science and healthcare sectors. Also, large organisations, with a revenue/budget of +1b Euro report a higher level of automation scores. The level of automation is a clear indicator for artificial intelligence maturity. However, it is fair to say that it is more straightforward to automate artificial intelligence than to implement proper artificial intelligence governance. However, organisations must focus on the implementation of proper governance to provide guiderails for automated artificial intelligence. The insights in artificial intelligence levels of automation and governance maturity levels are detailed in Fig. 8.

Initially organisations started to structure their artificial intelligence teams centrally. This was due to the scarcity of data scientists and data quality issues that many organisations faced. Clustering this capability was the preferred artificial intelligence operating model for most organisations. Over time, many organisations have improved and expanded their data science capabilities. Data citizens have made their entrance into artificial intelligence of many organisations, never more with the meteoric rise of platforms such ChatGPT. This has significant implications for the artificial intelligence operating model. From a central operating model, these organisations are transforming into a hybrid

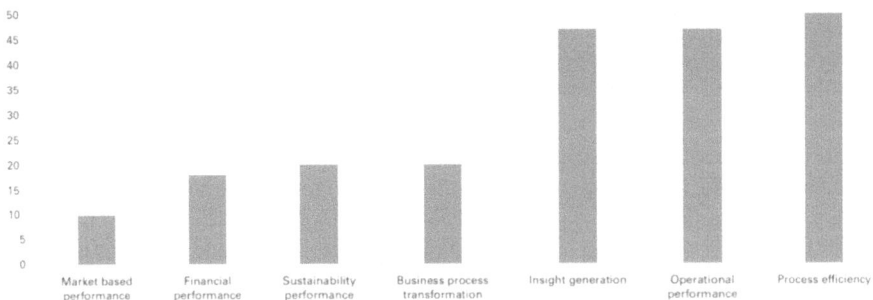

Fig. 7. Overview of purposes of artificial intelligence (N = 59)

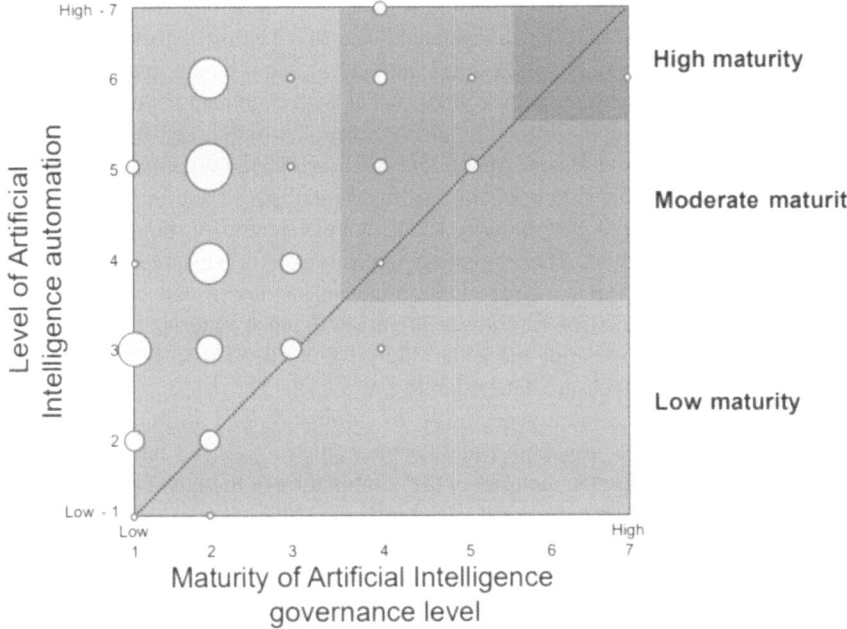

Fig. 8. The level of artificial intelligence automation and maturity of artificial intelligence governance level – Likert scale 1–7 (N = 59)

model. Currently there are a very limited number of organisations who have adopted a 100% decentralized model. It is also questionable if there will be organisations that face no synergies at all, and as a consequence refrain from having a central data science team. The reporting of both data scientists and data citizens is also important. Typically, data scientists are embedded in the technology and innovations teams of organisations. This also enables alignment and impact on artificial intelligence and data technology, and the enterprise and information technology architecture. Operating models support maintaining relationships with the business. Organisations might consider appointing a business sponsor for artificial intelligence. This will enable alignment and supports setting priorities. The data citizens are by nature embedded in the organisation, and outside the technology and innovation teams. This will also drive alignment with the business objectives of their organisational unit and support setting organisational-unit priorities. To ensure alignment with the central team, additional governance structures, including functional reporting into the central team and knowledge sharing sessions, have to be in place. Organisations can also structure their artificial intelligence operating model as fully decentralized. The implication is that there are no economies of scale, in effect artificial intelligence capabilities are in the DNA of all the relevant organisational units. In all fairness, the likelihood that this will happen in the foreseeable future on a large scale is very limited.

First of all, over 15% of the surveyed organisations don't even have an artificial intelligence operating model. This illustrates the maturity of these organisations, remarkably 40% of these organisations had a revenue/budget of +1b Euro. Most organisations have a hybrid operating model with a dominant central team, where just over 10% of the surveyed organisations reported a central model with dominant decentralized artificial intelligence teams supplemented by a central team, which is setting the standard to support the decentralised teams. About 25% of the surveyed organisations report a 100% central model. Neither their level of artificial intelligence automation, nor their artificial intelligence governance maturity levels, were different for the reported levels by all surveyed organisations. There was only one surveyed organisation that reported a 100% decentralized model – a large global financial institution with a high level of artificial intelligence automation but a low artificial intelligence maturity. For highly regulated organisation, this operating model has high risk profile. The insights in artificial intelligence operating models are detailed in Fig. 9.

The impact of artificial intelligence levels of automation and artificial intelligence governance maturity levels are about equal for operating models and business models, as detailed in Fig. 10, where the maturity of the combination of these two factors is low - over 80% of the surveyed organisations[2]. The remaining 20% of surveyed organisations report a moderate maturity for these two factors. Only one organisation, a large financial institution, reports a high maturity. The key question is the impact of an increase in the maturity of artificial intelligence governance on both operating models and business models. Obviously increasing the level of artificial intelligence automation should enable strengthening of governance. Especially for highly regulated organisations, it is important to be in control. Proper governance is a prerequisite to both operating models and business models. Also, upcoming legislation related to artificial intelligence in combination with moderate governance might hinder organisations in making the necessary changes to be in compliance. Moderate is not good enough, governance must be high to enable agile responses to changing and growing legislation.

---

[2] Both the level of artificial automation (automation) and artificial intelligence governance (governance) maturity are scored on a 1–7 Likert scale. The maturity of the combination of automation and governance is classified as follows: Low maturity if either automation or governance, or both have a score = < 3. Moderate maturity if both automation and governance are > 3 and < 6. High maturity if both automation and governance > = 6.

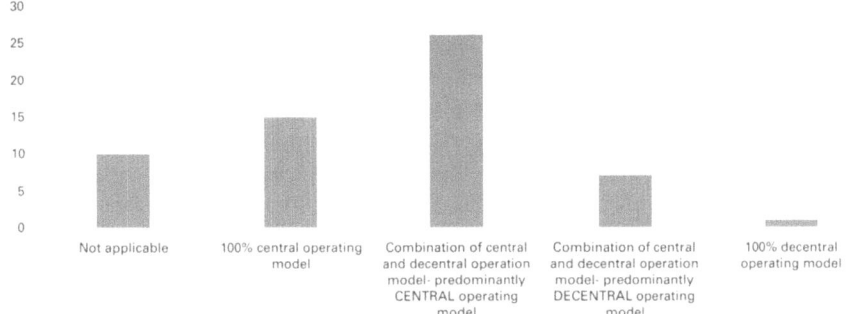

Fig. 9. Artificial intelligence operating models (N = 59)

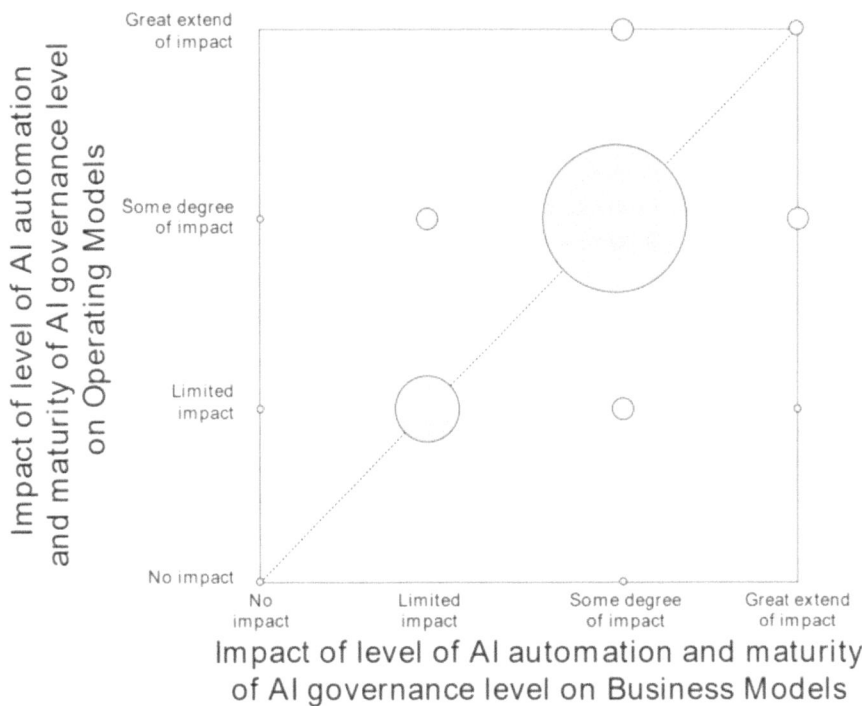

Fig. 10. The impact of level of artificial intelligence automation and maturity of artificial intelligence governance level on operating models and business models (N = 59)

Dealing with Ecosystem Dynamics

Innovation drives value chain dynamics as innovation opens up new opportunities. As a consequence, organisations consider setting up new ecosystems, participating in additional ecosystems and leaving ecosystems, as innovations present new opportunities. These decisions impact the market. Ecosystems that focus on innovation in combination with collectivism are impacted the least by value chain dynamics. Collectivism manifests itself best by keeping in mind and respecting the interests of all ecosystem partners. Attractiveness for all partners prevails. This requires a long-term perspective that is not always feasible, nevertheless any organisation should always consider the impact of any decision on the value creation of the ecosystem. Data sharing in more stable ecosystems is more straightforward as cross-organisation data governance and policies can be set. The alternative is that individual organisations contractually agree on data sharing. This is increasing not only the required contract effort, but also reduces the transparency in an ecosystem.

Furthermore, organisations will be less involved in ecosystems and, as a consequence, the value chain dynamics will be higher. All the above has a negative impact on value creation in end-to-end value journeys.

Negotiation power is related to the position in an ecosystem, the positions in other value chains, market circumstances, as well as opportunities to participate in other value chains and/or set up new value chains. In short it is very difficult, but also very important for organisations to understand their room to negotiate and to understand the position of their partners and competitors. This is where data sharing can be a key in collaboration. Exchanging data in ecosystems helps organisations better understand the requirements and interests of other partners.

The value chain dynamics are relatively high, as detailed in Fig. 11. On a 1–7 Likert scale the modus is 5. The surveyed organisations that report a value chain dynamic score of 5 or higher are predominantly large, +1b Euro revenue/budget, international organisations. In this category there are also three governmental organisations, which are all small organisations. This might be explained by the nature of their operations and the degree of engaging with non-governmental organisations. The reported negotiation power is quite balanced, some organisations reported low negotiation power, whereas other organisations reported strong negotiation power. As expected, size matters, the organisations that reported a high negotiation power score are predominantly large, +1b Euro revenue/budget, international organisations. Also three governmental organisations reported a high negotiation power score. This might be related to European tendering regulations in the European Union. The combination of the Likert score on value chain dynamics and negotiation power in end-to-end journeys is detailed in Fig. 12. The surveyed organisations reported they have more negotiation power than what they are facing in value chain dynamics for organisations to understand their room to negotiate and to understand the position of their partners and competitors. This is where data sharing can be key in collaboration. Exchanging data in ecosystems helps organisations better understand the requirements and interests of other partners.

Due to the increasing value chain dynamics, organisations must focus on agility and on expanding the number of active ecosystems. Agility will reduce the risks, as organisations are able to respond faster and better to changes in the market. On the other hand, value chain dynamics drive business model changes, as changes in ecosystem collaboration triggers the opportunities to explore additional/alternative value propositions. Furthermore, negotiation power can be used to enforce new business models, such as subscription models. The changes in business models will be beneficial for some ecosystem partners to the detriment of others.

The impact of value chain dynamics and negotiation power on operating models and business models is about equal, see Fig. 12. None of the surveyed organisations indicated there is no impact on both the operating model and the business model. For most organisations, there is some impact on both the operating model and the business model. Where the maturity of the combination of these two factors is moderate[3] for over 50% of the surveyed organisations. The remaining surveyed organisations report a low maturity for these two factors combined, expect for one organisation, a small financial institution, reports a high maturity.

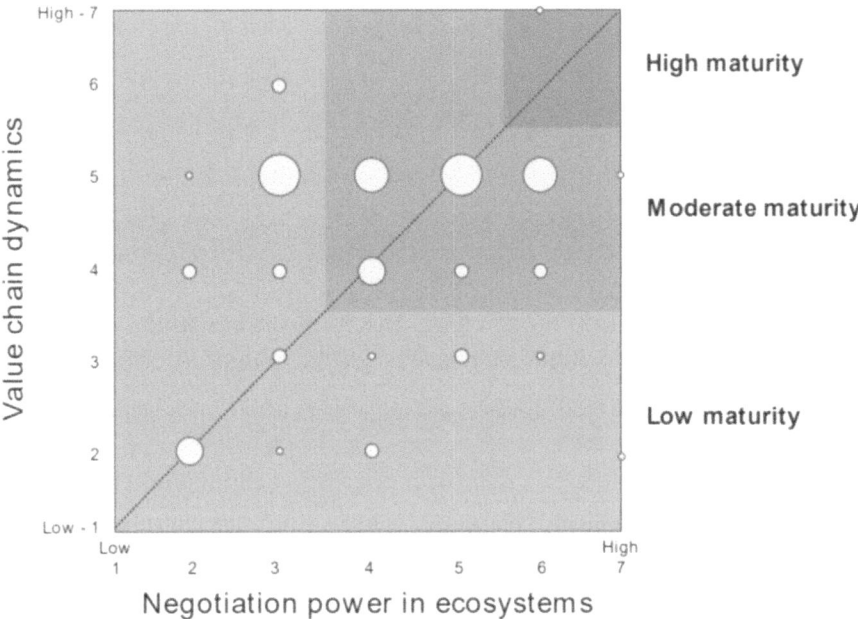

Fig. 11. The value chain dynamics and negotiation power in ecosystems – Likert scale 1–7 – where 1 = low and 7 = high (N = 58)

Co-creation

For the importance of creating Intellectual Property (IP) rights in ecosystems not of equal importance in all sectors. Typically for organisations that produce goods the creation of IP rights is more relevant than for services and governmental organisations. Also, the size of the organisation matters, as larger organisations have the ability to free up resources to focus on registering and maintaining and enforcing IP rights. Furthermore,

---

[3] Both the value chain dynamics and negotiation power are scored on a 1–7 Likert scale. The combination of value chain dynamics and negotiation power is classified as follows: Low maturity if either value chain dynamics or negotiation power, or both have a score = < 3. Moderate maturity if both value chain dynamics and negotiation power are > 3 and < 6. High maturity if both value chain dynamics and negotiation power > = 6.

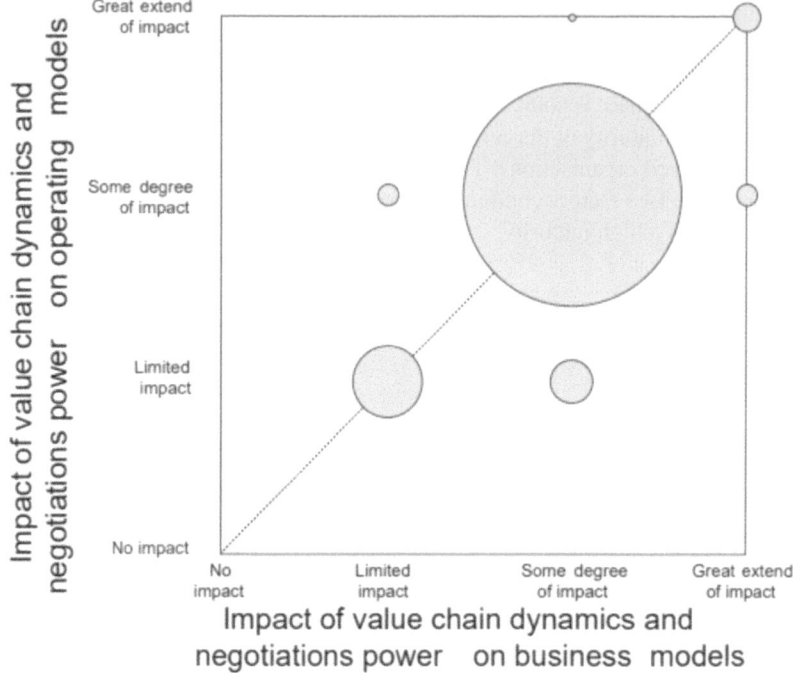

Fig. 12. The impact of value chain dynamics and negotiations power on operating models and business models (N = 58)

if organisations operate in highly competitive markets with a large number of ecosystems, IP rights can provide protection of both market position as well as margin. Data sharing supports innovation and therefore it can be worthwhile to consider registering and maintaining related IP rights.

The importance of creating IP rights in ecosystems, and in that context sharing data, varies across the surveyed organisations. The importance of creating IP rights in ecosystems and the contribution of data sharing to the creation of IP rights go hand in hand, e.g. if the importance of creating IP rights in ecosystems is high, then the importance of data sharing to the creation IP rights is also high. This is detailed in Fig. 13.

Furthermore, size matters, larger organisations report a high importance in both creating IP rights in ecosystems as well as in the contribution of data sharing to the creation of IP rights. The demarcation between international organisations and national organisations is less significant. Also remarkably, there are numerous service organisations and governmental organisations that report a high importance on both. Further research is required to understand these survey results better.

Organisations which are creating and maintaining IP rights need to set strategies, ranging from no strategy, a defensive strategy or a collaborative strategy, this is detailed in Fig. 14. The smaller the organisation, the harder it is to set strategies and implement defense mechanisms. Also organisations need to implement defense mechanisms which are aligned with their strategy. Good examples of effective defense mechanisms range from informal to formal/legal mechanisms. Organisations that would like to create value in end-to-end value journeys must consider the adoption of the collaborative IP strategy which combines a mix of informal, semi-formal and formal/legal mechanisms.

The intellectual property strategies have an impact on both the operating model as well as the business model. In the operating model, organisations can protect the production of their goods and services, whereas in the business model, organisations can monetise their IP rights. The latter is rarer than making reference to operating models.

Organisations report a comparable impact of IP strategies on operating models and business models. In twelve organisations there is no impact on both the operating model and the business model, this includes predominantly financial organisations and governmental organisations.

Also, the impact of IP strategies in larger organisations is bigger on operating models than in small organisations. The impact of Intellectual Property strategies on operating models and business models is detailed in Fig. 15.

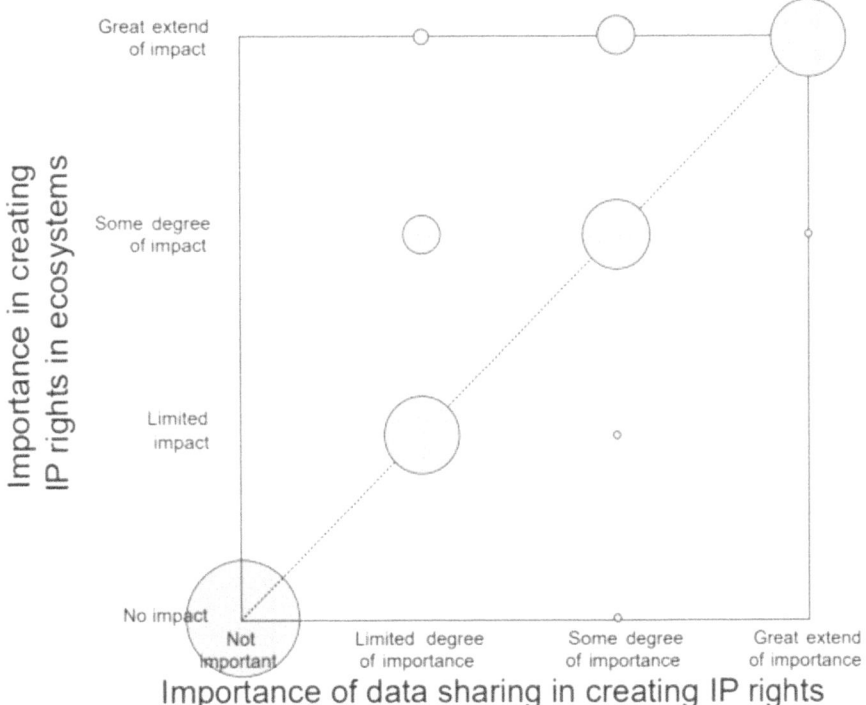

Fig. 13. The importance in creating IP rights in ecosystems versus the importance of data sharing in creating IP rights (N = 59)

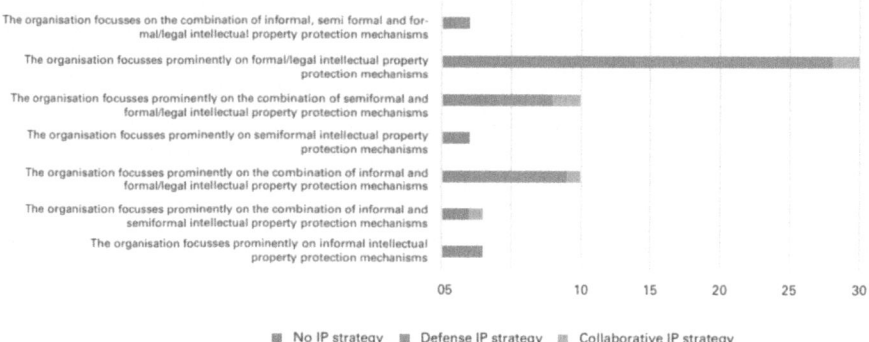

Fig. 14. The combination of IP strategies and the defense mechanism per strategy (N = 56)

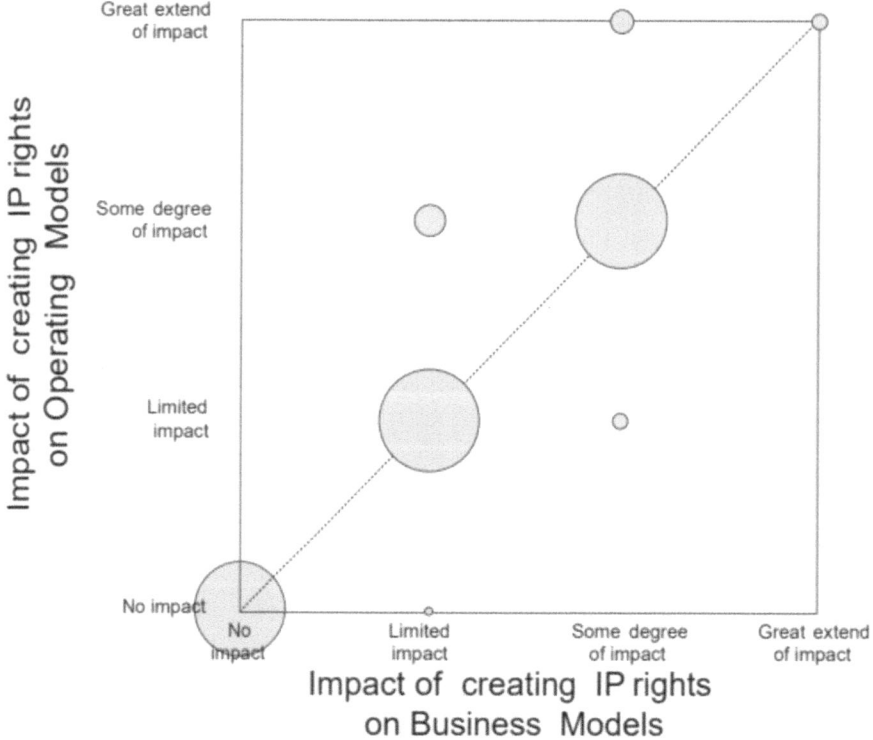

Fig. 15. The impact of creating intellectual property rights on operating models and business models (N = 56)

6   Recommendations

The survey results, the interviews and supplier subject matter expert contributions, and the round tables have provided valuable insights. Synthesizing these inputs resulted in nine recommendations that will keep organisations in check. The recommendations are clustered into three themes: 1. Strategic orientation, 2. Getting the basics rights and 3. Ecosystems.

The recommendations will strengthen the position of organisations in ecosystems and increase the value creation in end-to-end value journeys.

1. Strategic Orientation

Understanding the current market position of the organisation and any upcoming market developments and legislation is important. The following actions are typically allocated to representatives responsible for operations.

1.1 Market position: Assess in which end-to-end value journeys the organisation participates and identify the profitability, risks and strategic importance of each end-to-end value journey. Identify in which of the value chains the organisation has a pivotal role and in which value chains the organisation can be easily replaced by another partner and include the likelihood of being replaced over time in 12, 24, +24 months. In the assessment of the value chains also map out the partners and their contributions to the ecosystems, as input for painting the overall market position of the organisation.

1.2. Market developments: Assess the relevant innovations for the organisation and for the end-to-end value journeys the organisation is involved in at this moment or in the future. Also include in this assessment the anticipated responses of the current ecosystem partners and competitors, as this might have implications for the power balance in ecosytems, as well as in the market. Furthermore, it is important to keep an eye on potential new entrants. These can be start-ups but also organisations that are expanding into the market. Prepare scenarios on how to respond best to the potential outcomes of the assessments.

1.3. Regulatory developments: Assess the impact of upcoming relevant legislation on the organisation, the ecosystems the organisation operates in and on competition. The relevant legislation is not limited to national legislation, especially European Union legislations have a much broader impact. The assessment must be a balanced perspective, both risks, but also opportunities, must be taken into account. This helps organisations to anticipate upcoming legislation, which is beneficial for all partners in the ecosystems. Furthermore, organisations need to set a strategy for dealing with legislation. Organisations should always operate in full compliance; alternatively, an organisation can be more aggressive and operate more boldly by interpretating legislation.

2. Getting the Basics Right

Implementing proper date management and data governance is key to getting the basics right. The actions below are typically a joint responsibility of both the Chief Data Officer and the Chief Information Officer.

2.1. Data quality: Assess the data quality and the data governance of the organisation. This includes data policies and data ownership. The data ownership must be in the business, where data owners must be supported by data stewards, who are also positioned in the business. All of the above must be addressed by the Chief Data Officer. Furthermore, assessing data management tooling is important - what is the level of automation in the organisation? Addressing the data management tooling is with both the Chief Information Officer, related to the enterprise and IT architecture, and the Chief Data Officer, related to the information and insights requirements.

2.2. Data resilience: Monitor the quality and added value of data, especially for data and insights that the organisation shares with other partners in the ecosystem. As the volume of data and insights are continuously growing, this is not a one-off action, in an ideal situation monitoring is real time. Organisations need to implement processes and tools that are continuously monitoring. Data governance falls directly under the responsibility of the Chief Data Officer. With regards to insights, organisations need to keep a close eye on the algorithms and training data, which require data analytics policies and a rule board to assess artificial intelligence.

2.3. Data sharing: Agreeing on the exchange and conditions for exchanging data in the ecosystem is important. For conditions it is important to explore the commercial, as well as the compliance implications. Organisations need to be mindful that, due to changes in the market and/or in legislation, the impact is different over time. In order to implement this properly, data governance needs to be implemented across ecosystems. With the dynamics many end-to-end value journeys are facing, cross-ecosystem governance can be replaced by contractual commitments. Typically, contractual commitments reduce data sharing. The responsibility for this action is predominantly with the Chief Data Officers, who must align with their organisation to better understand the data needs of their organisations.

3. Ecosystems

Improve collaboration and drive innovation. The below actions are typically allocated to representatives responsible for operations and the Chief Data Officer.

3.1 Expand data sharing: Participate in initiatives that focus on improving and expanding data sharing in ecosystems. The initiatives are typically innovation related, and more fixated on adjusting business models than operating models and are driven by representatives responsible for the business models. In addition, it is important to focus on setting up governance bodies across the ecosystem. This also requires additional focus on improving data quality, which is typically driven Chief Data Officers.

3.2. Implement data-driven decision making: Implementing a combination of algorithms enabling repetitive, simple, and automated decision making and making data available for one-off, complex decision making, will enable data-driven decision making in ecosystems. This not only requires clean data, but also strong governance to ensure that the outcomes of both categories are correct. A step-by-step approach for the implementation of algorithms reduces risks, where making data available is more a matter of gradually improving data quality. Setting priorities for data quality improvements will benefit both categories.

3.3 Focus on talent management: Educating, recruiting, and retaining talent are essential in sharing data in ecosystems. Organisations need to build up their capabilities in data and data analytics in both the technology as well as in the operational domain. Nurturing data citizens is essential for expanding data sharing and implementing data-driven decisions. Furthermore, embedding data ownership in the operational domain also requires evangelisation. Understanding the benefits of true data ownership is helpful in embracing data ownership responsibilities. Furthermore, organising support, in the form of data stewards, for the data owner is essential.

7   Limitations and Future Research

Due to the nature of any survey, it is more difficult to understand the impact of data sharing. To better understand the impact, more qualitative research might be required, such as case studies or expert interviews. Furthermore, despite this research is conducted in the Netherland only this research includes 58% international respondents and 42% Dutch respondents. Finaly this research includes a low number of participants: 59 respondents. A larger and more international survey, as well as a higher response rate would have mitigated these concerns to a certain extend. Despite the subject matter expert contribution of suppliers, the supplier perspective of exit management also is missing in the survey. Suppliers might be able to add additional insights in exit management and co-creation in ecosystems.

Additional data also will enable to understand the relationship between the research topics better and to move beyond descriptive statistics. As a next step in this research both longitudinal studies and comparative analyses across regions must be considered.

8   Conclusion

Over the last decade data, data sharing and data analytics have already had a significant impact on value creation in end-to-end value journeys and ecosystems. The exponential growth of data has opened opportunities to optimize operations, enrich products and services with data, and monetise data.

Collaborating and sharing data in ecosystems enables further opportunities. Keep in mind this is only the start, as artificial intelligence, is still in its infant state. Setting up central data analytics teams and adding data citizens to organisational units will ensure artificial intelligence is also embedded in the organisations. For many organisations this implies that a significant effort is required to build up these capabilities. Also, for the foreseeable future, the artificial intelligence operating model will always have a central element. When the artificial intelligence capabilities mature, organisations might also consider having decentralised artificial intelligence resources. Having a fully decentralised artificial intelligence operating model is difficult to imagine. Large scale leveraging of artificial intelligence generates additional and advanced insights in end-to-end value journeys. Artificial intelligence also triggers innovation. It supports collaboration between ecosystem partners and enables an agile approach to innovation, as simulations and pathfinding are contributing to innovation success. However, organisations must acknowledge that increased data volumes and use of artificial intelligence increases the bar for both data management and data governance. These need to be implemented in organisations, as well as across the ecosystem. This is where tooling is essential, as this provides a foundation for improving the data quality and ensuring proper data usage by strict access management provisions. Also making templates and standard processes available enables the exchange of data and insights in ecosystems.

What ecosystems need are plug-and-play concepts to share data and insights. This must be the focus of the governance body across the ecosystem.

1. Operating Models

Data-driven approaches will adjust operating models of all organisations. Achieved efficiencies will enable investment in innovation. Sharing data and insights in ecosystems will result in innovations and new business models. The winner takes it all!

Some ecosystems are facing a lot of challenges by incumbent partners leaving the ecosystem, while on the other hand also new partners joining the ecosystem. These value chain dynamics jeopordise the sharing of data and the joint innovation. However, only anti-trust legislation can stop market dominance of a hand full of ecosystems. This is not challenging; legislation is a fact of life. Organisations must keep a close eye on legislation, including upcoming legislation, and make sure they understand the impact of the legislation on their organisations and the ecosystems in which they are operating.

It is important that organisations set a clear strategy for dealing with data and analytics related legislation, given its importance for creating value in end-to-end value journeys and the number and impact of expected upcoming relevant legislations. Some organisations adopted more risk averse strategies where other organisations adopted more aggressive strategies. For setting the strategy, the sector in which the organisation operates, and corporate values of an organisation, provide important guidelines.

Typically, highly regulated large organisations are more conservative, whereas new entrants, not limited to start-ups, are more aggressive. Deliberate decision making is important. However, organisations need to keep in mind that in turbulent times a too conservative approach to legislation potentially weakens the position of the organisation in ecosystems as well as competitiveness of entire ecosystems.

2. Business Models

In addition to changing operating models also business models will change due to sharing of data and insights. Due to the emerging developments in sharing data and insights, the impact is not as significant as the impact on operating models. It would be safe to assume that over time the impact on business models will exceed the impact on operating models. With respect to co-creation the outcomes in this study were different from expected. For organisations that manufacture products the expectation was that creating and registering intellectual property rights would be important in creating value in end-to-end value journeys. Most of the surveyed organisations didn't have a focus on creating and registering intellectual property rights and either had none or a defensive intellectual property strategy. The main arguments were that the registration effort is significant, and the protection is limited. Organisations consider the speed of innovation as a better strategy to stay ahead of the competition. With the continuous growth of data volumes and the potential of artificial intelligence, this is a defendable strategy, if not a better strategy.

In Conclusion

Sharing data and insights in ecosystems will continue to fuel innovation and enable value creation in end-to-end value journeys. In the next decade, organisations with strong capabilities in these areas will disrupt. This sets a clear agenda for the leadership of any organisation.

Acknowledgements. The author would like to thank Rob Beijleveld, Lenny Daams and Diego Nendissa and from ICT Media (www.ictmedia.nl) for inviting the members of the ICT Media community to participate in the survey and for facilitating the execution of the survey and the round tables. Furthermore also BCG and Wipro have contributed to this research by providing feedback to the survey, actively participating in the workshops and reviewing earlier versions of the market research report that is the basis for this publication (https://itexecutive.nl/hpdo/2023-hpdo-paper-sharing-data-in-ecosystems/). The author would like to thank Paul Verkerk, Malay Srivastava, Johan Stockmann and Marla Dans for reviewing draft versions of this market research report.

References

1. BCG. In Uncertain Times, Double Down on Business Ecosystems (2023). https://www.bcg.com/publications/2023/build-business-ecosystem-resilience-in-uncertain-times. Accessed 24 May 2025

2. BAIN. New technologies such as generative AI, quantum computing, and climate technology require unique but complementary managerial muscles – July (2024). https://www.bain.com/insights/taking-globally-orchestrated-approach-to-digital-disruption/. Accessed 24 May 2025

3. Tushman, M.L., Newman, W.H., Romanelli, E.: Convergence and upheaval: managing the unsteady pace of organizational evolution. Calif. Manage. Rev. **29**(1), 29–44 (1986)

4. Andal-Ancion, A., Cartwright, P.A., Yip, G.S.: The digital transformation of traditional business. MIT Sloan Manag. Rev. **44**(4), 34 (2003)

5. Matt, C., Hess, T., Benlian, A.: Digital transformation strategies. Bus. Inf. Syst. Eng. **57**, 339–343 (2015)

6. Gobble, M.M.: Digitalization, digitization, and innovation. Res. Technol. Manag. **61**(4), 56–59 (2018)

7. Sabbagh, K., Friedrich, R., El-Darwiche, B., Singh, M., Ganediwalla, S., Katz, R.: Maximizing the impact of digitization. Glob. Inf. Technol. Rep. **2012**, 121–133 (2012)

8. Parviainen, P., Tihinen, M., Kääriäinen, J., Teppola, S.: Tackling the digitalization challenge: how to benefit from digitalization in practice. Int. J. Inf. Syst. Proj. Manag. **5**(1), 63–77 (2017)

9. Walker, G., Weber, D.: A transaction cost approach to make-or-buy decisions. Adm. Sci. Q. 373–391 (1984)

10. Willcocks, L., Fitzgerald, G., Feeny, D.: Outsourcing IT: the strategic implications. Long Range Plan. **28**(5), 59–70 (1995)

11. Williamson, O.E.: Transaction cost economics: how it works; where it is headed. De Economist **146**, 23–58 (1998)

12. Beulen, E.: Contract renewal decisions in IT outsourcing: "Should I stay or should I go." J. Inf. Technol. Manag. **22**(4), 47–55 (2011)

13. Carmel, E.: Global software teams: collaborating across borders and time zones. Prentice Hall PTR (1999)

14. Carmel, E., Tjia, P.: Offshoring information technology: Sourcing and outsourcing to a global workforce. Cambridge university press (2005)

15. Beulen, E.: Long-held perceptions of the consequences of IT offshoring will become a reality: fewer IS jobs in developed countries. J. Inf. Technol. **25**, 376–377 (2010)

16. Oshri, I.: Offshoring strategies: Evolving captive center models. MIT Press (2011)

17. Beulen, E., Ribbers, P.: (Eds.). The Routledge companion to managing digital outsourcing. Routledge (2020)

18. Beulen, E.: Implementing and Contracting Agile and DevOps: A Survey in the Netherlands. In: Kotlarsky, J., Oshri, I., Willcocks, L. (eds.) Digital Services and Platforms. Considerations for Sourcing. Global Sourcing 2018. Lecture Notes in Business Information Processing, vol. 344. Springer, Cham (2019)
19. Bounfour, A.: Digital futures, digital transformation. Progress IS **10**, 978–973 (2016)
20. Pappas, I.O., Mikalef, P., Giannakos, M.N., Krogstie, J., Lekakos, G.: Big data and business analytics ecosystems: paving the way towards digital transformation and sustainable societies. IseB **16**(3), 479–491 (2018)
21. Subramaniam, M., Iyer, B., Venkatraman, V.: Competing in digital ecosystems. Bus. Horiz. **62**(1), 83–94 (2019)
22. Cennamo, C., Dagnino, G.B., Di Minin, A., Lanzolla, G.: Managing digital transformation: Scope of transformation and modalities of value co-generation and delivery. Calif. Manage. Rev. **62**(4), 5–16 (2020)
23. Ketonen-Oksi, S., Valkokari, K.: Innovation ecosystems as structures for value co-creation. Technol. Innovation Manag. Rev. **9**(2) (2019)
24. Siaw, C.A., Sarpong, D.: Dynamic exchange capabilities for value co-creation in ecosystems. J. Bus. Res. **134**, 493–506 (2021)
25. Carey, P.: Data protection: a practical guide to UK and EU law. Oxford University Press, Inc. (2018)
26. Sokol, D.D., Comerford, R.: Antitrust and regulating big data. Geo. Mason L. Rev. **23**, 1129 (2015)
27. Parker, G.G., Petropoulos, G., Van Alstyne, M.W.: Digital platforms and antitrust (2019)
28. Ifenthaler, D., Egloffstein, M.: Development and implementation of a maturity model of digital transformation. TechTrends **64**(2), 302–309 (2020)
29. Beulen, E.: Digital maturity: a survey in The Netherlands. In: Oshri, I., Kotlarsky, J., Willcocks, L.P. (eds.) Digital Technologies for Global Sourcing of Services. Global Sourcing 2019. Lecture Notes in Business Information Processing, vol. 410. Springer, Cham (2020)
30. Jacobides, M.G., Cennamo, C., Gawer, A.: Towards a theory of ecosystems. Strateg. Manag. J. **39**(8), 2255–2276 (2018)
31. Holgersson, M., Granstrand, O., Bogers, M.: The evolution of intellectual property strategy in innovation ecosystems: uncovering complementary and substitute appropriability regimes. Long Range Plan. **51**(2), 303–319 (2018)
32. Granstrand, O., Holgersson, M.: Innovation ecosystems: a conceptual review and a new definition. Technovation **90**, 102098 (2020)
33. Lundin, L., Kindström, D.: Digitalizing customer journeys in B2B markets. J. Bus. Res. **157**, 113639 (2023)
34. Cale, P., Allen-Diaz, B.H.: New models for ecosystem dynamics and restoration. Island Press (2013)
35. BCG. Company data champions driving resilience (2023). https://www.bcg.com/publicati ons/2023/company-data-champions-driving-resilience. Accessed 17 Nov 2024
36. Beulen, E., Dans, M.A.: Data Analytics and Digital Transformation. Taylor & Francis (2023)
37. Van Alstyne, M., Brynjolfsson, E., Madnick, S.: Why not one big database? Principles for data ownership. Decis. Support. Syst. **15**(4), 267–284 (1995)
38. Machado, I.A., Costa, C., Santos, M.Y.: Data mesh: concepts and principles of a paradigm shift in data architectures. Procedia Comput. Sci. **196**, 263–271 (2022)
39. Dosis, A., Sand-Zantman, W.: The ownership of data. J. Law Econ. Organ. **39**(3), 615–641 (2023)
40. Janssen, M., Brous, P., Estevez, E., Barbosa, L.S., Janowski, T.: Data governance: organizing data for trustworthy Artificial Intelligence. Gov. Inf. Q. **37**(3), 101493 (2020)
41. Malik, M., Kanwal, M.: Impacts of organizational knowledge sharing practices on employees' job satisfaction, J. Workplace Learn. (2018)

42. Azeem, M., Ahmed, M., Haider, S., Sajjad, M.: Expanding competitive advantage through organizational culture, knowledge sharing and organizational innovation. Technol. Soc. **66**, 101635 (2021)

43. Kugler, P., Plank, T.: Coping with the double-edged sword of data sharing in ecosystems. Technol. Innovation Manag. Rev. **11**(11–12) (2021)

44. Wang, P.: Connecting the parts with the whole: toward an information ecology theory of digital innovation ecosystems. MIS Q. **45**(1) (2021)

45. Oliveira, M.I., Barros Lima, G.D.F., Farias Lóscio, B.: Investigations into data ecosystems: a systematic mapping study. Knowl. Inf. Syst. **61**, 589–630 (2019)

46. Otto, B., Ten Hompel, M., Wrobel, S.: Designing data spaces: The ecosystem approach to competitive advantage, (p. 580). Springer Nature (2022)

47. Otto, B.: The evolution of data spaces. In: Designing data spaces: The ecosystem approach to competitive advantage, pp. 3–15. Springer International Publishing, Cham (2022)

48. Beulen, E., Plugge, A., van Hillegersberg, J.: Formal and relational governance of artificial intelligence outsourcing. Inf. Syst. E-Bus Manage. **20**, 719–748 (2022)

49. West, D.M., Allen, J.R.: How artificial intelligence is transforming the world. Brookings Institution (2018). https://www.brookings.edu/articles/how-artificial-intelligence-is-transforming-the-world/. Accessed 17 Nov 2024

50. Rawat, D.B., Doku, R., Garuba, M.: Cybersecurity in big data era: from securing big data to data-driven security. IEEE Trans. Serv. Comput. **14**(6), 2055–2072 (2019)

51. Pansara, R.R.: Cybersecurity measures in master data management: safeguarding sensitive information. Int. Numer. J. Mach. Learn. Robot. **6**(6), 1–12 (2022)

52. Pala, A., Zhuang, J.: Information sharing in cybersecurity: a review. Decis. Anal. **16**(3), 172–196 (2019)

53. Djotaroeno, M., Beulen, E.: Information security awareness in the insurance sector: cognitive and internal factors and combined recommendations. Information **15**(8), 505 (2024)

54. Beulen, E., Bode, R.: An information technology and innovation committee to guide digital transformations. Corporate Board: Role, Duties and Composition (2021)

55. Cantero Gamito, M., Marsden, C.T.: Artificial intelligence co-regulation? The role of standards in the EU AI Act. Int. J. Law Inf. Technol. **32**(1), eaae011 (2024).

56. BCG. The new tech tools in data sharing (2021). https://web-assets.bcg.com/a4/25/1764e5 1441a197b2c4393bdbe446/bcg-the-new-tech-tools-in-data-sharing-mar-2021.pdf. Accessed 17 Nov 2024

57. BAIN. The visionary CEO's guide to sustainability (2023). https://www.bain.com/globalass ets/noindex/2023/bain_report_the_visionary_ceos_guide_to_sustainability.pdf. Accessed 17 Nov 2024

58. Hopp, C., Antons, D., Kaminski, J., Oliver Salge, T.: Disruptive innovation: conceptual foundations, empirical evidence, and research opportunities in the digital age. J. Prod. Innovation Manag. **35**(3) (2018)

59. Brock, J.K.U., Von Wangenheim, F.: Demystifying AI: what digital transformation leaders can teach you about realistic artificial intelligence. Calif. Manage. Rev. **61**(4), 110–134 (2019)

60. Agrawal, A., Gans, J.S., Goldfarb, A.: Artificial intelligence adoption and system-wide change. J. Econ. Manag. Strategy **33**(2), 327–337 (2024)

61. Beulen, E., Ribbers, P.M.: Managing IT outsourcing. Third edition, Routledge (2021)

62. Wareham, J., Fox, P.B., Cano Giner, J.L.: Technology ecosystem governance. Organ. Sci. **25**(4), 1195–1215 (2014)

63. Ross, J. W., Weill, P., Robertson, D.: Enterprise architecture as strategy: Creating a foundation for business execution. Harvard Business Press (2006)

64. Timmers, P.: Business models for electronic markets. Electron. Mark. **8**(2), 3–8 (1998)

The AI-Driven Vendor: Impact of AI on Offshore Software Outsourcing

Erik Wende[1]([✉]), Rainer Alt[1] [ID], and Chi Toan Nguyen[2] [ID]

[1] University of Leipzig, Leipzig, Germany
{erik.wende,rainer.alt}@uni-leipzig.de
[2] Vietnamese-German University, Bến Cát, Vietnam
toan.nc@vgu.edu.vn

Abstract. The paper examines the transformative impact of artificial intelligence (AI) on offshore software outsourcing, with a focus on how AI-driven tools like GitHub Copilot and ChatGPT are reshaping development practices and vendor dynamics. These tools automate routine coding tasks, improve code quality, and accelerate development timelines, creating new value propositions for offshore vendors. This paper argues that the shift to AI demands a redefinition of vendor roles, emphasizing adaptability, knowledge integration, and higher-value contributions beyond traditional coding. Offshore vendors should now move up the value chain and embrace innovation, design, and consultancy roles to remain competitive. In combining theoretical insights with case-based observations, this paper proposes a future framework for AI-integrated outsourcing ecosystems. This framework addresses key challenges such as talent reskilling, collaboration models, and governance structures. Ultimately, the paper highlights that while AI presents efficiency gains, it also compels offshore vendors to evolve strategically and organizationally to sustain their relevance in an AI-dominated software industry.

Keywords: Artificial Intelligence · Offshore Software Outsourcing · Vendor Strategy

1 Introduction

The offshore software outsourcing landscape is rapidly transforming, with artificial intelligence (AI) playing an increasingly prominent role. AI-powered coding tools, such as GitHub Copilot and ChatGPT, are transforming software development by automating repetitive tasks, enhancing code optimization, and streamlining the development process. These AI-driven technologies are not only transforming the technical aspects of software development but are also reshaping the competitive dynamics within the offshore software vendor landscape. While existing research has explored the general impact of AI on various industries (e.g. [1, 2]), the specific implications of AI tools on the offshore software outsourcing sector remain largely unexplored.

An example is the Vietnamese offshore software development market (see [3–5]) which has emerged as a prominent player in the global outsourcing landscape, owing to its

M. Schreieck et al. (Eds.): DSPE 2025, LNBIP 563, pp. 126–139, 2026.
https://doi.org/10.1007/978-3-032-04512-6_7

skilled workforce, competitive cost advantages, and growing technological capabilities [6]. However, the specific ways in which AI-powered coding tools are reshaping the operations, competitiveness, and client-vendor relationships within this market have only little been analyzed.

This exploratory study investigates how AI-powered coding tools are transforming the Vietnamese offshore software outsourcing landscape from the perspective of offshore software vendors. By examining the perspectives of various personnel within strategically selected Vietnamese offshore providers, this research will explore the factors influencing AI tool adoption, the perceived impact on agility, adaptability, productivity, and the required skillsets within the IT industry. From a scientific view, the findings contribute to the offshoring literature and from a practical view, training programs in the offshore outsourcing sector may be enhanced.

This paper analyzes the multifaceted impact of AI-powered coding tools on the offshore software development industry in Vietnam. The Vietnamese software development market has gained emerged as a prominent hub for offshore software outsourcing due to factors such as the availability of a large pool of skilled and cost-effective technical talent, as well as the government's proactive efforts to develop the country's IT infrastructure ([6, 7]. The software offshoring market is characterized by a diverse range of offshore vendors, from large-scale enterprises to small and medium-sized firms [8]. These vendors cater to a global client base, offering a wide array of software development services, including web and mobile application development, enterprise software solutions, and specialized niche offerings. The present research aims to understand how novel tools based on generative AI [9] are influencing operational processes, competitiveness, and client-vendor relationships. It is guided by two central questions:

1. **How are AI-powered coding tools influencing the adoption, perceived agility, adaptability, code quality, productivity, and required skillsets within Vietnamese offshore software vendors?** This question addresses the core operational and competency-related aspects of AI integration. It aligns with existing literature that emphasizes the importance of technological capabilities and human capital in achieving organizational agility and responsiveness [4].

2. **How are AI tools reshaping client-vendor relationships in the context of offshore software outsourcing, specifically concerning collaboration, trust, and contractual agreements?** This question explores the broader implications of AI adoption on the collaborative dynamics between vendors and clients. It resonates with research that highlights the critical role of trust, communication, and contractual clarity in successful outsourcing partnerships [3].

By addressing these questions, this study aims to provide insights into AI's transformative potential in the offshore software development landscape and to offer guidance for vendors seeking to effectively leverage AI while navigating its associated challenges. By examining perspectives from personnel at randomly selected Vietnamese offshore providers, the findings shed light on AI tool adoption factors, perceived impacts on agility and adaptability, evolving metrics for code quality and productivity, and the evolving skill demands and competitive dynamics in the industry.

2 Literature Review

The following chapter summarizes several studies, which have explored the impact of AI on software development and offshore outsourcing. Based on the literature and existing applications in various industries, such as tourism [10] and human resources [11], it shows that the specific implications of AI tools on the offshore software outsourcing landscape remain largely unexplored.

2.1 AI in Software Development

As mentioned in the introduction, the rise of AI-powered tools, such as GitHub Copilot and ChatGPT, is significantly transforming the software development industry [12]. These powerful AI-powered assistants [13] leverage advanced machine learning algorithms to provide developers with a remarkable array of capabilities ranging from generating code snippets and detecting bugs, to suggesting code optimizations and completions [14, 15] and have the potential to increase efficiency, reduce risks, and enhance project success rates in agile software development [16, 17]. Research has consistently demonstrated that the integration of these AI coding tools can significantly enhance developer productivity and improve overall code quality [2]. Studies have shown that these tools can automate repetitive and time-consuming tasks, reduce error rates, and even identify opportunities for code optimization [2, 18]. Based on their survey of 207 software developers, Vaillant et al. found that 79.7% of respondents reported increased productivity due to ChatGPT, with 71.5% perceiving improvements in the quality of their work [19]. This leads to faster development cycles, improved software reliability, and greater efficiency in the software engineering process [20]. Furthermore, 87.9% of the surveyed developers believed that ChatGPT would have a significant impact on the software development industry in the coming years [19].

Additionally, AI promises to help in breaking down complex development processes for stakeholders, enabling more informed decision-making [17]. Existing research emphasizes the growing importance of factors like agility, adaptability, and building strong client-vendor relationships in driving success in IT outsourcing arrangements, rather than relying solely on cost advantages [3, 21, 22]. This shift aligns with the increased accessibility of AI tools, which can empower offshore vendors to better serve the evolving needs of their clients.

While research has highlighted the potential benefits of integrating AI coding tools, such as improved developer productivity and code quality, some studies have raised concerns about the long-term implications of these technologies [2, 15, 18]. Specifically, there are worries that the increased automation of certain software development tasks could lead to job displacement within the industry [12]. Additionally, the reliance on AI-powered tools may diminish the need for certain traditional software engineering skills, potentially reshaping the required skillsets for developers. Furthermore, the opaque nature of some AI systems raises questions about the transparency and interpretability of the code they generate, which could impact software maintainability and reliability in the long run [23]. Ultimately, the adoption of AI coding tools within the software development workflow requires careful consideration of the associated challenges and potential unintended consequences [2].

2.2 Offshore Outsourcing

Offshore software outsourcing has emerged as a widely adopted practice among businesses seeking to access skilled labor at competitive costs. This strategy enables enterprises to enhance their development capabilities and maintain a competitive edge in the market [24]. Traditionally, the success of IT outsourcing arrangements was primarily driven by the pursuit of cost advantages. However, recent research suggests a notable shift in focus, with critical factors such as agility, adaptability, and the cultivation of strong client-vendor relationships now taking on increased significance. This shift aligns with the growing recognition that sustainable success in offshore outsourcing requires more than cost savings. It necessitates the ability to respond swiftly to changing market demands, adapt to evolving client needs, and establish robust partnerships built on trust and effective communication. Establishing and maintaining trust, ensuring effective cross-cultural communication, and navigating the challenges posed by cultural differences have emerged as vital elements for cultivating successful offshore partnerships [25, 26]. However, the introduction of AI-powered tools like GitHub Copilot and ChatGPT is set to drastically transform the communication and collaboration dynamics between offshore vendors and their clients. These advanced AI assistants can streamline development processes, facilitate more seamless information sharing, and enable more efficient cross-cultural coordination [27].

As offshore vendors adapt to this AI-driven landscape, they must renegotiate various aspects of their client relationships. Factors like transparency, responsiveness, and the ability to address issues proactively will take on heightened importance, as AI tools can enhance vendor capabilities but also introduce new complexities. Offshore providers will need to invest in developing strong relational ties with clients, fostering a climate of trust and confidence that is crucial for the long-term viability and success of these software development collaborations, despite the transformative changes brought by AI integration [24]. Effective collaboration and coordination practices will remain key, as factors like the physical distance between the client and vendor may still influence the dynamics and outcomes of these outsourcing arrangements [26]. Building a shared understanding, aligning expectations, and developing robust communication channels has been recognized as essential for overcoming the logistical and cultural barriers inherent in these geographically dispersed partnerships [28], even as AI tools reshape the software development landscape.

3 Research Methodology

This study investigates the intersection of the growing adoption of AI-powered coding tools and the evolving landscape of offshore software outsourcing, focusing on the Vietnamese software development market. While existing research provides insights into AI in software development and offshore outsourcing separately, it aims to address this gap by conducting an in-depth investigation into how the introduction and adoption of transformative AI technologies, such as GitHub Copilot and ChatGPT, are impacting offshore software vendors in Vietnam. The research will delve into the ways these AI-powered tools and technologies are being integrated and utilized by Vietnamese offshore software providers, examining how the adoption of AI capabilities is affecting key aspects of the software development process, including developer productivity, code quality, adherence to best practices, and overall engineering workflow efficiency. Furthermore, the study will explore the influential role of AI in reshaping the dynamics of client-vendor relationships within the offshore outsourcing landscape. By focusing on the vendor perspective, often underrepresented, the research seeks insights into the challenges and opportunities associated with integrating AI capabilities into the offshore software development landscape. These insights shall contribute to academic understanding of this emerging trend and provide practical guidance to offshore vendors and their clients as they navigate the evolving landscape of AI-driven software development.

Based on exploratory endeavor, a qualitative research approach, conducting semi-structured interviews with personnel from Vietnamese offshore software providers, has been chosen. This approach enables an in-depth examination of individual experiences and perspectives. The participants included developers, project managers, team leads, and executives, providing insights from diverse roles and responsibilities within the organizations. The diversity of participants facilitated analysis of responses based on the interviewees' expertise and responsibilities within the organization.

3.1 Interview Methodology

The study selected twelve offshore vendors from different regions across Vietnam to ensure a well-rounded understanding of how regional variations may influence the adoption and impact of AI tools. This geographical diversity strengthens the study's generalizability and provides a comprehensive perspective on the factors shaping AI integration within the Vietnamese offshore software development landscape. It aims to provide guidance to both offshore software vendors and their clients, helping them navigate the evolving landscape of AI-powered software development and foster effective, adaptable, and beneficial partnerships. The semi-structured interview format followed a guideline designed to address key research questions, each grounded in existing literature:

- **Question Section 1: Background and Experience:** This section gathered background information on the interviewees, including their roles and experience in software development and offshore outsourcing. This helped understand their perspectives on AI adoption and its impact on their work. This approach aligns with prior studies that categorized participants by their roles within the IT organization [3]. Additionally, questions assessed the interviewees' familiarity with AI-powered coding tools like GitHub Copilot and ChatGPT, similar to research that has explored developers' perceptions and usage of such tools [19].
- **Question Section 2: Adoption Factors, Digital Platforms, Agility & Adaptability:** This section explored the various factors, both facilitating and impeding, that influence AI adoption by Vietnamese offshore software vendors. It echoed Davenport's concerns about the importance of organizational readiness and strategic alignment in successful AI integration [1]. The investigation went beyond technical considerations, delving into the organizational, cultural, and economic aspects of AI adoption. This comprehensive approach was valuable for understanding the broader context of AI adoption in the Vietnamese offshore software market. Notably, this research also examined how digital platforms, such as Upwork or Freelancer.com, might shape

the adoption of AI tools in the outsourcing context, potentially offering a novel contribution to the existing literature.

- **Question Section 3: Code Quality, Best Practices & Client Expectations:** This section addressed the aspect of code quality, a central theme in software engineering literature (e.g., [29, 30]). It explored how AI might impact existing quality assurance processes and the adherence to best practices, which helps to understand how AI tools can be integrated into existing workflows without compromising code quality or industry standards. Furthermore, it investigated how AI might affect communication and the understanding of client needs, recognizing that client expectations are paramount in the client-centric nature of outsourcing.

- **Question Section 4: Productivity Gains, Project Management & Competitiveness:** This section focused on the potential benefits of AI, aligning with research on AI's impact on productivity and efficiency (e.g., [11]). It investigated the practical benefits of AI in terms of time savings and project management enhancements, which is crucial for understanding the tangible benefits of AI adoption for offshore software vendors. It also explored the strategic implications of AI adoption, linking to the idea that AI can be a source of competitive advantage [1].

- **Question Section 5: Skills Evolution, Workforce Development & Freelancing:** This section addressed the aspect of workforce transformation in the face of AI, echoing the need for upskilling and reskilling emphasized in numerous studies. It explored the evolving skillset required for developers in the age of AI, aligning with the ongoing discussion about the future of work and the skills needed to thrive in an AI-powered world. It also addressed the potential impact of AI on the workforce, acknowledging the concerns about job displacement while emphasizing the importance of upskilling and retraining. Furthermore, it explored how AI might reshape the freelance landscape and create new opportunities or challenges for independent developers, which is particularly relevant to the Vietnamese context, given the prevalence of freelancing [12].

- **Question Section 6:** Client-Vendor Relationships, Trust & Contracts: This section examined the impact of AI on the client-vendor relationship, another important aspect of outsourcing success. It explored how AI might alter the dynamics of client-vendor collaboration, potentially leading to new models of interaction and project execution. It also addressed the ethical and legal implications of using AI in outsourcing, highlighting the importance of trust, transparency, and contractual clarity [3].

3.2 Data Collection and Analysis

The interviews, lasting between 45 and 60 min, were conducted partly in Vietnamese or English, based on the interviewees' preferences, and all interview records and reports were translated into English to facilitate analysis and reporting. This flexibility in language accommodates participant needs and ensures accurate data collection. The interview guide, comprising 6 question sections (listed in the previous section) and 13 detailed questions, was designed to deeply explore the research questions outlined in the introduction. The collected interview data were analyzed using rigorous thematic analysis techniques to identify the key themes and patterns directly relevant to addressing the research questions. Through a systematic and in-depth examination of the interview transcripts, the research team was able to uncover meaningful insights that shed light on the multifaceted impact of AI tools on the Vietnamese offshore software outsourcing industry.

The interview data were analyzed using thematic and interpretive analysis techniques [31]. The transcripts were initially coded to identify recurring themes and patterns related to the research questions. This involved carefully examining the interviewees' responses to identify key concepts, ideas, and opinions. Following the initial coding, the identified themes were further analyzed and interpreted to understand their significance and implications in the context of the research questions. This interpretive analysis involved a deeper reflection on the meaning of the themes, considering the various perspectives and experiences shared by the interviewees. The analysis specifically focused on factors influencing AI tool adoption, the impact of these tools on agility and adaptability, methods for measuring code quality, quantification of productivity gains, implications for workforce development, and transformation of client-vendor relationships. The final step integrated the key findings from the thematic and interpretive analysis into a cohesive narrative that addressed the research questions and provided insights into the impact of AI on the offshore software vendor landscape in Vietnam. The findings are presented in the next section, supported by illustrative quotes from the interviewees, which provide rich qualitative insights into the experiences and perspectives of the Vietnamese offshore software vendors regarding the adoption and impact of AI tools.

4 Findings

The interview data provided a multifaceted depiction of how Vietnamese offshore software vendors adopt AI technology. It shows that individual developers and testers have enthusiastically embraced AI tools, primarily motivated by personal efficiency gains and the ability of these tools to act as personal assistants. However, this enthusiasm has not yet translated into a strategic vision at the organizational level, with many companies lacking a cohesive strategy for AI implementation. This disconnect raises concerns about missed opportunities to harness the full potential of AI for broader business objectives. Additionally, the interviews highlight several ethical considerations that need to be addressed to ensure responsible and transparent AI adoption.

4.1 Individual Use of AI Tools

On the individual level, the interviews revealed a widespread and enthusiastic adoption of AI-powered coding assistants, such as GitHub Copilot and ChatGPT, among developers. This is evident from the statement by one of the interviewees: *"For the developers, I think they are looking for some suggestions in coding."* The interview data indicated that these AI tools were used on a daily basis by employees across the Vietnamese software outsourcing industry, with both developers and testers leveraging them for a variety of tasks, including code generation, bug detection, and code optimization. This finding highlights the growing prominence and integral role of AI tools in the daily work of software development professionals within these offshore vendors.

However, the interviews also suggested that the adoption of AI tools is not yet standardized, and the extent of their use varies significantly among individuals and companies. Some interviewees reported extensive use of AI tools for tasks like code generation, bug detection, and testing, while others had only experimented with them or not used them at all. This variation in adoption and usage patterns may be attributed to several factors, including awareness and understanding of the tools, cost and resource considerations, concerns about the reliability and quality of AI-generated code, organizational culture, employee acceptance, and security and legal implications.

Despite this variation, there was a general consensus among the interviewees that AI tools have the potential to significantly benefit the software development process. They cited benefits such as increased efficiency, improved code quality, idea generation to solve problems, and reduced development time. However, they also acknowledged the importance of using AI tools thoughtfully and strategically, ensuring that they complement rather than replace human expertise. As one interviewee aptly stated, *"I would like to apply AI for, but it is not for all the people here."*.

4.2 Role of Personal Efficiency and Benefits

A key theme emerging from the interviews was the significant role personal motivation plays in adopting AI tools. Developers and testers were primarily driven by the desire to enhance their own efficiency and streamline their individual workflows. They saw AI tools as a means to alleviate tedious tasks, improve code quality, and ultimately become more productive in their daily work. This focus on individual efficiency was evident in several interviewees' remarks. One developer highlighted the time-saving benefits of AI tools, stating, "Tools like GitHub Copilot can automatically complete code snippets based on the current context, which helps programmers write code faster and minimize errors." This sentiment was echoed by another interviewee who praised the ability of AI to "suggest more efficient ways to write code, ultimately helping to optimize application performance." These quotes illustrate the appeal of AI tools in empowering developers to work more efficiently and effectively.

At the same time, the interviews revealed that the use of AI tools was not without its challenges. One developer noted that while AI tools like Copilot and CodeVista can help generate code quickly and accurately, they sometimes struggle to comply with specific client patterns. *"This shortcoming requires programmers to manually modify and resolve the code, as they cannot rely on AI to provide the necessary patterns."* Despite these challenges, the overall sentiment was that AI tools are valuable assets for enhancing personal efficiency and productivity.

The emphasis on individual efficiency and benefits raised important questions about the broader implications of AI tool adoption. While individual developers and testers were eager to embrace these tools, it was important for companies to consider how to leverage this enthusiasm to achieve strategic goals and promote company-wide benefits. This includes providing adequate training and resources, establishing clear guidelines for AI usage, and fostering a culture of responsible and ethical AI adoption.

4.3 AI Tools as Personal Assistants

A key theme emerging from the interviews was the contrast between the enthusiastic use of AI tools by individual developers and testers and the lack of a cohesive, company-wide strategy for their implementation. Developers and testers saw AI as valuable personal assistants, capable of enhancing their efficiency and effectiveness in various tasks. They appreciated the ability of AI to *"suggest more efficient ways to write code, helping to optimize application performance"* and to *"detect non-optimal code snippets and suggest alternatives."* The appeal of AI tools was seen in their capacity to augment individual capabilities and streamline workflows, allowing developers to focus on more complex and creative aspects of their work. This is further exemplified by the appreciation for AI's ability to automate code generation: *"AI can convert natural language descriptions into source code. For example, a programmer only needs to describe the function they want, and the AI will automatically generate the corresponding code."*

However, this individual enthusiasm has not yet translated into a strategic vision at the organizational level. While developers were eager to leverage AI for personal productivity gains, companies appeared to be lagging in formulating comprehensive strategies for AI adoption and integration. One manager said *"I can say that we are in the very initial phase of experimenting with the AI tools. We know the few AI tools that could be beneficial for our work...we have seen that our developers, some of the developers already employs those kinds of tools, but mostly for their personal work."* This disconnect raises concerns about missed opportunities to harness the full potential of AI for broader business objectives. The absence of a holistic approach suggests that companies may not be adequately addressing the challenges and implications of AI adoption, such as data security, ethical considerations, and the need for workforce retraining. This lack of strategic direction could hinder the long-term benefits that AI could bring to the Vietnamese software outsourcing industry.

4.4 Lack of Strategic or Holistic View

Another finding pertains to the lack of strategic focus on the use of AI tools at the organizational level. While individuals were utilizing AI tools to enhance their efficiency and streamline tasks, there was limited evidence suggesting that companies have been implementing these tools holistically or strategically to achieve broader business objectives. This indicates a potential gap between individual adoption and organizational strategy in leveraging AI's transformative potential. One interviewee, when asked about their company's approach to AI implementation, stated, *"I can say that we are in the very initial phase of experimenting with the AI tools... Not in an actual project due to some restriction."* This statement highlights the tentative and limited approach many companies are taking towards AI adoption. Another interviewee, representing a small company, revealed a reliance on traditional methods for quality control, stating, *"As a small company, we use Peer Review processes to measure the quality of code. For the released product, we have an in-house QA team."* This suggests a lack of exploration into how AI tools could be integrated into existing workflows to potentially enhance quality control processes.

Furthermore, the interviews suggested that companies were missing opportunities to leverage AI tools for broader applications beyond coding and testing. When asked about using AI for predicting customer needs, one interviewee simply responded, *"No"*. Similarly, another interviewee, when asked about the potential of AI tools to support broader development processes, also responded with *"No"*. This lack of awareness or initiative in exploring AI's potential beyond individual tasks indicates a missed opportunity for companies to leverage AI for broader business objectives. It underscores the need for companies to develop a company-wide AI strategy that outlines how AI tools can be used to achieve broader business objectives, such as improving efficiency, productivity, and competitiveness. This strategy should go beyond simply allowing employees to use AI tools for individual tasks and instead focus on integrating AI into various aspects of the software development lifecycle. As one interviewee suggested, AI tools may be used to enhance flexibility and agility in meeting changing customer requirements. However, when asked for a specific example, the interviewee simply stated, *"I describe it as doing what I want it to do."* This highlights the need for companies to guide and strategize AI adoption to ensure it aligns with broader organizational goals and objectives.

4.5 Ethical Considerations

The integration of AI tools in software development brings forth a range of ethical considerations. Transparency with clients is paramount and companies should disclose the usage of AI tools, their functions, and their potential impact on projects. This ensures trust and manages client expectations. Additionally, developers need to understand the AI's process to prevent over-reliance on its output. Open communication about AI usage addresses potential trust concerns from clients worry of AI-generated code. In addition, data security and privacy are ethical concerns. Robust security measures and explicit consent for data usage in AI applications are necessary. Companies should prioritize data protection and regulatory compliance to maintain client trust and avoid legal repercussions. Intellectual property rights in AI-generated code require clear policies to prevent infringement. Ownership and usage rights should be discussed with clients, especially in outsourcing scenarios. Establishing contractual agreements and ownership protocols is essential.

Finally, accountability for AI-assisted development is vital. Roles and responsibilities for developers, testers, and managers must be defined to ensure the quality, accuracy, and ethical implications of AI-generated code. Clear guidelines and accountability mechanisms ensure compliance with client requirements and ethical standards. By proactively addressing these ethical considerations, companies can promote responsible AI adoption, ensuring these tools benefit both the company and clients while aligning with ethical principles and societal values.

5   Discussion and Implications

This study's findings contribute to the understanding of AI's influence on offshore software development by highlighting a potential disconnect between individual enthusiasm for AI tools and the lack of strategic organizational implementation. While individual developers are eager to use AI for personal efficiency gains, most of the surveyed companies lack a cohesive strategy for AI adoption and integration. This observation aligns with previous research that has emphasized the importance of organizational capabilities and strategic alignment in achieving successful technology implementation. For instance, Søderberg et al. (2013) have highlighted the significance of organizational commitment, knowledge transfer, and interconnectedness between client and vendor activities for successful outsourcing outcomes [27]. The lack of such strategic alignment in the context of AI adoption, as observed in this study, may impede the full realization of AI's potential benefits. This study also found that AI tools are currently underutilized in critical areas like requirements analysis and communication, despite their potential to improve efficiency and bridge geographical and cultural gaps in offshore outsourcing. This suggests that vendors may be missing opportunities to leverage AI's capabilities beyond just code generation, which could lead to more holistic benefits for both the vendor and the client.

Overall, the study's findings emphasize the necessity for a deeper understanding of the ethical ramifications of artificial intelligence (AI) in offshore software development. The potential of AI to enhance communication and requirements analysis in offshore outsourcing offers a new perspective on AI's ability to bridge geographical and cultural gaps. Effective communication is known to be crucial in offshore relationships, as it can help to build trust, reduce misunderstandings, and ensure that projects are completed successfully. AI can positively support communication in several ways. For example, AI-powered translation tools can help to overcome language barriers and cultural misunderstandings.

Additionally, AI can be used to analyze communication patterns and identify areas for improvement. By leveraging AI to enhance communication, businesses can improve the efficiency and effectiveness of their offshore relationships. However, the introduction of AI-powered coding tools raises various ethical concerns that vendors should address. These include data security, intellectual property rights, algorithmic bias, and accountability for AI-generated outputs. To maintain client trust and social responsibility, vendors must proactively develop and implement ethical frameworks to ensure the responsible and transparent use of these technologies.

The lack of strategic focus on AI at the organizational level raises concerns about missed opportunities to harness AI's full potential for broader business objectives. Companies may not adequately address the challenges and implications of AI adoption, such as data security, ethical considerations, and the need for workforce retraining. This lack of strategic direction could hinder the long-term benefits that AI could bring to the Vietnamese software outsourcing industry. Based on the findings of this study, the following recommendations are proposed for Vietnamese offshore software vendors to effectively leverage AI while mitigating potential risks:

1. **Develop a Company-wide AI Strategy:** Move beyond ad hoc individual usage and establish a clear, organization-wide AI strategy that aligns with business objectives.
2. **Invest in Training and Development:** Provide comprehensive training programs to upskill the workforce on AI tools and technologies, ethical considerations, and best practices.
3. **Prioritize Data Security and Privacy:** Implement robust security measures to protect client data and ensure compliance with relevant regulations.

4. **Promote Transparency and Communication:** Maintain open communication with clients regarding AI usage, addressing potential concerns and building trust.
5. **Foster a Culture of Responsible AI Adoption:** Encourage the ethical and responsible use of AI, emphasizing human oversight and continuous learning.

6   Conclusion

This exploratory research investigated the impact of AI on offshore software vendors in the Vietnamese market, focusing on the adoption of AI-powered coding tools and their broader implications for the industry. Two key research questions guided this investigation: 1) How are AI-powered coding tools influencing the operations and strategic decisions of Vietnamese offshore software vendors? and 2) How are these AI tools reshaping the dynamics and relationships between clients and vendors in the offshore outsourcing industry?

Regarding the first research question, the finding that developers primarily use AI tools for personal benefit rather than strategically leveraging them for broader company-wide benefits is surprising. Although the use of these tools is widespread, developers and testers viewed them primarily as personal assistants that enhance their productivity and code quality. This enthusiastic adoption by individuals, however, contrasts with the lack of a cohesive, strategic approach to AI implementation at the organizational level. Companies are lagging in formulating comprehensive strategies for AI adoption and integration, raising concerns about missed opportunities to harness the full potential of AI for broader business objectives.

Regarding the second research question AI tools have reshaped client-vendor relationships by introducing new complexities and considerations. While AI has the potential to improve communication and collaboration, it also necessitates discussions on data security, intellectual property rights, and ethical implications. The lack of a cohesive AI strategy at the organizational level may hinder the full realization of these benefits, underscoring the need for companies to proactively address the transformative influence of AI on client-vendor dynamics.

Beyond the research questions, the study also revealed that AI tools are currently underutilized in critical areas like requirements analysis and communication, despite their potential to improve efficiency and bridge geographical and cultural gaps in offshore outsourcing. This suggests that vendors may be missing opportunities to leverage AI's capabilities beyond just code generation, which could lead to more holistic benefits for both the vendor and the client. This suggests a need for companies to actively guide how these tools may be employed along the entire software development process and how this aligns with organizational goals and objectives. In particular, companies need to address the ethical implications of AI in offshore software development. Companies should prioritize transparency with clients regarding AI usage, data security, intellectual property rights, and potential bias in AI outcomes. Clear lines of accountability and responsibility must be established for AI-assisted development.

The study has several limitations. First, the small sample size of the study limits the ability to generalize the findings to the broader Vietnamese offshore software vendor population. Second, the qualitative nature of the study makes it difficult to quantify the precise impact of AI tools on factors such as developer productivity and code quality.

Finally, the study's focus on the Vietnamese market may restrict the generalizability of the findings to other offshore outsourcing markets around the world.

To address these limitations, future research should take a more quantitative approach, conducting studies with larger sample sizes. This would help provide a more comprehensive understanding of the impact of AI tools within the offshore software development industry. Additionally, future research could expand the geographical scope of the investigation, exploring the influence of AI tools in different offshore outsourcing markets beyond Vietnam. This would offer valuable comparative insights and a more global perspective on the transformative impact of these technologies. Furthermore, future studies could delve deeper into the long-term implications of AI tools on the skills and knowledge required of software developers in the offshore outsourcing industry. As these technologies continue to evolve, it is key to understand how they may reshape the competencies and job roles within this sector, enabling vendors to adapt their workforce development strategies accordingly.

References

1. Davenport, T.H.: From analytics to artificial intelligence. J. Bus. Anal. **1**, 73–80 (2018). https://doi.org/10.1080/2573234X.2018.1543535
2. Ajiga, D., Okeleke, P.A., Folorunsho, S.O., et al.: Enhancing software development practices with AI insights in high-tech companies. Comput. Sci. IT Res. J. **5**, 1897–1919 (2024) https://doi.org/10.51594/csitrj.v5i8.1450
3. Venumuddala, V.R., Kamath, R.: Evolving client–vendor relationship: as manifested through an artificial intelligence research unit of an Indian IT Organization. Vikalpa: J. Decis. Makers 49:157–166 (2024). https://doi.org/10.1177/02560909241254998
4. Jang, S., Lee, H., Ko, K.: Becoming a fast learner in offshore software outsourcing: the case of Vietnam's FPT software. Int. Area Rev. **13**, 183–203 (2010). https://doi.org/10.1177/2233 86591001300110
5. Vu, D.A., Bui, Q.H., Pham, T.Q.: Critical success factors for Vietnamese software companies: a framework for investigation. JSR **3** (2012). https://doi.org/10.5296/jsr.v3i2.2307
6. Hung, P.D., Cuong, L.G., Bach, N.L.: Offshore development center management in action. In: Proceedings of the 2020 5th International Conference on Intelligent Information Technology. ACM, New York, NY, USA, pp. 77–85 (2020)
7. Nguyen, P.T., Babar, M.A., Verner, J.M.: Critical factors in establishing and maintaining trust in software outsourcing relationships. In: Osterweil, L.J., Rombach, D., Soffa, M.L. (eds.) Proceedings of the 28th International Conference on Software Engineering. ACM, New York, NY, USA, pp. 624–627 (2006)
8. Gallaugher, J., Stoller, G.: Software outsourcing in Vietnam: a case study of a locally operating pioneer. E. J. Info. Sys. Dev. Countries **17**, 1–18 (2004). https://doi.org/10.1002/j.1681-4835. 2004.tb00110.x
9. Banh, L., Strobel, G.: Generative artificial intelligence. Electron Markets **33** (2023). https://doi.org/10.1007/s12525-023-00680-1
10. Solakis, K., Katsoni, V., Mahmoud, A.B., et al.: Factors affecting value co-creation through artificial intelligence in tourism: a general literature review. JTF **10**, 116–130 (2024). https://doi.org/10.1108/JTF-06-2021-0157
11. Zel, S., Kongar, E.: Transforming digital employee experience with artificial intelligence. In: 2020 IEEE / ITU International Conference on Artificial Intelligence for Good (AI4G). IEEE, pp. 176–179 (2020)

12. Sauvola, J., Tarkoma, S., Klemettinen, M., et al.: Future of software development with generative AI. Autom. Softw. Eng. **31** (2024). https://doi.org/10.1007/s10515-024-00426-z

13. Schmidt, R., Alt, R., Zimmermann, A.: Assistant platforms. Electron Markets **33** (2023). https://doi.org/10.1007/s12525-023-00671-2

14. Anantrasirichai, N., Bull, D.: Artificial intelligence in the creative industries: a review. Artif. Intell. Rev. **55**, 589–656 (2022). https://doi.org/10.1007/s10462-021-10039-7

15. Marar, H.W.: Advancements in software engineering using AI. Comput. Soft Media Appl. **6**, 3906 (2023). https://doi.org/10.24294/csma.v6i1.3906

16. Sergeyuk, A., Golubev, Y., Bryksin, T., et al.: Using Ai-Based Coding Assistants in Practice: State of Affairs, Perceptions, and Ways Forward (2024)

17. Mahboob, M., Ahmed, M.R.U., Zia, Z., et al.: Future of Artificial Intelligence in Agile Software Development (2024). https://doi.org/10.48550/ARXIV.2408.00703

18. Talamadupula, K.: Applied AI matters: AI4Code. AI Matters **7**, 18–20 (2021). https://doi.org/10.1145/3465074.3465080

19. Vaillant, T.S., Almeida de, F.D., Neto, P.A.M.S., et al.: Developers' Perceptions on the Impact of ChatGPT in Software Development: A Survey. arXiv (2024)

20. Sushma, T.N.: Automation of Software Development using DevOps and its enefits. IJERT V9 (2020). https://doi.org/10.17577/IJERTV9IS060369

21. Kotlarsky, J., Rivard, S., Oshri, I.: Building a reputation as a business partner in information technology outsourcing. MISQ **47**, 901–922 (2023). https://doi.org/10.25300/MISQ/2022/15554

22. Keshta, I., Odeh, A.: Critical barriers in software outsourcing vendor organizations and their impacts on software outsourcing clients: a systematic literature review. J. Comput. Sci. **16**, 1346–1354 (2020). https://doi.org/10.3844/jcssp.2020.1346.1354

23. Ozkaya, I.: The next frontier in software development: AI-augmented software development processes. IEEE Softw. **40**, 4–9 (2023). https://doi.org/10.1109/MS.2023.3278056

24. Khan, S.U., Niazi, M., Ahmad, R.: Factors influencing clients in the selection of offshore software outsourcing vendors: an exploratory study using a systematic literature review. J. Syst. Softw. **84**, 686–699 (2011). https://doi.org/10.1016/j.jss.2010.12.010

25. Niazi, M., Ikram, N., Bano, M., et al.: Establishing trust in offshore software outsourcing relationships: an exploratory study using a systematic literature review. IET softw **7**, 283–293 (2013). https://doi.org/10.1049/iet-sen.2012.0136

26. Poston, R.S., Simon, J.C., Jain, R.: Client communication practices in managing relationships with offshore vendors of software testing services. CAIS **27** (2010). https://doi.org/10.17705/1CAIS.02709

27. Søderberg, A.-M., Krishna, S., Bjørn, P.: Global software development: commitment, trust and cultural sensitivity in strategic partnerships. J. Int. Manag. **19**, 347–361 (2013). https://doi.org/10.1016/j.intman.2013.04.004

28. Ali, S., Khan, S.U.: Critical success factors for software outsourcing partnership (SOP): A systematic literature review. In: 2014 IEEE 9th International Conference on Global Software Engineering. IEEE, pp. 153–162 (2014)

29. Cross, S.E.: A quality doctrine for software: do it right the first time. In: Ninth Asia-Pacific Software Engineering Conference, 2002. IEEE Comput. Soc, pp. 187–194 (2002)

30. Lenarduzzi, V., Lomio, F., Moreschini, S., et al.: Software Quality for AI: Where We Are Now? In: Winkler, D., Biffl, S., Mendez, D., et al. (eds.) Software Quality: Future Perspectives on Software Engineering Quality, vol. 404, pp. 43–53. Springer International Publishing, Cham (2021)

31. Knox, S., Burkard, A.W.: Qualitative research interviews. Psychother. Res. **19**, 566–575 (2009). https://doi.org/10.1080/10503300802702105

The Entrepreneurial Language and Strategic Patterns of Initial Coin Offerings

Benjamin Barraza$^{(\boxtimes)}$ [ID], Kiron Ravindran [ID], and Álvaro Arenas [ID]

IE Business School, Maria de Molina 11-13-15, Madrid, Spain
benjamin.barraza@student.ie.edu, {kiron.ravindran,
Alvaro.Arenas}@ie.edu

Abstract. Initial Coin Offerings (ICOs) present blockchain entrepreneurs an alternative avenue to funding their initiative while simultaneously supporting the platform imperative of igniting their transactional market. White papers have been a component of blockchain and cryptocurrency initiatives since the advent of Bitcoin. These documents play a key role in signaling to potential token buyers the purpose, competitive position, and expected strategic trajectory of the firm. We build 5 research propositions around the practice of ICOs and white papers as key strategic instruments. These research propositions aim to further our understanding of the practice and implications of actions that are within managers' control. Propositions explore strategic decisions related to organizational form, token allocation patterns, post-ICO fundraising planning, risk disclosure, and technological alignment. Implications for researchers support further differentiation in ICOs as fundraising mechanisms and support token buyers as a novel class of investors.

Keywords: Initial Coin Offering · white papers · cryptocurrency · strategic language

1 Initial Coin Offerings and White Papers

Blockchain's novel form of fundraising, the Initial Coin Offering (ICO) continues to be an important channel for entrepreneurial activity and startup fundraising. In the first 4 months of 2025, 112 ICOs had received anywhere from $0–$350M in fundraising totaling nearly $1.5B in funding with an average ICO yield of $13M [4]. Cryptocurrency prices and ICO outcomes tend to be correlated with Bitcoin prices [5]. As Bitcoin has achieved an all-time high spot price in 2025 [6], we expect renewed interest in cryptocurrency and ICO practices. While ICOs have similarities to other forms of fundraising such as IPOs and crowdfunding, many believe that they fill a unique gap. Akbarpour [7] notes that ICOs disrupt traditional venture capital and nicely fill a small gap in the $1M to $3M range. They argue that ICOs open the door for entrepreneurs that are often overlooked by traditional capital.

Earlier portions of this study were presented at the 2023 International Conference on Information Systems in Hyderabad, India, the 2024 European Conference on Information Systems in Paphos, Cyprus, and the 16th Digital Sourcing, Platforms, and Ecosystems Workshop, Obergurgl, Austria [1–3]

M. Schreieck et al. (Eds.): DSPE 2025, LNBIP 563, pp. 140–152, 2026.
https://doi.org/10.1007/978-3-032-04512-6_8

"White papers" play a key strategic role in the ICO practice as they serve to frame the business plan, market opportunity, and to educate potential investors on the unique aspects of their platform offering. As documents primarily geared towards fundraising, they are of key interest to researchers on financial outcomes. Formal requirements, if any, of white papers vary across markets although some mimetic practices have emerged. Documents can take the form of an academic paper, as was the case with the initial proposal for Bitcoin, to technical and econometric treatises, to utopian descriptions of future markets. Founders signal to potential investors, advisors, and other ecosystem stakeholders their strategic intentions through the white paper practice. Among the key messages observed is the founder's intended distribution of tokens to various groups including the allocations to the ICO sale, founders, advisors, developers, and functional pools such as liquidity or company reserves. *What are the implications of entrepreneurial language and strategic patterns disclosed in white papers prior to a firm's ICO?*

1.1 Language, Risk, and Entrepreneurship

Risk and entrepreneurship have been explored through multiple lenses and literatures. Strategic Management researchers suggest that effective risk disclosure requires a balance between sufficient and relevant information, using clear and concrete language, and considering the context and predispositions of the audience [8–10]. The MIS literature on crowdfunding similarly explores risk and disclosure utilizing the context of social media and crowdfunding campaigns. Havakhor et al., [11] explore how the language of early disclosures has a significant effect on venture capital. Others have analyzed the language utilized in required risk disclosures on crowdfunding websites such as Kickstarter finding that relevancy and authenticity with a balanced tone has a significant effect on donations [12].

1.2 ICO Funding in Blockchain Cryptocurrency Projects

Initial Coin Offerings (ICOs) constitute one of the unique channels through which funds find their way into blockchain markets. An ICO is akin to an Initial Public Offering (IPO) in that it is a key moment for investors to purchase tokens directly from the company. Signals during the lead-up and buying phases of the ICO are sent to small-cap crowdfunding type investors, more sophisticated venture and investment capitalists, and transaction-oriented buyers that are interested in the real-market side of the cryptocurrency's economy. The principal tool for this initial strategic communication has been the white paper. This document typically serves as a public discourse of the business plan, a description of technologies involved, confidence and trust building in the founding team, and a breakdown of the tokens to be offered in the ICO. Some researchers have explored strategic aspects of white papers [13, 14], and others the effectiveness of the ICO practice [5, 15, 16]. Empirical analyses of ICOs have considered explicit factors such as the availability of the source code, a presale of tokens, and when the tokens have a definite utility value [17].

While ICOs have similarities to other forms of fundraising such as IPOs and crowdfunding, many believe that they fill a unique gap and fill a niche often overlooked by traditional venture capital [7]. O'Dair and Owen [18] examine the practice through the lens of a specific industry noting that the ICO is an opportunity to push back against traditional fundraising empowering a different class of founders and investors. However, Anson [19] notes that token holders have essentially zero rights and constitute "subordinated equity", suggesting that while the ICO practice may give rise to a new class of investors, the rights of those investors should be more closely examined. Koeppl and Kronick [20] also see the opportunity for new investors and a funding gap, but they recommend regulation sooner rather than later to build protections and confidence in the practice.

Some of the inquiry of investor perceptions and behaviors explores the nature of the ICO relative to other forms of fundraising and fintech. Choi [21] examined the ICO practice against established patterns of fintech lending such as peer-to-peer and crowdfunding finding novelty and utility in ICOs. Garratt and van Oordt [22] theoretically examined ICOs relative to traditional bank financing concluding that the is ICO a legitimate funding vehicle, even optimal in some cases, relative to the stage of development and operations of the firm. Benedetti and Kostovetsky [23] conducted a year-long panel study finding that, in their dataset of 2,390 tokens, the ICO practice does generate "solid" returns for investors which seem to hold for a year. To that end, authors describe most ICOs as underpriced, meaning they are sold at a significant discount relative to their future value. The underpricing effect does not seem to be related to information asymmetry like IPO underpricing. The underpricing phenomenon may be related to the heyday hype of ICOs as others have found that there are significant outliers on both sides of the general trend and a significant correlation with Bitcoin prices [24]. Felix and von Eije [25] show that companies that issue a large number of tokens or have a pre-ICO distribution tend to perform better in the ICO, suggesting that the informational lead-up and informational gains from word of mouth are key factors in signaling value.

Many blockchain firms that utilize the ICO model of early fundraising are quick to point out that it is not an equity offer [26]. But from a more fundamental perspective, investment advisors recognize that assets are flowing into the firm with the expectation that there will be a return of some sort either in the way of future value transactions or increased value of coins on third-party exchanges [27]. Researchers and regulators bring a more critical approach to the practice, often finding that tokens do represent a security, albeit without the typical protections of other investments [28–31]. For example, in 2018 the U.S. SEC "…has issued over 100 subpoenas on ICOs and the federal government recently formed a task force to increase cooperation for money laundering and financial crimes including from digital currency [32]."

1.3 How Coins are Distributed

Coins are distributed through a few key mechanisms. There is a lot of flexibility for owners regarding when and how many coins they want to distribute. For example, Bitcoin generated a certain number of coins that were retained by founders and utilized in early experimentation. But Bitcoin is best known for its "mining" distribution mechanism. With Bitcoin, the total number of coins to be distributed was known at inception. Modern coins based on Ethereum standards typically specify the total quantity of coins to be made available at inception. Other chains permit an inflationary approach with no limit to the number of tokens that may be minted. Our preliminary review of ICO white papers finds that most cryptocurrencies present readers with idiosyncratic patterns of coins to be held, distributed, and total quantities (Table 1).

Table 1. Timing of Token Distributions

Stage	Distribution
Pre-ICO and Pre-operational	During the early phase of launching the endeavor, the platform owner may allocate coins as a type of owner's equity prior to any public involvement or market operations. Additionally, coins are often sold Pre-ICO at a discount to generate interest and gain early adopters
ICO and Pre-operational	Platform owners may opt to sell coins to the public through an ICO. However, the coins still do not have any operational utility. Coins that grant governance rights may create an opportunity for token holders to participate in governance
Post-ICO and Operational	After the ICO, firms may distribute coins as recompense for carrying out the work necessary to facilitate the transactional infrastructure, typically "mining." Additionally, firms may have held a reserve of coins for strategic uses such as compensation or market liquidity

2 Research Propositions

2.1 Governance Affordances

Some organizations have emerged that more deliberately articulate governance rights and affordances granted to token holders. Examples include Distributed Autonomous Organizations (DAO), Security Token Offerings (STO), and Governance Tokens. Early DAOs focused on charity and democratic investment decisions, content curation, and commodities trading [33]. Researchers have called for more inquiry on DAOs highlighting some of the decentralization, automation, and general evaluation of DAOs as an organizational form [34]. Others have noted that although some token based governance approaches appear on the surface to be democratic, the low barrier to entry and tendency to concentrate control yields organizations that function similar to other equity based forms [35]. ICOs often serve as a means to funding liquidity to support next stage growth [15].

However, as speculative buyers purchase and hold tokens, we quickly confront classic agency problems. Fama and Jensen [36] establish that efficient governance forms, typically advisory boards, should emerge when those that are financing the next stage of growth when organizational structures seem to follow open corporations or financial mutuals as is the case with many cryptocurrency offerings. However, it seems to be the case that organizational forms that have emerged from the cryptocurrency ecosystem have eschewed representative governance preferring the extremes of operating as private holdings (e.g. most Ethereum based cryptocurrencies), completely distributed (e.g. most DAOs), or as a tightly controlled technological regime (e.g. Bitcoin). There is a long list of cryptocurrency projects that have failed to deliver on their premises. As of Q2 2025, Forbes' cryptocurrency listing covers 13,600 different coins and shows a total market cap of $3.55 trillion [37]. However, 4,738 of these coins have a market cap of $0 and 9,985 have a market cap of less than $1M. The juxtaposition of effectively failed coins against others that represent trillions of dollars in value—even if only speculative—suggests a somewhat efficient market where users and investors alike have rejected the majority of offerings. We believe that this ecosystem would benefit from further inquiry of Fama and Jensen's predicted organizational structures to see if the technological affordances and claims of blockchain have upended or reinforced Fama and Jensen's predicted organizational forms.

Proposition 1. Differences in organizational form with respect to token holders and governance rights or affordances granted to them may shape managerial decision-making influencing competitive market position.

2.2   Internal, External, and Strategic Allocation Patterns

There is a prevalent libertarian tradition in cryptocurrencies that eschews centralized governance of monetary policy [38, 39]. This critical perspective of central banks may be supported by the timing around the development of Bitcoin and the embedded message in the first block of Bitcoin. The Satoshi Nakamoto writings began in Fall of 2008 just after the Lehman Brother's collapse and the initial policy responses to what would become known as The Great Recession. The genesis block in Bitcoin has an embedded message that alludes to a headline article in the British newspaper, The Times: "The Times 03/Jan/2009 Chancellor on the brink of the second bailout for banks." We expect that investors would prefer tokens that have a strong external distribution allocation pattern empowering individual holders rather than institutional and centralized paradigms. Although token holders are rarely granted governance rights, the ability of the community of token holders to influence the may allow for token holder organization and influence [35].

Within white papers, firms have task of disclosing the organizational and economic expectations of the tokens to be sold in the ICO. Discussions of the token frequently consist of the total number of tokens to be released, technical descriptions (e.g. ERC-20 attributes), sale price and discounts, and relational value to underlying tokens such as Ethereum or Bitcoin. A disclosure of interest is the strategic token allocation pattern made by founders. Figure 1 is a typical example from the CVProof/FileProof token white paper [40]. In this case, 40% of the total token economy is to be dedicated to the ICO. However, the two allocations to "financing", are tokens to be held in reserve and utilized for the firm-specific strategic initiative to raise funds and finance operations and startups. 15% of the tokens held in reserve for the founders and team are a type of equity compensation. And finally, 5% of tokens are intended to be either used to compensate developers that fix bugs, advisors providing direction, and fund marketing campaigns.

Whereas Fig. 2 shows the token distribution plan from the Game Ace Token (GAT) [41]. While there are similarities between the two, note that GAT makes no investment

FILEPROOF.ORG TOKEN DISTRIBUTION

TOTAL TOKENS CREATED	1,000,000,000	100%	
TOKEN SALE	400,000,000	40%	
CVPROOF FINANCING	160,000,000	16%	
START-UPS FINANCING	240,000,000	24%	
FOUNDERS & TEAM	150,000,000	15%	*24 months lock-in (30% released upon closing the crowdsale)*
TOKEN SALE COST	50,000,000	5%	*bounty, advisors, marketing campaigns*

Fig. 1. FileProof.org Token Distribution

in community development or funding startup costs. 50% of tokens are dedicated to some sort of public sale (Pre-ICO and ICO). 14% are reserved to be sold publicly but at a premium over ICO prices. And 22% of non-ICO tokens are dedicated to founders, partners, and advisors. And finally, 14% or reserved for operational, in-application use.

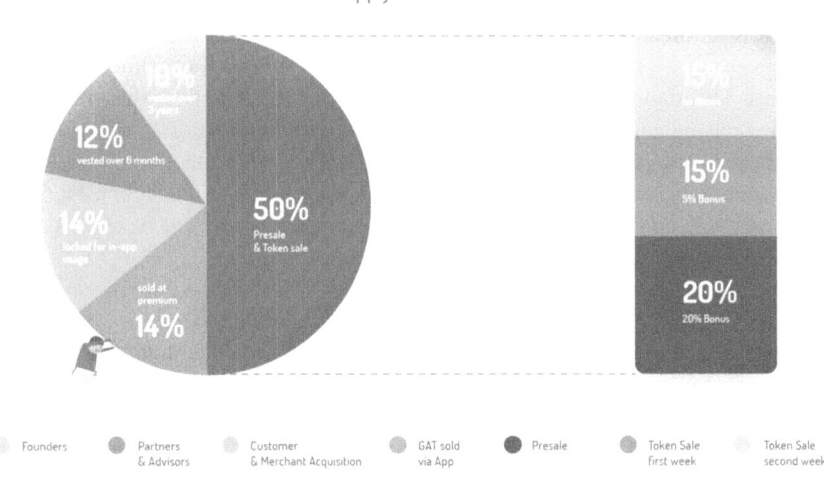

Fig. 2. GAT coin token distribution

Often firms make several allocations within the same organization to groups of people that may refer to the same individuals, but operating in different roles at different times, for example, founders, owners, team, company, and contributors are common categories but could refer to the same small set of individuals that are the core of the company.

Many firms hold onto reserves intended to serve as liquidity for their markets, with the implication that they would find some administrative channel to disperse tokens to actors primarily interested in operational transactions or other liquidity policies. These reserves and other internal, uncertain pools of tokens may dampen investor enthusiasm in market participation if they are perceived as increasing strategic uncertainty. Contrasted with organizations that articulate more specific utilization of tokens such as community building, ecosystem support, or as compensation for specific activities that may facilitate the ignition or healthy operations of the community including bug bounties and referral bonuses.

Some researchers have found that token reserves are positively correlated with ICO fundraising outcomes implying that average investors do not have a preference for a pure market ecosystem, but rather, prefer signals that originate from firms indicating a market control orientation [42]. Public and Reserve allocation of tokens typically represent how the majority of coins are intended to be distributed. However, there are a number of other token allocation categories that, when taken together, may combine to represent strategic archetypes that represent competitive orientations that are more successful.

Proposition 2. Differing token allocation patterns may inform token buyers of organizational strategies thereby influencing ICO fundraising.

2.3   Post Fundraising Decisions

Similar to the token allocation patterns articulated in white papers is the less typical, but not rare practice of disclosing how funds raised would be used to facilitate the growth of the organization. Categories often include marketing and advertising, software development, technology purchase, and other startup costs typical for technology platform companies. This underscores the fundraising utility of the ICO and similarities of IPO companies raising capital for next-stage growth. Figure 3 shows a distribution of how funds raised in the ICO are expected to be used. This representative example shows typical technology startup costs of IT infrastructure, administration, legal fees, development, marketing, and contractors constitute 50% of how funds will be used, while the other 50% are held in reserve.

Figure 4 from the CVPROOF white paper shows their intended use of funds. While there are some similarities, they disclose quantities allocated to salaries. In this case, the broad categorization of "Product Development" is vague enough that the reader can project their notion of how that money raised will be applied. Will it be compensation for executives that define the road map? Salaries for developers and product designers? Depending on the specificity of the description, potential investors may see different strategic applications of funds raised. But unfortunately, these same investors are not likely to have any control over how funds are utilized.

Treating ICO token buyers as investors, whether they be speculative investors anticipating increased value through resale or claims to residuals, or they be utility-oriented users anticipating a healthy transactional ecosystem of which they will benefit, both expect that the future transactional value of the firm is higher than at the time of purchase. Fama and Miller treated this as an investor growth expectation in future periods stating,

Budget Distribution

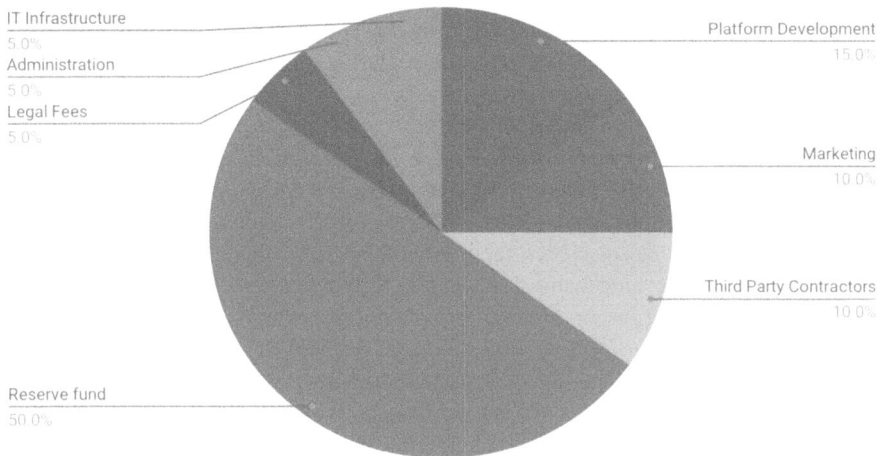

Fig. 3. Example Budget Distribution

CVPROOF USE OF FUNDS

Category	Share of budget	Activities
Product Development	**28%**	*Product development as per roadmap*
Ecosystem	**20%**	*Incentive INK tokens to attract users and develop services, partnerships, loyalty program, and platform cost*
Operations	**46%**	*Salaries, operating costs*
Legal	**6%**	*Contracts, corporate formation*

Fig. 4. CVProof use of funds

"For a given level of resources in period 1, the consumer always prefers more to less resources in period 2. And similarly, given the level of resources in period 2, more resources in period 1 are always preferred to less [43]."

With this inherent expectation of growth and efficient application of funds raised, we expect that investors will respond to firms that disclose post-ICO application of funds, and that the categorical allocation patterns of these disclosures will similarly matter to how investors perceive the growth trajectory of the firm.

Proposition 3. Differing patterns of post-ICO fund application may reveal firm maturity and growth strategies thereby impacting ICO purchase decisions and fundraising performance.

2.4   White Papers, Risk Disclosure, and Entrepreneurial Language

The white paper serves as a primary signaling device to both sophisticated and unsophisticated investors. It is of greatest importance during the period just prior to the ICO and during the ICO as that is when funds are expected to flow into the platform and will serve to establish operations and legitimacy.

Signaling within ICO markets has been a highly mimetic process. The original cryptocurrency, Bitcoin, was initiated through a series of "white papers" written under the pseudonym Satoshi Nakamoto. This tradition of introducing a new cryptocurrency through a white paper has also been incorporated by firms that are creating coins that serve a unique purpose, sidechains that extend the functionality of basic blockchains, new general use blockchains, or other utilities intended to enhance the market. However, within the cluster of coins that create novel targeted markets, the white paper activity has incorporated several other signaling devices including descriptions of the value proposition, the scope of the target traditional market, legal and regulatory disclaimers, technical descriptions of tokens, internal market economics of tokens, allocation patterns for pre-ICO token distribution, key contributors and advisors, partnerships, intended uses of the funds raised, general blockchain education, transaction flows and processes, and technological signals [44–46].

The white paper practice, while pervasive, is not wholly reliable. As regulation is unevenly paced and not all ICOs are subject to risk disclosures, a broad ethical spectrum of risk disclosures in papers can be seen [13, 47]. This is somewhat expected from a self-reported document that is more a market signaling device than it is a technical or fiduciary disclosure. Some white papers have been publicly exposed to have been using pictures of celebrities instead of the founding team [48]. Many white papers are pseudo-academic in nature following the initial Bitcoin paper; others are glossy commissioned documents produced by reputable consulting firms. Regardless of the authorship, the strategic utility of the white paper is apparent as an introduction of the firm to purchasers of tokens and parties interested in the business of the firm.

Some researchers have taken up the topic of ICO risk disclosure in the absence of regulation finding that firms that engage in voluntary disclosure, especially in the presence of complementary risk mitigation actions and third party ratings agencies, benefit from the transparency [49]. The language of risk and both informal and regulatory disclosures in ICOs has changed over time. Just as with Kickstarter and its "regulatory" change by requiring projects to begin incorporating a formal risk statement [12], we expect that ICO risk disclosure and the language of risk to evolve over time. Given the highly mimetic ecosystem in cryptocurrencies and the introduction of new language text analysis tools such as LLMs and updated LIWC dictionaries, are there new dimensions to risk disclosure and risks particular to cryptocurrencies and ICOs that merit further inquiry?

Proposition 4. Differing approaches to the general language of entrepreneurship and risk disclosure within white papers may have an impact on token buyer perceptions and influence ICO fundraising outcomes. Next generation tools and techniques may yield nuanced insights.

2.5 Smart Contracts and Oracles

Central to most Ethereum based cryptocurrencies is the smart contract. This is the code that underpins most core value transactions conducted on Ethereum's blockchain. These smart contracts however do not access outside data and primarily rely on the data necessary at the time of the transaction [50]. Treating the smart contract as an agent, these contracts do have access to external information by way of consuming data produced by oracles. Ethereum characterizes oracles as, "…applications that produce data feeds that make off-chain data sources available to the blockchain for smart contracts [51]." The code-level details of the smart contract and the information contained in the Oracle's feed are often publicly available, but not always. Some authors of white papers bring transparency to their offering by describing the nature of the smart contract, sharing code, and pointing interested readers to source code repositories. Additionally, they often describe how external data finds its way into their system through oracles or other off-chain schemes. Externally, some large scale projects have attempted to explore and categorize the code-level nature of smart contracts finding that there exists a rich diversity of offerings and approaches [52, 53].

Intermediaries in the broader ecosystem have emerged to help individuals explore the source code of smart contracts. In particular, Etherscan (etherscan.io) contains a suite of tools specific to smart contracts that facilitate the public disclosure and verification of smart contract details, allows for comparative analysis, and searchers across contracts. Referring back to our earlier discussion of the broader ecosystem of cryptocurrencies and the high number of failed projects, we believe that similar to an analysis of risk disclosure practices, inquiry that analyzes the reliability of smart contracts in operational versus failed projects may yield insights as to the strategic governance of technological resources and technological posturing of cryptocurrency firms. In more practical terms, are the claims made in white papers reflected in the code and how does that align with the overall posture of the company?

Proposition 5. Alignment in smart contract code and oracle data with white paper claims are likely to be perceived as indicators of firm reliability and may impact a firm's market performance.

3 Conclusion

Tokens purchased in an ICO have some significant departures from other forms of equity and fundraising mechanisms. For example, investor claims to an alienable asset, a lack of voting rights afforded to investors, firm disclosure of strategic categorization of asset holders, and tokenized compensation to some classes of stakeholders. We expect that fundraising behavior will reflect investor preferences of strategic behaviors and decisions that can be exposed through white paper language and patterns. Additionally, we expect that when firms disclose patterns that support key strategic initiatives related to the start-up and early operational phase of the project, that investors will support the clarity in next steps articulated by firms. We expect that these investor behaviors will be seen in the short-term through ICO funds raised and the medium-term market cap position of the firm relative to its competitors.

This suite of proposals would contribute to our understanding of Initial Coin Offerings as a novel fundraising practice. Prior research has established that there exist unique behaviors of token purchasers in response to actions taken by firms. Future research would benefit studies that employ a variety of methodologies including quantitative, qualitative, and mixed approaches where founders are surveyed in addition to evaluation of their white papers to tease out alignment in strategic thinking and observed behavior. This agenda would further our understanding of ICO buyers as a new class of investors. Additionally, furthering this line of inquiry would provide key considerations for managers creating white papers or other fundraising documents and increasing the likelihood of onboarding early investors while maximizing firm flexibility even in the face of dogmatic market values.

Disclosure of Interests. The authors have no competing interests to declare that are relevant to the content of this article.

References

1. Barraza, B., Ravindran, K., Arenas, A.: Initial coin offerings. In: ICIS 2023 TREOS (2023)
2. Barraza, B., Ravindran, K., Arenas, A.: The entrepreneurial language and outcomes of initial coin offerings. In: ECIS 2024 TREOS (2024)
3. Barraza, B.: The entrepreneurial language and strategic patterns of initial coin offerings. In: 16th Digital Sourcing, Platforms, and Ecosystems Workshop. , Obergurgl, Austria (2025)
4. ICO Drops - Ended ICOs. http://icodrops.com/category/ended-ico/. Accessed 21 Apr 2025
5. Domingo, R.-S., Piñeiro-Chousa, J., Ángeles López-Cabarcos, M.: What factors drive returns on initial coin offerings? Technol. Forecast. Soc. Chang. **153**, 119915 (2020). https://doi.org/10.1016/j.techfore.2020.119915
6. Malwa, S., Van Straten, J.: Bitcoin price news: BTC sets record high above $109,000 ahead of donald trump inauguration. https://www.coindesk.com/markets/2025/01/20/bitcoin-surges-to-109-k-hits-record-high-ahead-of-donald-trumps-inauguration. Accessed 21 Apr 2025
7. Akbarpour, S.: Blockchain start-ups to venture out from venture capital! Are ICOs here to stay? J. Invest. **28**, 32–44 (2019). https://doi.org/10.3905/joi.2019.1.078
8. Pan, L., McNamara, G., Lee, J.J., Haleblian, J. (John), Devers, C.E.: Give it to us straight (most of the time): top managers' use of concrete language and its effect on investor reactions. Strat. Manage. J. **39**, 2204–2225 (2018). https://doi.org/10.1002/smj.2733
9. Shrestha, P., Thewissen, J., Arslan-Ayaydin, Ö., Parhankangas, A.: A sense of risk: responses to crowdfunding risk disclosures. Strateg. Entrep. J. **17**, 925–970 (2023). https://doi.org/10.1002/sej.1480
10. Hyde, S.J., Bachura, E., Bundy, J., Gretz, R.T., Sanders, W.G.: The tangled webs we weave: examining the effects of CEO deception on analyst recommendations. Strat. Manage. J. **45**, 66–112 (2024). https://doi.org/10.1002/smj.3546
11. Havakhor, T., Golmohammadi, A., Sabherwal, R., Gauri, D.: Do early words from new ventures predict fundraising? A comparative view of social media narratives. Manag. Inf. Syst. Q. **47**, 611–638 (2023)
12. Kim, K., Park, J., Pan, Y., Zhang, K., Zhang, X.: (Michael): risk disclosure in crowdfunding. Inf. Syst. Res. **33**, 1023–1041 (2022). https://doi.org/10.1287/isre.2021.1096
13. Momtaz, P.P.: Entrepreneurial finance and moral hazard: evidence from token offerings. J. Bus. Ventur. (2020). https://doi.org/10.1016/j.jbusvent.2020.106001

14. Momtaz, P.P.: CEO emotions and firm valuation in initial coin offerings: an artificial emotional intelligence approach. Strateg. Manag. J. **42**, 558–578 (2021). https://doi.org/10.1002/smj. 3235

15. Howell, S.T., Niessner, M., Yermack, D.: Initial coin offerings: financing growth with cryptocurrency token sales. Rev. Finan. Stud. **33**, 3925–3974 (2020). https://doi.org/10.1093/rfs/ hhz131

16. Thies, F., Wallbach, S., Wessel, M., Besler, M., Benlian, A.: Initial coin offerings and the cryptocurrency hype - the moderating role of exogenous and endogenous signals. Electron Markets. **32**, 1691–1705 (2022). https://doi.org/10.1007/s12525-021-00460-9

17. Adhami, S., Giudici, G., Martinazzi, S.: Why do businesses go crypto? An empirical analysis of initial coin offerings. J. Econ. Bus. (2018). https://doi.org/10.1016/j.jeconbus.2018.04.001

18. O'Dair, M., Owen, R.: Financing new creative enterprise through blockchain technology: opportunities and policy implications. Strateg. Chang. **28**, 9–17 (2019). https://doi.org/10. 1002/jsc.2242

19. Anson, M.: Initial coin offerings: economic reality or virtual economics? J. Private Equity. **21**, 41–52 (2018). https://doi.org/10.3905/jpe.2018.21.4.041

20. Koeppl, T., Kronick, J.: Tales from the crypt – How to regulate initial coin offerings. Commentary - C.D. Howe Institute. 0_1, 0_2, 1-19 (2018)

21. Choi, T.-M.: Financing product development projects in the blockchain era: initial coin offerings versus traditional bank loans. IEEE Trans. Eng. Manage. **69**, 3184–3196 (2022). https:// doi.org/10.1109/TEM.2020.3032426

22. Garratt, R.J., van Oordt, M.R.C.: Entrepreneurial incentives and the role of initial coin offerings. J. Econ. Dyn. Control **142**, 104171 (2022). https://doi.org/10.1016/j.jedc.2021. 104171

23. Benedetti, H., Kostovetsky, L.: Digital tulips? Returns to investors in initial coin offerings (2018)

24. Hu, A.S., Parlour, C.A., Rajan, U.: Cryptocurrencies: stylized facts on a new investible instrument. Financ. Manage. **48**, 1049–1068 (2019). https://doi.org/10.1111/fima.12300

25. Felix, T.H., von Eije, H.: Underpricing in the cryptocurrency world: evidence from initial coin offerings. Manag. Financ. **45**, 563–578 (2019). https://doi.org/10.1108/MF-06-2018-0281

26. Bernstein, B.: Cryptocurrencies are money, not equity. https://tokeneconomy.co/cryptocurrencies-are-money-not-equity-30ff8d0491bb. Accessed 15 July 2023

27. Hyatt, J.: Decoding crypto: what it is, how it works, and how to get started. https://www.nasdaq.com/articles/news-and-insights/what-is-cryptocurrency-and-how-it-works. Accessed 15 July 2023

28. Boreiko, D., Ferrarini, G., Giudici, P.: Blockchain startups and prospectus regulation. Eur. Bus. Organ. Law Rev. **20**, 665–694 (2019). https://doi.org/10.1007/s40804-019-00168-6

29. Exercise caution with crypto asset securities: investor alert (2023). https://www.sec.gov/oiea/ investor-alerts-and-bulletins/exercise-caution-crypto-asset-securities-investor-alert

30. Maume, P., Fromberger, M.: Regulation of initial coin offerings: reconciling U.S. and E.U. Securities Laws. Chicago J. Int. Law. **19**, 548–585 (2019)

31. Tiwari, N.: The commodification of cryptocurrency. Michigan Law Rev. **117**, 611–634 (2018). https://doi.org/10.36644/mlr.117.3.commodification

32. Cryptocurrency taxes to soar amid tighter rules. International Tax Review. N.PAG-N.PAG (2018)

33. Wang, S., Ding, W., Li, J., Yuan, Y., Ouyang, L., Wang, F.-Y.: Decentralized autonomous organizations: concept, model, and applications. IEEE Trans. Comput. Soc. Syst. **6**, 870–878 (2019). https://doi.org/10.1109/TCSS.2019.2938190

34. Santana, C., Albareda, L.: Blockchain and the emergence of Decentralized Autonomous Organizations (DAOs): an integrative model and research agenda. Technol. Forecast. Soc. Chang. **182**, 121806 (2022). https://doi.org/10.1016/j.techfore.2022.121806

35. Bakos, Y., Halaburda, H.: Will blockchains disintermediate platforms? The problem of credible decentralization in DAOs. The Problem of Credible Decentralization in DAOs (2022)
36. Fama, E.F., Jensen, M.C.: Agency problems and residual claims. J. Law Econ. **26**, 327–349 (1983)
37. Cryptocurrency prices, market cap and charts. https://www.forbes.com/digital-assets/crypto-prices/. Accessed 29 May 2025
38. Lustig, C., Nardi, B.: Algorithmic authority: the case of bitcoin. In: 2015 48th Hawaii International Conference on System Sciences, pp. 743–752 (2015). https://doi.org/10.1109/HICSS.2015.95
39. Sotirakopoulos, N.: Cryptomarkets as a libertarian counter-conduct of resistance. Eur. J. Soc. Theory **21**, 189–206 (2018). https://doi.org/10.1177/1368431017718534
40. CVProof white paper. https://web.archive.org/web/20180725174944/http://www.cvproof.com/white-paper.html. Accessed 9 June 2023
41. Alchemy toys whitepaper (2018). https://alchemy.toys/whitepaper.pdf
42. Davydiuk, T., Gupta, D., Rosen, S.: De-crypto-ing signals in initial coin offerings: evidence of rational token retention. Manage. Sci. **69**, 6584–6624 (2023). https://doi.org/10.1287/mnsc.2022.4631
43. Fama, E.F., Miller, M.H.: The Theory of Finance. Holt Rinehart & Winston, Hinsdale, Ill (1972)
44. Barraza, B.: The worth of words: how technical white papers influence ICO blockchain funding. MIS Q. Executive **18**, 281–285 (2019). https://doi.org/10.17705/2msqe.00021
45. Kasatkin, S.: The legal content of a white paper for an ICO (Initial Coins Offering). Inf. Commun. Technol. Law. **31**, 81–98 (2022). https://doi.org/10.1080/13600834.2021.1950382
46. What is a white paper? A beginner's guide on how to write and format one. https://cointelegraph.com/learn/what-is-a-white-paper-a-beginners-guide-on-how-to-write-and-format-one. Accessed 15 July 2023
47. Chen, S.: Why you can't trust more cryptocurrency white papers (2018). https://www.wired.com/story/why-you-cant-trust-most-cryptocurrency-white-papers/
48. Serrels, M.: Fake cryptocurrency lists "Ryan Gosling" as its graphic designer. https://www.cnet.com/news/ryan-gosling-cryptocurrency/. Accessed 8 Sep 2018
49. Bourveau, T., De George, E.T., Ellahie, A., Macciocchi, D.: The role of disclosure and information intermediaries in an unregulated capital market: evidence from initial coin offerings. J. Account. Res. **60**, 129–167 (2022). https://doi.org/10.1111/1475-679X.12404
50. Introduction to smart contracts. https://ethereum.org/en/developers/docs/smart-contracts/. Accessed 29 May 2025
51. Oracles. https://ethereum.org/en/developers/docs/oracles/. Accessed 29 May 2025
52. Ferreira, J.F., Cruz, P., Durieux, T., Abreu, R.: SmartBugs: a framework to analyze solidity smart contracts. In: Proceedings of the 35th IEEE/ACM International Conference on Automated Software Engineering, pp. 1349–1352. Association for Computing Machinery, New York, NY, USA (2021). https://doi.org/10.1145/3324884.3415298
53. Pinna, A., Ibba, S., Baralla, G., Tonelli, R., Marchesi, M.: A massive analysis of ethereum smart contracts empirical study and code metrics. IEEE Access. **7**, 78194–78213 (2019). https://doi.org/10.1109/ACCESS.2019.2921936

How to Innovate Through Crowdsourcing: Integrating Organizational and Crowd Perspectives

Lily Haffner⬥ and Julia Kotlarsky(✉) ⬥

University of Auckland Business School, Auckland 1010, New Zealand
{lily.haffner,j.kotlarsky}@auckland.ac.nz

Abstract. Crowdsourcing has been claimed to help organisations innovate by leveraging crowd knowledge to generate novel ideas, products and services. The extant literature emphasises external and internal organizational crowdsourcing as strategic efforts toward innovation, highlighting the importance of a comprehensive crowdsourcing strategy for innovation success. However, there is limited knowledge about how to simultaneously manage internal and external crowdsourcing efforts to improve organizational innovation outcomes. Based on a systematic review of the information systems and management literatures on crowdsourcing and innovation, this paper makes a theoretical contribution in the form of an integrated framework of external and internal crowdsourcing factors for innovation from the firm, platform and crowd-level perspectives. Managerial recommendations are then outlined based on these multi-level factors for crowdsourcing innovation success.

Keywords: Innovation · Crowdsourcing · Organizational Strategy

1 Introduction

In an organizational context, innovation – in the form of unique ideas that lead to gradual or radical change – aims to provide value to individuals inside and outside the environment in which it is implemented [1, 2]. These ideas typically emerge internally, from a firm's Research and Development (R&D) department [3]. Internal R&D activities are thus directly associated with an organization's innovativeness. However, in today's fast-paced business environment, there is growing pressure on organisations to search for innovation beyond firm boundaries, to increase innovation opportunities, profitability and process efficiency through external knowledge contributions [4]. This organizational shift in focus from internal R&D activities to external efforts for achieving innovation is referred to as 'open innovation' [5] With technological advancements enabling the creation of online communities, organisations can embrace open innovation by capturing innovative ideas and solutions from individuals outside their boundaries [6–9]. Open innovation contests are open calls targeting the public crowd, or those crowd members who are part of a specific community relevant to the organisation [8]. Reaching out to the crowd is referred to as 'crowdsourcing' – a form of open innovation that is enabled through digital technologies [10, 11]. Innovation through crowdsourcing generates organizational value from the crowd's knowledge and experience, as reflected in idea and problem-solving submissions [9, 12]. This crowdsourcing value is the level of organizational learning generated from crowd contributions, which is then incorporated into the internal R&D process [3]. The crowd's knowledge enhances existing firm capabilities, thus increasing organizational innovativeness [13].

Crowdsourcing – the endeavor of outsourcing an activity commonly performed by an entrusted individual through an open call to a public crowd [14] – has been used to complement internal organizational efforts of various kinds, from simple tasks for routine procedures, to more complex problem-solving and creative tasks for generating innovative ideas [15]. Relying on online platforms that can be firm owned (internal) or managed by an external intermediary [2, 16], organisations (consumers or seekers) aim to capture value from crowd submissions [12, 16] by connecting to members of the crowd (creators or solvers) who generate ideas and problem solutions. Therefore, a crowdsourcing community denotes a large group of diverse individuals who choose to participate in an organization's problem-solving efforts for a specific period of time [17]. Typically, crowdsourcing is associated with reaching an external crowd outside organizational boundaries, but firms may also engage with an internal crowd (i.e., employees). To distinguish between these two scenarios, we refer to the former as external crowdsourcing and the latter as internal crowdsourcing.

While both external and internal crowdsourcing configurations have apparent benefits, they also present a number of potential challenges, suggesting that facilitating crowdsourcing contests requires careful assessment. To harness the benefits and address the potential challenges of crowdsourcing, firms must understand and adeptly manage crowdsourcing ventures. Such understanding, however, necessitates a multi-level perspective that allows firms to identify and manage all key drivers of innovation success in crowdsourcing. In this paper we therefore aim to provide innovation-seeking organisations that are considering tapping into crowdsourcing with an understanding of these influential factors. For this purpose we undertook a systematic literature review guided by the research question: *Under what conditions can internal and external crowdsourcing support the organizational search for innovation?* The review integrates insights from the innovation and crowdsourcing literature streams to identify key factors that are important for the success of crowdsourcing initiatives in pursuit of innovation. In the following sections, we first present an overview of the benefits and challenges specific to both external and internal crowdsourcing. Next, we delve into our systematic review process and offer insights into the use of coding as an analysis technique. Subsequently, we discuss our review findings and present an integrated framework to answer our research question. Finally, we touch on theoretical contributions and offer managerial recommendations, along with opportunities for future work.

2   Overview of Crowdsourcing Configurations

2.1   Trade-Off Between External and Internal Crowdsourcing

Unlike internal R&D efforts, external crowdsourcing outcomes are derived from the ideas of individuals outside the firm [13]. Participants in external crowdsourcing provide the solution-seeking organisation with a diverse knowledge repertoire for a specified problem [18]. While engaging a crowd with distant knowledge [19] enables organisations to more thoroughly grasp their external environment [20], ideas from scattered and diverse sources can introduce uncertainty into the crowdsourcing outcome [13]. Organizational attention to external ideas may also diminish when overloaded with information, which is known as crowding [19]. In other words, the width and diversity of the crowd's knowledge may negatively impact the efficiency of an organization's solution search [6]. Recognizing the multiple challenges associated with external outreach, some organisations have experimented with internal crowdsourcing [20], targeting a range of internal employees who possess knowledge situated within the firm's boundaries. One advantage is that the ideas submitted by internal crowd members undergo faster implementation, promptly affecting the organization's operations and market performance [21]. However, given the less diverse nature of internal crowds compared to external crowds, proposed ideas are likely to align more closely with the organization's existing knowledge, resulting in fewer radically new ideas and inhibiting long-lasting organizational competitiveness [22]. Identifying the organizational challenges and benefits associated with external and internal crowdsourcing (as summarized in Table 1), Ruiz and Beretta [23] suggest a concurrent integration of both internal and external crowdsourcing efforts by organisations. This joint effort seeks to enhance the heterogeneity of incoming ideas for the innovation process.

Table 1. Key challenges and benefits in external and internal crowdsourcing.

	External crowdsourcing	Internal crowdsourcing
Challenges	• Information overload and handling of diverse ideas [18, 19] • Lack of topic-specific crowd knowledge [21] and problem-solving ability [24] • Crowding [6, 13, 25] • Uncertain outcomes due to diverse crowd knowledge [13] • Suggestions with high value and innovation potential [26]	• Employee engagement and participation [21] • Competitive organizational nature hinders employee collaboration [21] • Lack of innovative [21, 22] and effective ideas [27] • Employee bias leading to short-term solutions [22]
Benefits	• Access to and consideration of diverse solutions [13, 19, 28] • Suggestions with high value and innovation potential [26]	• Expert-specific knowledge [21] • Accelerated idea development and implementation [21] • Fewer intellectual property issues [21]

2.2 Challenges and Benefits of External Crowdsourcing

One prevalent issue in external crowdsourcing is crowding, which is the information overload resulting from the considerable number of crowd submissions an organisation receives [19]. When crowding occurs, organizational resource constraints prevent firms from attending to all appropriate solution suggestions [19]. External crowd submissions may also display a lack of topic-specific knowledge, which is critical for generating implementable solutions [21]. Consequently, the crowding issue calls for resource-heavy filtering of submitted solutions [6, 13, 25]. Compared to internal R&D processes, organisations also face more uncertainty when relying on external suggestions [13]. General crowds without specific background knowledge are restricted in their ability to solve problems that require specialist knowledge as they have no in-depth understanding of the problem context [24]. Furthermore, the crowd's diversity may lead to widely varying idea suggestions, making it difficult for an organisation to detect clear patterns across numerous crowd submissions [18]. Additionally, the web based nature of crowdsourcing means that organisations are physically distant from the crowd, so participant engagement is challenging to achieve [29].

On the other hand, the knowledge diversity of an external crowd provides firms with access to a broad range of solutions to consider for implementation [13, 19] compared to a knowledge-limited internal solution search [28]. External crowdsourcing further allows organisations to quickly trial a wide variety of proposed solutions, many of which will lie outside the range of solutions considered by the firm's internal R&D unit [28]. Due to the large crowd it reaches, external crowdsourcing can also draw the public's attention to a specific problem, leading to an increase in idea submissions, and potentially more valuable and innovative suggestions [26].

2.3 Challenges and Benefits of Internal Crowdsourcing

Internal crowdsourcing efforts also give rise to several potential challenges for organisations in their search for innovation. Firstly, other time commitments and poor understanding of the purpose behind internal crowdsourcing may prevent employee engagement and participation [21]. Similarly, the competitive nature of the organizational environment complicates employee collaboration in crowdsourcing contests [21]. Organizational employees also form a less diverse knowledge network than external crowds, leading to less innovative [21] and effective ideas [27]. Furthermore, an employee's familiarity with the firm's strategic approaches and resources can lead to biased decisions and the selection of more short-term and surface-level solutions for implementation, thus potentially hindering a firm's competitive success in the long run [22]. Such employee bias also occurs in the idea evaluation phase [27].

Despite these challenges, the varying cognitive perspectives present within an organisation can still lead to innovative ideas and approaches [21]. Employees' expert specific knowledge can accelerate the process of developing and identifying ideas that are implementable in the firm's existing strategies and innovation system [21]. Further, firms engaged in internal crowdsourcing also face fewer intellectual property rights issues than those involved in external crowdsourcing [21].

3   Research Design and Methodology

We followed Okoli's [30] IS-specific and stepwise guide to conducting a standalone systematic literature review that is explicit, comprehensive and reproducible in its methodological approach. In line with this approach, the research design can be divided into four overarching stages: (i) planning, (ii) selection, (iii) extraction, and (iv) execution (see Fig. 1).

3.1   Review Planning

In the planning stage, the following research question was formulated to clarify the aim of the review: *Under what conditions can internal and external crowdsourcing support the organizational search for innovation?* The review topic required the integration of insights from two literature streams − innovation and crowdsourcing. To allow for the search and selection of relevant articles, the researchers further agreed to use the keyword "crowd*" (or "crowd" for journals that do not accept the asterisk "*") in combination with "innovation".

3.2   Literature Selection

For the literature selection, it was important to include studies published in IS, innovation and general management outlets in order to cover research at the intersection of innovation and crowdsourcing. Therefore, the journals searched for this literature review were chosen from these three distinct research fields (see Table 7 in Appendix 1). Specifically, mainstream IS journals were complemented by seven Innovation journals and six journals from the field of General Management. The selection of Innovation and General Management journals was informed by the 2021 Academic Journal Guide provided by the Chartered Association of Business Schools (CABS), and limited to those journals ranked 3, 4 or 4* and 4*, respectively. Further, to ensure the retrieved set of articles was relevant and manageable within the contextual and time boundaries of this study, the keyword search was limited to the title and abstract of an article, and only articles written in English were included. While an initial search produced a total of 46 articles, 18 articles found to be off-topic (i.e., not focused on crowdsourcing and innovation) were eliminated after an initial analysis of their content, reducing the number of articles from the initial top journal search to 28. An additional 11 articles were identified using backward (five articles) and forward reference searching (six articles), as recommended by Webster and Watson [31]. A record of all the selected journals and the respective number of articles extracted from each during the initial literature search is provided in Table 7 in Appendix 1.

3.3   Data Extraction

For the purpose of systematically extracting data from the selected articles, information about each article was recorded in a spreadsheet. The spreadsheet included the journal name, the article's author(s), publication date, title and abstract, its perspective on

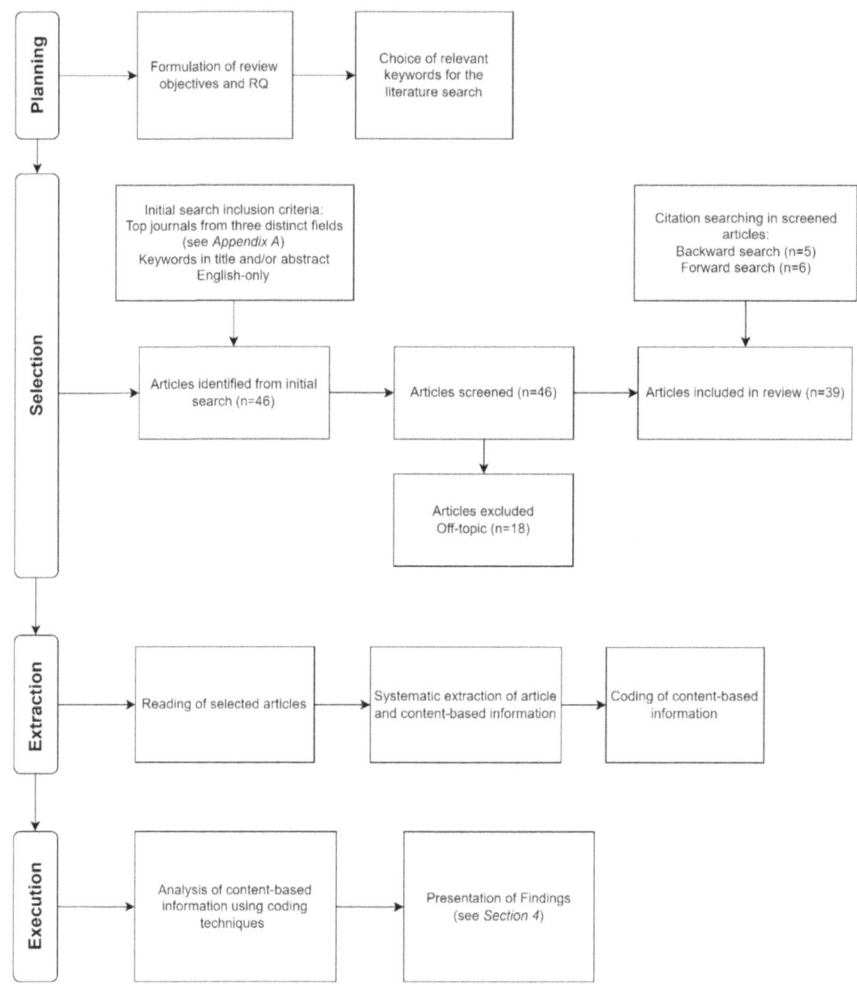

Fig. 1. Four stage systematic literature review process.

crowdsourcing (firm, crowd or platform) and the research focus and study findings. In addition, the following content-based information was captured and coded: relevant key definitions, research method, crowdsourcing configuration (internal or external), advantages and disadvantages associated with the crowdsourcing approach, the structure of the organisation under study, involved stakeholders, managerial implications and relevant figures.

3.4 Review Execution

During the execution stage, the selected innovation and crowdsourcing articles were analysed following Wolfswinkel et al.'s [32] grounded theory techniques, as adapted for literature reviews. Specifically, the articles were analysed using the open coding method, through which codes emerged that briefly described the content-based information from the respective articles [33]. Over several iterations that involved reviewing emerging codes, articles were then linked to other articles with related codes. These articles were further grouped into categories representing the perspectives of the different stakeholder groups – firm, crowd and platform – on crowdsourcing for innovation. The categories were finally grouped into themes concerning the respective crowdsourcing configuration covered by an article (e.g., external, internal, or internal & external crowdsourcing, as shown in Table 2). Finally, we conducted an in-depth analysis of the articles associated with each stakeholder group, for internal and external crowdsourcing, followed by a comparison of similarities and differences between the identified factors. Based on this analysis, an integrative framework was developed (see Fig. 4).

Table 2. Overview of themes, categories and codes.

Themes (crowdsourcing configuration)	Categories (stakeholder groups)	Codes (specific factors related to innovation)
External crowdsourcing	Firm	Governmental vs. organizational crowdsourcing Supporting integration mechanisms Use for business model innovation Organizational learning through crowdsourcing Firm reputation IP rights configuration
	Crowd	Innovation-furthering crowd characteristics Crowd motivation Crowd fairness expectations Knowledge and idea sharing Requirements for co-creation Idea implementation Reusing and remixing ideas Crowd-based idea filtering Idea filtering Idea appropriateness
	Platform	Platform support for crowdsourcing success Selection of platform type Suitable platform designs Design principles

(*continued*)

Table 2. (*continued*)

Themes (crowdsourcing configuration)	Categories (stakeholder groups)	Codes (specific factors related to innovation)
Internal crowdsourcing	Firm	Objectives for internal crowdsourcing Crowdsourcing practices
	Employee (crowd)	Employee characteristics
External & internal crowdsourcing	Firm	Integration of external crowdsourcing into the firm's innovation system Design decisions for successful integration External crowdsourcing vs. established internal practices Simultaneous management of external and internal innovation
	Crowd	Comparison of crowd knowledge

In the following section, we present our systematic analysis of the literature, focusing on each crowdsourcing configuration in turn, and following the themes listed in Table 2. Within each theme we discuss insights associated with the specific stakeholder groups (firm, crowd and platform).

4   Literature Analysis

4.1   External Crowdsourcing for Innovation

Previous studies have laid out various firm, platform, and crowd-level factors that impact external crowdsourcing for innovation. See Fig. 2 for an illustration of these factors.

Firm-Level Factors.   An important factor influencing the innovation outcomes of firms' external crowdsourcing initiatives is **organizational reputation**. High organizational brand value and investment opportunities increase crowd submissions, thus improving the quality of innovative ideas and generating higher firm profits [13].

In addition to organizational reputation, **crowdsourcing project management** plays a vital role in innovation success [3, 19, 34–38]. Piezunka and Dahlander [19] argue that strategic idea processing is crucial to ensure project efficiency. They propose preventative actions for effective idea processing as follows: (1) limiting the number of accepted submissions, (2) filtering ideas for relevance, (3) including diverse ideas, and (4) prioritizing distant knowledge ideas. Klein and Garcia [25] suggest a crowd-based filtering process to accelerate the firm's idea selection process. This filtering process is supported by setting out specific selection criteria and rewarding participants who closely follow them [25]. Managing the implementation of external crowdsourcing projects into the firm's internal innovation system is another crucial objective [3, 34, 36, 37]. Fayard et al. [34] report that

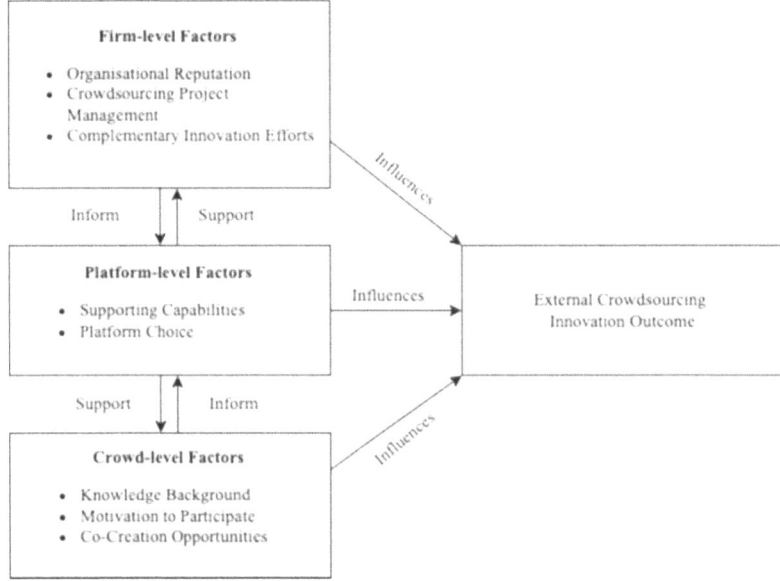

Fig. 2. Influential factors for innovation outcomes in external crowdsourcing.

organisations with existing internal innovation processes adjust external crowdsourcing efforts to align with their established practices, suggesting that external innovation efforts should be configured to match a company's internal innovation processes. In a similar vein, Randhawa et al. [37] argue that organizational-level strategies should precede and complement a firm's project-level activities to ensure successful implementation. Pollok et al. [36] emphasise the development of organizational capacity for successfully managing crowdsourcing for innovation. This can be achieved through the interplay of formal and informal employee roles and established knowledge management practices, including employee training and communication of external crowdsourcing strategies, as well as establishing guidelines and documentation to help employees better understand the firm's crowdsourcing approach. Furthermore, successful project management and implementation require a well-defined crowdsourcing plan with clearly defined objectives [3, 35], as well as appropriate configuration of task communication and the crowd's degree of involvement in the innovation process. These factors will vary depending on whether an innovation search is conducted in the firm's local or distant knowledge environment [3]. Organizational management of crowdsourcing projects also requires integration mechanisms. In this respect, Ruiz et al. [38] propose combining internal and external integration mechanisms to support the development of a firm's absorptive capacity, namely the process of detecting, absorbing and realizing external innovative ideas. Internal integration mechanisms bring together employees from different organizational functions, whereas external mechanisms include crowd attraction, third-party collaboration, and creating a collaborative environment for knowledge sharing and idea development [38].

Innovation success also depends on **complementary innovation efforts**, that is, the firm's efforts in addition to external crowdsourcing activities [7, 11]. Schlagwein and Bjørn-Andersen [11] identify that the interplay between organizational and external crowd activities results in corporate learning, enhancing the innovative crowdsourcing outcome. Further, the involvement of both internal experts and crowd members can assist in achieving organizational learning objectives [11]. External crowdsourcing for business model innovation also benefits from internal R&D efforts [7].

Platform-Level Factors. A platform must possess specific **supporting capabilities** to contribute value to a firm's external crowdsourcing efforts [12, 29, 35, 39]. Specifically, for innovation success, a platform should offer features that enable both firm-crowd collaboration and interaction between crowd members [35]. Such platform-enabled crowd engagement and collaboration can be improved by: (1) managing the intermediary knowledge domain, (2) managing the network that facilitates crowd interaction, and (3) transferring authority to the crowd [39]. Feller et al. [29] claim that an effective crowdsourcing platform should improve knowledge sharing, enhance a firm's ability to convert crowdsourced ideas into profitable output, and ensure a stable crowdsourcing process. Further, supportive platforms offer idea filtering processes, manage IP transfers, and provide dual incentives for the participating organisations and crowd [29]. Process transparency, efficiency and confidentiality guarantees are additional supporting capabilities [29]. Kohler and Chesbrough [12] find that a value-capturing platform design prioritizes (1) idea quality, (2) a crowd incentive system that is independent of the contest outcome, (3) interaction between crowdsourcing parties, and (4) a model based on quality control and firm expectation management.

A firm's **platform choice** should also be guided by a structured decision-making process [15]. Schenk et al. [15] highlight contextual, strategic and operational considerations for identifying the optimal crowdsourcing platform for an organisation. Relevant considerations include (1) crowdsourcing-related transaction costs and a firm's ability to generate a large number of crowd submissions without any external support, (2) the strength of the firm-crowd relationship, and (3) availability of resources relevant to the external crowdsourcing process [15].

Crowd-Level Factors. The crowd's **knowledge background** is recognised as a deciding factor in external crowdsourcing innovation outcomes [8, 24, 40, 41]. Mack and Landau [8] report that some domain-relevant knowledge is associated with more innovative and feasible ideas. Boons and Stam [40] further argue that ideas from individuals with educational backgrounds that align with the organization's crowdsourcing problem topic are more often selected. Individuals adopting an unrelated perspective can submit good ideas, but only in combination with a related perspective [40]. Taking a slightly different tack, Ren et al. [24] show that ideas from a general, non-expert crowd are more practical and innovative for solutions that do not require expert knowledge. However, for solutions requiring expert knowledge, crowd members with suitable knowledge provide more implementable, but not necessarily more novel, ideas [24]. Finally, ideas submitted by crowd members are also more suitable if the individual has had past success and experience with idea submissions [41].

Additionally, a crowd's **motivation to participate** has been linked to the innovativeness of idea submissions [6, 8, 17, 41, 42]. The literature reports mixed findings for extrinsic and intrinsic motivation in terms of increasing crowd participation, and thus furthering innovation generation [6, 8, 42]. For example, Bakici [42] identifies intrinsic motivation as the primary driver of crowd participation, and further notes variations in the prevalence of extrinsic motivation drivers between third-party and firm-owned crowdsourcing platforms. However, Mack and Landau [8] contest extrinsic motivation as associated with more innovative and implementable ideas. Adding to the debate, Acar [6] find that extrinsic and intrinsic motivation increase the appropriateness of crowdsourcing ideas in innovation contests, whereas internalized motivation has a negative impact. Similarly, another study reports that ideas are more suitable if the individual has received negative feedback in the past and is intrinsically motivated to improve [41]. Perceived fairness and recognition are also motivating factors for participation. Franke et al. [17] argue that crowd members are less likely to participate if they perceive the contest as unfair due to higher financial gains for the crowdsourcing firm, or they perceive a lack of recognition for the crowd's submissions. If the firm claims full IP rights, this negatively influences the crowd's incentive to participate [17, 43].

A third crowd-level consideration concerns the **co-creation opportunities** for crowd members, which can enhance innovation outcomes for the crowdsourcing firm [9, 18, 26]. Majchrzak and Malhotra [9] suggest the following supporting factors for successful crowd co-creation: (1) detaching co-creation from idea development, (2) enhanced accessibility of co-created knowledge, (3) a larger and more diverse crowd, perhaps through mixing internal with external participants, and (4) physical separation of idea submission and idea discussion on the crowdsourcing platform. A subsequent study by Majchrzak and Malhotra [18] highlights that both the type of shared knowledge and the sharing sequence influence the crowdsourcing outcome. They argue that the sharing of knowledge, socially validated through other crowd members and addressing a problem with seemingly paradoxical objectives results in the most innovative outcomes. Additionally, Han et al. [26] propose the reuse of previously generated innovation knowledge, suggesting that a knowledge remixing process improves the efficiency of idea generation through collaboration between crowd members with varying perspectives and skills, and using existing ideas to allow for more in-depth knowledge creation. Successfully reusing knowledge for crowdsourcing innovation outcomes relies on a remix that contains topics crowd members are familiar with and explains the integration of chosen ideas in detail, thus providing them with more insights into idea development [26].

4.2   Internal Crowdsourcing for Innovation

Previous studies have addressed firm, platform, and crowd-level factors that influence internal crowdsourcing for innovation. See Fig. 3 for a visual depiction of these factors.

Firm-Level Factors. Crowdsourcing project management, the strategic management of an internal crowdsourcing project, is seen as vital to success [21, 27, 44–46]. Ashurst [44] suggests that crowdsourcing project leaders should also take on the role of facilitating internal innovation activities. Furthermore, Campos-Blázquez et al. [45], Malhotra et al. [21], and Pohlisch [27] highlight idea processing management as a strategic

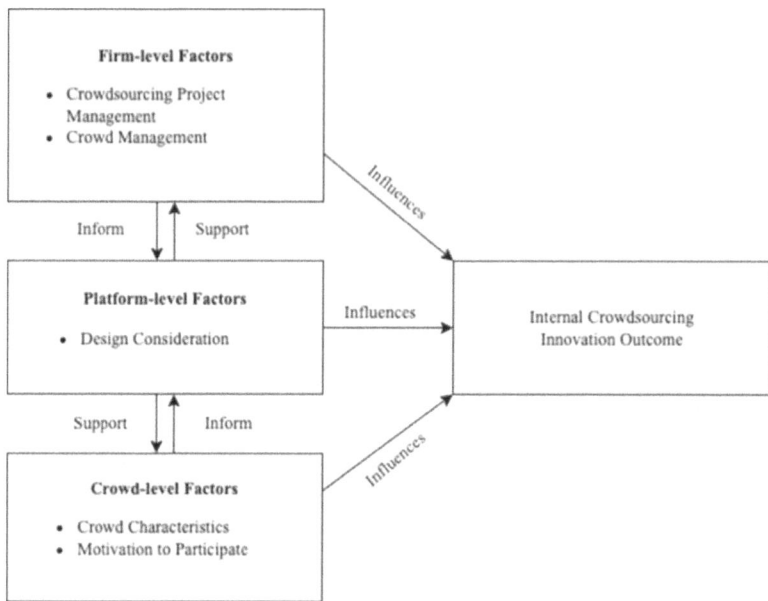

Fig. 3. Influential factors for innovation outcomes in internal crowdsourcing.

imperative for firms seeking innovation through internal crowdsourcing. An optimal idea selection process will focus on ideas that enhance long-term organizational performance and transparent selection criteria [21]. It is also recommended that idea evaluation be delegated to experts who are less biased than the firm's employees, and thus more capable of selecting valuable ideas [27]. Campos-Blázquez et al. [45] offer stepwise guidance on the organizational crowdsourcing process for innovation, emphasizing the benefits of thorough process planning.

Strategic **crowd management** can further enhance the internal crowdsourcing contest [16, 21, 27, 46–48]. Malhotra et al. [21], Malhotra et al. [46], and Pohlisch [27] highlight the importance of managerial communication and crowdsourcing participation during regular work hours to keep employees engaged. Malhotra et al. [21] and Malhotra et al. [46] further claim that permitting anonymous participation and knowledge sharing amongst employees can increase engagement. Additionally, Ashurst [44] underscore the importance of creating an environment that encourages the sharing of ideas and fosters a constructive approach to providing feedback. Further strategy considerations include a loose approach to idea generation, managerial support for participating employees and granting employees idea ownership [27]. Additional efforts are regulating the influence of expert employees on idea generation [21], enhancing feedback provision by implementing ideas into existing processes, and involving lower-level management in these implementation decisions [46]. Further, Chen et al. [47] and Zhu et al. [48] argue that providing feedback to idea developers enhances idea quality, and thus the likelihood that ideas will be implemented in the firm's innovation system. Chen et al. [47] also suggest less frequent feedback provision, with a focus on offering feedback later in the crowdsourcing contest. Zhu et al. [48] offer criteria for feedback, including (1) varying the feedback, (2) providing useful and appropriate feedback, and (3) concerning the degree of communication exchange between idea evaluator and developer.

Platform-Level Factors. Beretta et al. [48] and Deichmann et al. [50] identify platform **design considerations** for facilitating internal crowdsourcing, highlighting the influence of managerial motivations for implementing a crowdsourcing platform in the firm. The most successful platform design seeks to leverage innovation opportunities within the firm boundaries but outside the R&D department [49] by (1) adopting successful external design practices, (2) aligning the platform with the firm's existing innovation efforts, (3) engaging many employees to generate diverse ideas, and (4) focusing on idea processing, feedback provision, and transparent idea evaluation [49]. Particular focus should be placed on idea evaluation and participant communication [49]. Deichmann et al. [50] claim that a mutual commitment to other crowd participants' ideas increases the attention developers receive for their own ideas. Accordingly, they recommend (1) a focus on participant collaboration and exposure to others' ideas, (2) opportunities for participants to engage with other developers' ideas prior to organizational idea processing, and (3) a reward system for collaborative efforts regarding internal crowdsourcing platform design.

Crowd-Level Factors. Various **crowd characteristics** play a decisive role in internal crowdsourcing for innovation outcomes [22, 51–53]. Asplund et al. [22] argue that the frequency of employee participation and the knowledge they possess are critical factors. With regard to internally sourced innovative solutions to a firm problem that require expert knowledge, sporadically participating employees prefer easily implementable rather than innovative ideas. These employees should thus be encouraged to participate more frequently to develop an open mind towards novel ideas [22]. Zhu et al. [53] find in their study that creativity and pro-activity are linked to innovative behaviour. Creative individuals are more likely to submit ideas in an internal crowdsourcing contest, whereas pro-active individuals submit more implementable ideas [53]. Co-creation between individuals with either one of these characteristics can enhance innovation outcomes [53]. Crowd diversity can also improve internal crowdsourcing success [51, 52]. Employees from diverse backgrounds contribute value by producing innovative ideas or voting for and commenting on other ideas [51].

Further, intrinsic and extrinsic factors can enhance a crowd's **motivation to participate** in internal crowdsourcing [51, 52]. Beretta and Søndergaard [51] report that employees partaking in internal crowdsourcing are often intrinsically motivated to contribute to firm innovativeness, while others may have an extrinsic motivation to exhibit their skills and expertise and learn from the contest outcomes. Similarly, Gallus et al. [52] assert that managerial recognition can extrinsically motivate employees. Recognition from other employees only motivates employees who are regarded as less noticeable [52].

5 Discussion

In this section we discuss similarities and differences between influential factors for external and internal crowdsourcing configurations, and then propose an integrated framework depicting the factors that influence crowdsourcing for innovation at the firm, platform and crowd level.

5.1 A Comparison of External and Internal Crowdsourcing for Innovation

The literature focuses on two divergent crowdsourcing configurations, namely internal and external crowdsourcing for innovation. Various factors can influence the innovation outcome for either configuration; some of these overlap while others are only relevant for one of the two crowdsourcing approaches. The following section contrasts and compares those factors highlighted in the crowdsourcing and innovation literature from the established perspectives of firm, platform and crowd.

Firm-Level Differences. Firms engaged in crowdsourcing for innovation are actively involved in the innovation-generating contest. However, given the variation in project boundaries and participating actors between external and internal contests [6, 13, 21] there are some differences in firm-level factors (see Table 3). Firstly, because external crowds often lack contest awareness and prior connections to the innovation-seeking firm, organizational reputation can aid firms engaged in external crowdsourcing efforts to attract crowd members situated outside firm boundaries [13]. Conversely, with internal crowdsourcing the crowd encompasses firm employees who are familiar with the company [21], making engagement easier and diminishing the importance of firm reputation. Secondly, whereas the importance of a comprehensive management strategy is emphasized in both the internal and external crowdsourcing literature [3, 21, 27, 34, 36, 37, 46], the strategic focus differs significantly. For external crowdsourcing, emphasis is placed on the integration of the crowdsourcing project into the firm's existing internal innovation system and processes [3, 34, 36–38]. This focus highlights the challenges organisations face when facilitating external innovation activities that are more difficult to control and manage [13]. Firms that crowdsource internally are not concerned with project implementation and integration management because the contest comprises an internal employee crowd and runs within organizational boundaries [21]. Instead, engaging with the employee crowd [21, 27, 46] and providing feedback [47, 48] play a vital role in internal crowd management. The focal organisation benefits from the minimal time and cost resources needed to engage with the employee crowd. Lastly, a firm's internal innovation efforts can supplement external crowdsourcing and be employee [11] or department-specific [7]. However, internal crowdsourcing usually spans the entire organisation [21], thus eliminating the need for further internal support.

Platform-Level Differences. A crowdsourcing platform facilitates communication between the innovation-seeking firm and its participating crowd [12, 15]. External crowds are more distant from innovation-seeking firms [18, 19], thus requiring distinct platform capabilities that support managerial objectives and activities in terms of crowd collaboration [39], crowd engagement [29, 39], and crowd selection [29]; idea

Table 3. Firm-level differences between external and internal crowdsourcing for innovation.

	External crowdsourcing	Internal crowdsourcing
Organizational reputation	Relied upon given the lack of firm-crowd relationship	Not needed to attract the internal employee crowd
Strategic focus	Efficient implementation and integration of the external contest into the internal innovation system	Engaging and communicating with the participating crowd
Resources	Internal innovation efforts can complement the external development of innovative outcomes	The development of innovative ideas takes place in-house and spans the entirety of the firm

processing [12, 29]; process transparency and efficiency [29]; and firm-crowd interaction [12]. In contrast, due to already established relationships, internal crowds simplify collaboration and engagement, rendering certain platform capabilities redundant. Further, internal crowd engagement can be facilitated through managerial support and a firm-wide strategy [21, 27, 46]. Additionally, because the internal crowd is smaller and less diverse [22], idea processing is less resource heavy. Lastly, the ease of communication makes internal crowdsourcing more transparent and efficient, requiring little support from the crowdsourcing platform. The choice of an appropriate platform for external crowdsourcing is also contingent on transaction costs and the firm's ability to autonomously generate sufficient crowd submissions, the firm-crowd relationship, and any relevant resources [15]. Choosing an internal crowdsourcing platform likely entails different criteria. Since idea implementation and realization are more efficient using internal crowds [21], project costs play a minor role. Additionally, resource predictability is higher, and the choice between internally and externally managed platforms, as emphasized by Schenk et al. [15], is also redundant. Instead, the literature highlights a proven, engaging and transparent design [49], as well as a collaborative, interactive and reward-based platform [50].

Crowd-Level Differences. External and internal crowds usually differ in their knowledge backgrounds and proximity to the firm [13, 19, 21]. While external crowds typically consist of anonymous individuals with little to no connection to the crowdsourcing firm, internal crowds are knowledgeable about the firm's processes, capabilities and challenges. As a result, several differences exist between crowd-level factors for internal and external crowdsourcing (see Table 4). Firstly, the knowledge background of an external crowd influences the contest outcome [8, 24, 40, 41]. Existing firm-related knowledge [8, 40], past crowdsourcing experience and success [41], and the trade-off between general and expert knowledge should be considered [24]. Internal crowds with firm-relevant knowledge [21] eliminate the need to select participants with suitable knowledge backgrounds. Secondly, although the crowd's knowledge background is not an organizational focus, the literature highlights participation frequency and expertise [22] and creativity and pro-activity [53] as crucial crowd characteristics in internal crowdsourcing. The potential lack of creativity in small-sized internal crowds [22] and participant similarity explains the firm's emphasis on creativity. Thirdly, a firm's contest set-up (e.g., regarding IP ownership configuration) can influence the willingness of an external crowd to participate [17, 43]. Unlike internal crowds, external crowds usually lack a connection to the innovation-seeking firm, heightening their skepticism toward the firm. In other words, the crowd's trust cannot be taken for granted, making crowd participation more challenging to attain. Lastly, co-creation opportunities are relevant for external crowdsourcing efforts [9, 18, 26]. External crowds situated outside the firm boundaries [13] complicate efficient collaboration due to inherent differences. In contrast, internal crowd members are familiar with working alongside their co-employees, in-person and in real time, thus minimizing the organizational need to provide co-creation opportunities.

Table 4. Crowd-level differences between external and internal crowdsourcing for innovation.

	External crowdsourcing	Internal crowdsourcing
Knowledge background	More diverse given the size and distribution of the crowd participants	Employees are assumed to have appropriate firm knowledge
Crowd characteristics	Crowd diversity and creativity are assumed given the crowd size and distribution	Crowd diversity, participation frequency, creativity and pro-activity determine innovation
Motivation to participate	Crowd trust is difficult to obtain and maintain given the lack of pre-existing relationships between firm and crowd	The crowd has an established relationship with the organisation
Co-create opportunities	Crowd trust is difficult to obtain and maintain given the lack of pre-existing relationships between crowd members	In-person collaboration between co-workers is easy to achieve

5.2 Similarities Between External and Internal Crowdsourcing for Innovation

Despite apparent differences between internal and external crowdsourcing for innovation in terms of firm, platform and crowd-level factors, some similarities exist between influential success factors. Firm-level research highlights the importance of strategic idea processing, specifically through idea filtering using a set of selection criteria that directly contribute to effective contest facilitation and innovation outcomes [19, 21, 25, 27, 45]. At the crowd level, external crowd motivations resemble those of internal employees. Intrinsic and extrinsic motivational factors are seen as improving crowd participation, thus furthering innovation generation in both external [6, 8] and internal crowdsourcing [51, 52]. Table 5 summarizes external and internal crowd motivations by comparing motivational triggers and their visibility.

Table 5. Comparing external and internal crowd motivations.

	External crowdsourcing	Internal crowdsourcing
Motivational Triggers	Negative feedback received for past crowdsourcing idea submissions [41]	Managerial recognition and (in some cases) recognition from other employees [52]
Visibility of extrinsic motivation	Submission of more appropriate and innovative ideas [6, 8]	Aim to add to the firm's innovation processes [51]
Visibility of intrinsic motivation	Submission of more appropriate and innovative ideas [6]	Desire to display and obtain new skills and knowledge through participation [51]

5.3   Innovation Through Crowdsourcing: An Integrated Framework

Having looked at the differences and similarities between factors that influence the success of internal and external crowdsourcing, we derive a combined framework of factors for achieving innovation through crowdsourcing (see Fig. 4). The framework, which builds on the analysis of innovation and crowdsourcing literature, distinguishes between three levels (firm, platform, and crowd) arranged in descending order according to the amount of control a crowdsourcing organisation has over the factors that influence the crowdsourcing innovation outcomes on each level. Influential factors are either unique to a crowdsourcing configuration (external or internal) or overlap between these two configurations. Table 8 in Appendix 2 provides additional insights for crowdsourcing organisations by offering guiding questions for each identified factors. These questions can serve as both managerial considerations and potential avenues for future research.

An organizational view of crowdsourcing starts with a consideration of the firm-level factors, which encompass the strategic management of resources, capabilities and processes that impact the success of innovation outcomes for both configurations. Thereby, external crowdsourcing demands a reflection on the organization's reputation (for example, by asking *What is the impact of organizational reputation on idea submissions in this crowdsourcing contest, and how can organizational reputation be improved to enhance crowd participation?*, see Table 6) and the coordination of firm-internal innovation efforts to complement external crowdsourcing engagement. Both configurations require a comprehensive crowdsourcing project management strategy, which, in the case of external crowdsourcing, can be guided by the assessment of the firm's reputation. For internal crowdsourcing, project management is followed by crowd management, which entails engagement and communication with the innovating crowd. Formulated firm-level objectives and strategies can inform the organization's view regarding influential platform-level factors. That is, external crowdsourcing platforms facilitate the firm's interaction with a large, often global audience, which is reflected in the consideration of supporting capabilities that precede the choice of a suitable crowdsourcing platform. In contrast, for internal crowdsourcing, several design factors can enhance the implemented platform, prompting firms to ask: *Which design factors of crowdsourcing platforms are most critical for enhancing the success of crowdsourcing contests?*

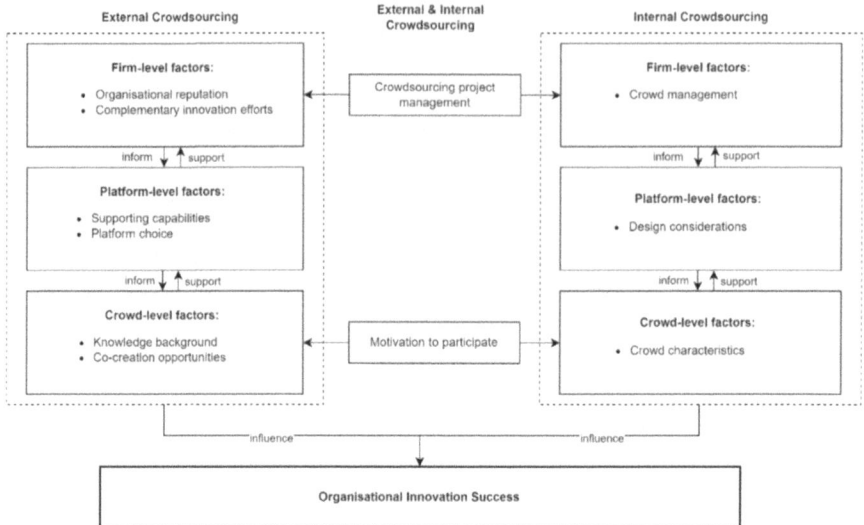

Fig. 4. An integrated framework of key factors driving innovation through crowdsourcing.

Table 6. Key considerations/questions for achieving innovation through crowdsourcing.

	External crowdsourcing	External & internal crowdsourcing	Internal crowdsourcing
Firm	**Organizational reputation:** *What is the impact of organizational reputation on idea submissions in crowdsourcing contests, and how can organizations improve their reputation to enhance crowd participation?* **Complementary innovation efforts:** *What are the strategies for complementing external crowdsourced innovation with internal firm efforts, and how can these strategies be effectively implemented to maximize innovation outcomes?*	**Crowdsourcing project management:** *What are the key strategic actions required for processing and implementing ideas generated during the contest?*	**Crowd management:** *What are effective methods for actively managing the participating crowd in organizational crowdsourcing processes?*

(continued)

Table 6. (*continued*)

	External crowdsourcing	External & internal crowdsourcing	Internal crowdsourcing
Platform	**Supporting capabilities:** *Which supporting capabilities of crowdsourcing platforms are most critical for enhancing the success of crowdsourcing contests?* **Platform choice:** *What are the key contextual, strategic and operations factors that influence the decision-making process of choosing a suitable crowdsourcing platform?*		**Design considerations:** *Which design factors of crowdsourcing platforms are most critical for enhancing the success of crowdsourcing contests?*
Crowd	**Knowledge background:** *What selection and screening processes can organisations employ to target individuals with the right knowledge background for their crowdsourcing objectives?* **Co-creation opportunities:** *How can organisations identify and exploit co-creation opportunities in amongst geographically dispersed crowd members?*	**Motivation to participate:** *What motivational triggers drive individuals to submit innovative ideas to crowdsourcing contests?*	**Crowd characteristics:** *What selection and screening processes can organisations employ to target individuals with the right knowledge background for their crowdsourcing objectives?*

(see Table 6). Lastly, the crowdsourcing platform facilitates interaction between the innovation-seeking organisation and participating crowd members, who ultimately determine the innovation success of the firm's contest. Organisations participating in external crowdsourcing should, therefore, select a suitable crowd, as informed by the crowd's knowledge background, and also identify any co-creation opportunities between crowd members. Internally crowdsourcing firms can conduct a broader search for suitable crowd participants. Another deciding factor regards the crowd's motivation to participate, which is shared by both crowdsourcing approaches and provokes the following question: *What motivational triggers drive individuals to submit innovative ideas to crowdsourcing contests?* (see Table 6). Finally, the innovation success of organizational crowdsourcing efforts is also determined by a firm's consideration of the interconnected factors and guiding questions.

6   Contributions and Conclusion

6.1   Theoretical Contribution

Previous research on crowdsourcing for innovation has predominantly focused on the issues, benefits, and success factors of organizational crowdsourcing, clearly distinguishing between the adoption of external and internal crowdsourcing configurations. As a result, there is only limited insight regarding the simultaneous management of internal and external crowdsourcing efforts as a means of improving crowdsourcing outcomes for innovation seeking organisations [23]. This research gap highlights the necessity of combining insights from the external and internal crowdsourcing literature to obtain a more well-rounded understanding of the influential factors of crowdsourcing for innovation success from an organizational perspective. Consequently, in this paper, we have integrated literature insights from external crowdsourcing with those from internal crowdsourcing for innovation to derive a theoretical framework that combines and contrasts success factors for innovation from these two distinct crowdsourcing configurations. Specifically, the derived framework adds to existing research by outlining influential crowdsourcing factors from three perspectives: the firm, platform, and crowd level. This integrated perspective on crowdsourcing for innovation and the formulated questions for each influential factor can also guide future research on the success and failure of innovation-driven organizational crowdsourcing ventures. From the derived framework, we further develop a set of practical recommendations for managers of organizational crowdsourcing endeavors, which specify the conditions for innovation success through crowdsourcing (see Table 8 in Appendix 2).

6.2   Conclusion and Future Work

We carried out a systematic review to shed light on the potential benefits of facilitating crowdsourcing contests for organizational innovation and the importance of a comprehensive crowdsourcing strategy for innovation success. By integrating insights from two distinct literature streams, innovation and crowdsourcing, our aim was to enhance knowledge of when and how internal and external crowdsourcing configurations can support an organization's search for innovation. Previous research in the field makes a clear distinction between the adoption of external and internal crowdsourcing configurations, leaving a critical gap in the existing literature, which lacks an integrated perspective on internal and external crowdsourcing in the context of organizational innovation. To bridge this gap, we offer a multi-level framework that outlines influential factors underlying successful crowdsourcing initiatives across the firm, platform, and crowd levels. The derived framework draws on and combines insights from both external and internal crowdsourcing to offer a more holistic view of crowdsourcing in the context of organizational innovation. It further provides a practical roadmap for organisations seeking to harness crowdsourcing for innovation. Future empirical research studies could further analyse how the multi-level factors identified in this integrated perspective influence the success of organizational efforts to improve their innovation capabilities through crowdsourcing. There is an opportunity to build on this review to further advance understanding of how organisations can effectively leverage crowdsourcing for innovation in an ever evolving and highly competitive business landscape.

Disclosure of Interests.   The authors have no competing interests to declare that are relevant to the content of this article.

Appendix

Appendix 1

Table 7. Overview of included IS, innovation and general management journals.

Research field	Journal name	Number of articles
IS	Decision Support Systems	2
	Information System Frontiers	1
	Information Systems Journal	1
	Information Systems Research	2
	International Journal of Information Management	3
	Journal of the AIS	2
	Journal of Strategic Information Systems	2
	European Journal of Information Systems Information & Management Information and Organization Journal of Information Technology Journal of Management Information Systems MIS Quarterly	0
	Total	*13*
Innovation	Journal of Product Innovation Management	2
	R&D Management	6
	Research Policy	3
	Technological Forecasting and Social Change	2
	Industry and Innovation Technovation The Journal of Technology Transfer	0
	Total	*13*
General Management	Academy of Management Journal	1
	Organization Science	*1*
	Academy of Management Review Administrative Science Quarterly Journal of Management The Academy of Management Annals	*0*
	Total	*2*
Total		**28**

Appendix 2

Table 8. Managerial recommendations for innovation success through crowdsourcing.

	Managerial recommendations
Firm-level	(1) To successfully generate organizational innovation from crowdsourcing efforts, organisations should consider firm-level factors that can influence this innovation approach. When tasked with facilitating and managing the crowdsourcing contest, managers should first **evaluate the impact of organizational reputation on idea submissions** in terms of generating crowd submissions for the firm's innovation contest. In external crowdsourcing competitions, an insufficient or bad reputation may affect the crowd's willingness to support the innovation-seeking organisation through their participation. Well known or popular organisations are likely to attract large crowds given their reputation. Therefore, firms should aim to improve their reputation prior to implementing a crowdsourcing strategy
	(2) **Formulating a comprehensive crowdsourcing project management strategy** is the second cornerstone of a firm's crowdsourcing campaign. Projects that are not guided by organizational-level objectives are doomed to fail. This can result in high resource costs for the crowdsourcing organisation that could have been prevented through strategic pre-planning of the contest. Relevant strategic actions concern the processing of ideas generated during the crowdsourcing contest as well as their implementation into the firm's innovation system, if not already guaranteed as in internal crowdsourcing
	(3) The third firm-level factor is **supporting external innovation with internal firm efforts** Having formulated a project management strategy, the innovation-seeking organisation is advised to complement external crowdsourcing crowd innovation with internal firm efforts, where possible. Complementary innovation activities can be conducted at the employee or departmental level and may involve employees from all backgrounds, or those with specific expert knowledge
	(4) Fourth is **actively managing the participating crowd.** Given their proximity to the firm, internal crowds are easy to reach during organizational crowdsourcing processes, and management should have strategies in place to effectively engage and communicate with them. Managerial feedback is a crucial tool for driving quality idea submissions and creating a positive learning experience for internal crowd members, given that many employees may return to participate in subsequent crowdsourcing contests

(*continued*)

Table 8. (*continued*)

	Managerial recommendations
Platform-level	(1) Smooth contest facilitation is also determined by the platform, which connects all involved crowdsourcing actors. Organisations that align their strategic crowdsourcing objectives with design objectives for the associated platform can increase their chances of obtaining innovative ideas suitable for implementation in their systems. Consequently, managers are urged to **identify appropriate design factors and supporting capabilities** Organisations should seek platform capabilities that support the external crowdsourcing contest. An appropriate platform will not only support crowd collaboration and engagement but also enhance the firm's idea processing capabilities, leading to more efficient and implementable crowdsourcing outcomes. Similarly, selecting a suitable platform design is pivotal for firms engaged in internal crowdsourcing. Besides basic functionalities (e.g., storing and processing idea submissions), managers should focus on a proven and collaborative design that allows for interaction between crowdsourcing actors, a transparent contest and an effective incentive systems
	(2) Our second recommendation **is to base platform choice on firm resources and capabilities** Organisations seeking external crowdsourcing innovation are advised to base their ultimate platform choice on existing firm capabilities and resources and their relationship with the crowd. Managers need to understand that platform choice involves a decision-making process that takes into account various factors, including contextual, strategic and operational considerations
Crowd-level	(1) As the origin of innovative outcomes in a crowdsourcing contest, extensive organizational attention should be directed towards the participating crowd. To select appropriate participants for the firm's crowdsourcing activity, crowdsourcing managers need to first **utilize crowd information.** Managerial attention should be devoted to the crowd's knowledge background, which is a decisive factor in idea development, in turn influencing the innovation success of a crowdsourcing contest. This requires the organizational facilitation of a crowd screening or pre-selection process, targeting individuals with a suitable knowledge background to support the organizational crowdsourcing objectives. Prior to the contest, the firm can either obtain specific information about the crowd's knowledge background or assume given capabilities based on other available crowd information. For internal crowdsourcing where more information about the employee crowd is accessible to the firm, managers may want to engage in a more comprehensive screening and selection process considering various crowd characteristics. Organizational focus should be directed to attracting a crowd with characteristics that optimally align with the specific crowdsourcing objectives formulated in the firm's strategy, and which are supported and carried out by the chosen crowdsourcing platform

(*continued*)

Table 8. (*continued*)

	Managerial recommendations
	(2) The second crowd-level recommendation is **understanding and leveraging the motivational triggers of crowdsourcing participants** Crowdsourcing managers need to understand what motivates individuals to submit their innovative ideas to the contest. Motivational triggers can differ depending on the targeted crowd, but extrinsic and intrinsic motivation triggers are both effective in encouraging crowd members. The organization's task is to identify such triggers and utilize them to maximize crowd submissions. An individual's underlying motivation is reflected in their behaviour during the contest and can thus also inform future crowdsourcing activities by the organisation
	(3) Finally, it is important to **identify co-creation opportunities where collaboration is difficult to achieve** Firms need to recognise the difficulty of enabling collaboration amongst external crowd members, given their distance from each other. Managerial efforts can drive crowd co creation by recognizing opportunities and leveraging such opportunities through strategic actions and platform design features

References

1. Amabile, T.M.: A model of creativity and innovation in organisations. Res. Organ. Behav. **10**, 123–167 (1988)
2. Marjanovic, S., Fry, C., Chataway, J.: Crowdsourcing based business models: in search of evidence for innovation 2.0. Sci. Public Policy **39**(3), 318–332 (2012). https://doi.org/10.1093/scipol/scs009
3. Jespersen, K.R.: Crowdsourcing design decisions for optimal integration into the company innovation system. Decis. Support. Syst. **115**, 52–63 (2018). https://doi.org/10.1016/j.dss.2018.09.005
4. Cassiman, B., Valentini, G.: Open innovation: Are inbound and outbound knowledge flows really complementary? Strateg. Manag. J. **37**, 1034–1046 (2016). https://doi.org/10.1002/smj.2375
5. West, J., Salter, A., Vanhaverbeke, W., Chesbrough, H.: Open innovation: the next decade. Res. Policy **34**(5), 805–811 (2014). https://doi.org/10.1016/j.respol.2014.03.001
6. Acar, O.A.: Motivations and solution appropriateness in crowdsourcing challenges for innovation. Res. Policy **48**(8), 2–54 (2019). https://doi.org/10.1016/j.respol.2018.11.010
7. Bagheri, S.K., et al.: Using the crowd for business model innovation: the case of Digikala. R&D Management **50**(1), 3–17 (2020). https://doi.org/10.1111/radm.12353
8. Mack, T., Landau, C.: Submission quality in open innovation contests – An analysis of individual-level determinants of idea innovativeness. R&D Management **50**(3), 47–62 (2020). https://doi.org/10.1111/radm.12345
9. Majchrzak, A., Malhotra, A.: Towards an information systems perspective and research agenda on crowdsourcing for innovation. J. Strat. Inf. Syst. **22**(4), 257–268 (2013). https://doi.org/10.1016/j.jsis.2013.07.004
10. Bogers, M., et al.: The open innovation research landscape: established perspectives and emerging themes across different levels of analysis. Ind. Innov. **24**(1), 8–40 (2017). https://doi.org/10.1080/13662716.2016.1240068

11. Schlagwein, D., Bjørn-Andersen, N.: Organisational learning with crowdsourcing: the revelatory case of LEGO. J. AIS **15**(11), 754–778 (2014). https://doi.org/10.17705/1jais. 00380

12. Kohler, T., Chesbrough, H.: From collaborative community to competitive market: the quest to build a crowdsourcing platform for social innovation. R&D Management **49**(3), 356–368 (2019). https://doi.org/10.1111/radm.12372

13. Cappa, F., Oriani, R., Pinelli, M., De Massis, A.: When does crowdsourcing benefit firm stock market performance? Res. Policy **48**(9), 1–39 (2019). https://doi.org/10.1016/j.respol.2019. 103825

14. Howe, J.: Crowdsourcing: How the Power of the Crowd is Driving the Future of Business. Random House, New York (2008)

15. Schenk, E., Guittard, C., Penin, J.: Open or proprietary? Choosing the right crowdsourcing platform for innovation. Technol. Forecast. Soc. Chang. **144**, 303–310 (2019). https://doi.org/ 10.1016/j.techfore.2017.11.021

16. Schenk, E., Guittard, C.: Towards a characterization of crowdsourcing practices. J. Innov. Econ. Manage. **7**(1), 93–107 (2011). https://doi.org/10.3917/jie.011.0093

17. Franke, N., Keinz, P., Klausberger, K.: "Does this sound like a fair deal?": antecedents and consequences of fairness expectations in the individual's decision to participate in firm innovation. Organ. Sci. **24**(5), 1495–1516 (2013). https://doi.org/10.1287/orsc.1120.0794

18. Majchrzak, A., Malhotra, A.: Effect of knowledge-sharing trajectories on innovative outcomes in temporary online crowds. Inf. Syst. Res. **27**(4), 685–703 (2016). https://doi.org/10.1287/ isre.2016.0669

19. Piezunka, H., Dahlander, L.: Distance search, narrow attention: how crowding alters organisation's filtering of suggestions in crowdsourcing. Acad. Manag. J. **58**(3), 856–880 (2015). https://doi.org/10.5465/amj.2012.0458

20. Stieger, D., Matzler, K., Chatterjee, S., Ladstaetter-Fussenegger, F.: Democratising strategy: how crowdsourcing can be used for strategy dialogues. Calif. Manage. Rev. **54**(4), 1–36 (2012). https://doi.org/10.1525/cmr.2012.54.4.33

21. Malhotra, A., Majchrzak, A., Kesebi, L., Looram, S.: Developing innovative solutions through internal crowdsourcing. MIT Sloan Manag. Rev. **58**(4), 73–79 (2017)

22. Asplund, F., Björk, J., Magnusson, M.: Knowing too much? On bias due to domain-specific knowledge in internal crowdsourcing for explorative ideas. R&D Management, 1–15 (2021). https://doi.org/10.1111/radm.12517

23. Ruiz, E., Beretta, M.: Managing internal and external crowdsourcing: an investigation of emerging challenges in the context of a less experienced firm. Technovation **106**(3), 2–23 (2021). https://doi.org/10.1016/j.technovation.2021.102290

24. Ren, J., Han, Y., Genc, Y., Yeoh, W., Popovič, A.: The boundary of crowdsourcing in the domain of creativity. Technol. Forecast. Soc. Chang. **165**, 1–14 (2021). https://doi.org/10. 1016/j.techfore.2020.120530

25. Klein, M., Garcia, A.C.B.: High-speed idea filtering with the bad of lemons. Decis. Support. Syst. **77**(6), 1–27 (2015). https://doi.org/10.1016/j.dss.2015.06.005

26. Han, Y., Ozturk, P., Nickerson, J.V.: Leveraging the wisdom of the crowd to address societal challenges: revisiting the knowledge reuse for innovation process through analytics. J. AIS **21**(5), 1128–1152 (2020). https://doi.org/10.17705/1jais.00632

27. Pohlisch, J.: Internal open innovation - Lessons learned from internal crowdsourcing at SAP. Sustainability **12**(10), 4245 (2020). https://doi.org/10.3390/su12104245

28. Martinez, M.G., Walton, B.: The wisdom of crowds: The potential of online communities as a tool for data analysis. Technovation **34**(3), 203–214 (2014). https://doi.org/10.1016/j.tec hnovation.2014.01.011

29. Feller, J., Finnegan, P., Hayes, J., O'Reilly, P.: 'Orchestrating' sustainable crowdsourcing: a characterisation of solver brokerages. J. Strat. Inf. Syst. **21**(3), 216–232 (2012). https://doi.org/10.1016/j.jsis.2012.05.002

30. Okoli, C.: A guide to conducting a standalone systematic literature review. Commun. Assoc. Inf. Syst. **37**, 879–910 (2015). https://doi.org/10.17705/1CAIS.03743

31. Webster, J., Watson, R.T.: Analyzing the past to prepare for the future: writing a literature review. MIS Q., 13–23 (2002). https://doi.org/10.25300/MISQ/2002/26.2.03

32. Wolfswinkel, J.F., Furtmueller, E., Wilderom, C.P.M.: Using grounded theory as a method for rigorously reviewing literature. Eur. J. Inf. Syst. **22**(1), 45–55 (2013). https://doi.org/10.1057/ejis.2011.51

33. Myers, M.D.: Qualitative Research in Business & Management, 3rd edn. Sage Publications, Thousand Oaks (2020)

34. Fayard, A., Gkeradakis, E., Levina, N.: Framing innovation opportunities while staying committed to an organisational epistemic stance. Inf. Syst. Res. **27**(2), 302–323 (2016). https://doi.org/10.1287/isre.2016.0623

35. Pacauskas, D., Rajala, R., Westerlund, M., Mäntymäki, M.: Harnessing user innovation for social media marketing: case study of a crowdsourced hamburger. Int. J. Inf. Manage. **43**, 319–327 (2018). https://doi.org/10.1016/j.ijinfomgt.2018.08.012

36. Pollok, P., Lüttgens, D., Piller, F.T.: How firms develop capabilities for crowdsourcing to increase open innovation performance: the interplay between organizational roles and knowledge processes. J. Prod. Innov. Manag. **36**(4), 412–441 (2019). https://doi.org/10.1111/jpim.12485

37. Randhawa, K., Wilden, R., West, J.: Crowdsourcing without profit: the role of the seeker in open social innovation. R&D Management **49**(3), 298–317 (2019). https://doi.org/10.1111/radm.12357

38. Ruiz, E., Brion, S., Parmentier, G.: Absorbing knowledge in the digital age: the key role of integration mechanisms in the context of crowdsourcing for innovation. R&D Management **50**(1), 63–74 (2020). https://doi.org/10.1111/radm.12379

39. Yuan, S.D., Hsieh, C.: An impactful crowdsourcing intermediary design - A case of a service imagery crowdsourcing system. Inf. Syst. Front. **20**(4), 841–862 (2018). https://doi.org/10.1007/s10796-016-9700-8

40. Boons, M., Stam, D.: Crowdsourcing for innovation: How related and unrelated perspectives interact to increase creative performance. Res. Policy **48**(7), 1758–1770 (2019). https://doi.org/10.1016/j.respol.2019.04.005

41. Liu, Q., Du, Q., Hong, Y., Fan, W., Wu, S.: User idea implementation in open innovation communities: evidence from a new product development crowdsourcing community. Inf. Syst. J. **30**(5), 899–927 (2020). https://doi.org/10.1111/isj.12286

42. Bakici, T.: Comparison of crowdsourcing platforms from social-psychological and motivational perspectives. Int. J. Inf. Manage. **54** (2020). https://doi.org/10.1016/j.ijinfomgt.2020.102121

43. Mazzola, E., Acur, N., Piazza, M., Perrone, G.: "To own or not to own?" A study on the determinants and consequences of alternative intellectual property rights arrangements in crowdsourcing for innovation contests. J. Prod. Innov. Manag. **35**(6), 908–929 (2018). https://doi.org/10.1111/jpim.12467

44. Ashurst, C., Freer, A., Ekdahl, J., Gibbons, C.: Exploring IT-enabled innovation: a new paradigm. Int. J. Inf. Manage. **32**, 326–336 (2012). https://doi.org/10.1037/t34019-000

45. Campos-Blázquez, J.R., Morcillo, P., Rubio-Andrada, L.: Employee innovation using ideation contests: seven-step process to align strategic challenges with the innovation process. Res. Technol. Manag. **63**(5), 20–28 (2020). https://doi.org/10.1080/08956308.2020.1790237

46. Malhotra, A., Majchrzak, A., Bonfield, W., Myers, S.: Engaging customer care employees in internal collaborative crowdsourcing: managing the inherent tensions and associated challenges. Hum. Resour. Manage. **59**(2), 121–134 (2020). https://doi.org/10.1002/hrm.21952

47. Chen, Q., Magnusson, M., Björk, J.: Collective firm-internal online idea development: exploring the impact of feedback timeliness and knowledge overlap. Eur. J. Innov. Manage. **23**(1) (2019). https://doi.org/10.1108/EJIM-02-2018-0045

48. Zhu, H., Kock, A., Wentker, M., Leker, J.: How does online interaction affect idea quality? The effect of feedback in firm-internal idea competitions. J. Prod. Innov. Manag. **36**(1), 24–40 (2019). https://doi.org/10.1111/jpim.12453

49. Beretta, M., Frederiksen, M., Wallin, M., Kulikovskaja, V.: Why and how firms implement internal crowdsourcing platforms. IEEE Trans. Eng. Manage. (2021). https://doi.org/10.1109/TEM.2020.3045118

50. Deichmann, D., Gillier, T., Tonellato, M.: Getting on board with new ideas: an analysis of idea commitments on a crowdsourcing platform. Res. Policy **50**(9), 104320 (2021). https://doi.org/10.1016/j.respol.2021.104320

51. Beretta, M., Søndergaard, H.A.: Employee behaviours beyond innovators in internal crowdsourcing: what do employees do in internal crowdsourcing, if not innovating, and why? Creat. Innov. Manage. **30**(3), 542–562 (2021). https://doi.org/10.1111/caim.12449

52. Gallus, J., Jung, O.S., Lakhani, K.R.: Recognition incentives for internal crowdsourcing: a field experiment at NASA. Harvard Business School Technology & Operations Management Unit Working Paper (2020)

53. Zhu, H., Djurjagina, K., Leker, J.: Innovative behaviour types and their influence on individual crowdsourcing performances. Int. J. Innov. Manage. **18**(6) (2014). https://doi.org/10.1142/S1363919614400155

Governing Ecosystem Transformations – The Case of Microsoft Azure

Maximilian Schreieck[1]([✉]) [iD], Tobias Riasanow[2], Thorsten Schwaab[3],
Markus Böhm[4] [iD], Philipp W. Yetton[5] [iD], and Helmut Krcmar[6] [iD]

[1] University of Innsbruck, Innsbruck, Austria
maximilian.schreieck@uibk.ac.at
[2] SAP SE, Munich, Germany
[3] Microsoft Deutschland GmbH, Munich, Germany
[4] University of Applied Sciences Landshut, Landshut, Germany
[5] Deakin University, Victoria, Australia
[6] Technical University of Munich, Munich, Germany

Abstract. Microsoft's rollout of its cloud platform, Microsoft Azure, required a fundamental transformation of its partner ecosystem. Before the rollout, most partners were either resellers who focused on selling licenses for Microsoft's on-premises products or development partners who co-created on-premises products and services to expand Microsoft products. After the rollout, Microsoft aimed to foster an ecosystem with partners who would develop applications on the cloud platform to address the needs of customers and that would potentially scale on the platform. In a case study based on the introduction of the Azure platform, we lay out the challenges that Microsoft and its resell and development partners faced during the ecosystem transformation. Drawing on the responses to these challenges by Microsoft and its partners, we derive four governance mechanisms for enterprise software vendors during ecosystem transformation (e.g., establishing innovation clusters for specific target markets) and three adaptation mechanisms for ecosystem partners (e.g., developing their own IP). These mechanisms can guide incumbent companies and their partners as major technological shifts affect their ecosystems.

Keywords: Ecosystem Transformation · Partner Ecosystem · Cloud Platform · Partner Governance · Governance Mechanism · Microsoft Azure

1 Introduction

Enterprise software vendors like Microsoft, SAP, IBM, and Oracle have traditionally established large partner ecosystems [1, 2]. Partners in their ecosystem resell their products and services, develop complementary products, and offer additional services such as consulting, training, and maintenance [3, 4]. With this approach, enterprise software vendors could serve customers across the globe and address the needs of companies from diverse industries. Thus, partners have emerged as a critical success factor for enterprise software vendors. The vendors have developed capabilities to orchestrate their partner ecosystems, for example, through partner programs, certifications, and joint go-to-market strategies [5].

The enterprise software industry has changed significantly in the last decade, transforming from on-premises software products to cloud services [6]. With the increasing capabilities of cloud computing technologies, software vendors have, on the one hand, moved their core products to the cloud, replacing "packaged" ERP solutions that were implemented at the customers' premises and customized to their specific needs. For example, SAP's latest generation ERP (SAP S/4) is available via private and public cloud. On the other hand, they introduced cloud platforms to allow partners to develop and distribute cloud services. For example, SAP introduced the SAP Cloud Platform (now labeled SAP Business Technology Platform), Oracle introduced the Oracle Cloud Platform, and Microsoft introduced the Azure platform.

However, as the enterprise software vendors launched these cloud platforms, a significant challenge arose: convincing ecosystem partners to go along with the transformation of the ecosystem from a focus on on-premises solutions to cloud services. Critically, transforming an on-premises partner ecosystem into a cloud platform ecosystem involves a major discontinuous organizational transformation that could risk the business's survival.

To manage such a transformation of a partner ecosystem, the focal firm needs to apply governance, i.e., it has to orchestrate the ecosystem of partners and steer them towards the transformed ecosystem. However, there is little guidance on how to do so because the information systems literature has primarily focused on the governance of ecosystems with homogeneous third-party developers on a technology platform. Also, this "platform governance" [7] has mostly been studied in emerging or stable ecosystems and not in ecosystems that undergo a transformation. Addressing this gap, we thus pose the question of how enterprise software vendors can govern partner ecosystems during major transformations and how partners can adapt to this governance.?

This question is gaining importance because, first, more and more incumbent organizations explore the opportunities of cloud technologies to transform their on-premises partner ecosystems. Second, ecosystem transformation can be triggered by other major technological shifts, such as the introduction of generative artificial intelligence as an innovation platform in the ecosystem [8].

To better understand the challenges of ecosystem transformation, we analyze the transformation of Microsoft's partner ecosystem following the introduction of the cloud platform Azure. Like other incumbent enterprise software vendors, Microsoft had built an on-premises software business in which partners developed software solutions for customers, installed and maintained that software on the customers' premises, and charged customers a license fee for each machine that ran the software. For the Azure platform to be successful, Microsoft had to move its partners to the cloud and help them develop the capabilities required to leverage the digital platform features to grow both Microsoft's and their partners' businesses.

By observing Microsoft's ecosystem transformation over time, we identified four governance mechanisms: (1) establish innovation clusters for specific target markets, (2) implement scalable partner enablement, (3) apply 'carrot-and-stick' governance to incentivize transformation, and (4) align the internal partner organization with ecosystem-level goals. We also derived adaptation mechanisms from partners that engaged in the transformation along with Microsoft, namely: (1) build a unique experience in relevant target markets, (2) develop own IP, and (3) engage in partner communities. These mechanisms can be helpful for incumbent companies in the enterprise software industry and beyond who need to transform their partner ecosystem due to technological shifts, as well as for partners that plan to remain part of or join the ecosystem.

The paper is structured as follows. First, we briefly recap the role of partner ecosystems in the enterprise software industry. Second, we provide background to the Microsoft Azure case and, third, describe challenges that Microsoft and its partners faced during the ecosystem transformation. Then, we derive the governance mechanisms based on how Microsoft navigated the transformation and the adaptation mechanisms based on how partners reacted to the transformation. We conclude with a discussion of these mechanisms and their implication for practitioners.

2 Background

2.1 Partner Ecosystems in the Software Industry

Moore [9] established the notion of business ecosystems, which he described as companies working "cooperatively and competitively to support new products, satisfy customer needs, and eventually incorporate the next round of innovation." In his seminal article, he referred to Apple and IBM as orchestrators of software and hardware ecosystems, which included suppliers and partners.

Soon, the term ecosystem, often partner ecosystem, became well-established in the software industry. In particular, when the fast-growing enterprise software industry transformed from monolithic to modular software architectures in the late 1990s and early 2000s, the ecosystems grew as more and more partners offered extensions to the core enterprise software products or additional services [10–12]. For example, IBM established the "IBM Software Development Platform Partner Ecosystem" in 2004:

> *Today, an ecosystem of hundreds of IBM partners adds value to the IBM Software Development Platform. These companies provide complementary technology and services for Eclipse, WebSphere® Studio Workbench, WebSphere Studio, and Lotus® Domino® software, as well as for the Rational® suite of products.* [13].

In this era of modular on-premises enterprise software (also referred to as "packaged" enterprise software), partners have become increasingly important. Examples of such packaged enterprise software include SAP's enterprise resource planning system R/3, launched in 1992, becoming the most successful packaged enterprise software, and Oracle's E-Business Suite, introduced in 1987 and expanded throughout the 1990s. Ecosystem partners co-created value with the vendors mainly by taking over sales, implementing, and customizing the packaged enterprise software [3, 4].

While on-premises enterprise software still flourished in the 2000s, the steadily increasing success of Salesforce, a cloud-native vendor of customer relationship management software, was a precursor of a broader shift toward cloud computing [14, 15].

By offering a core product as software-as-a-service via the cloud, it became even easier for partners to build complementary applications. These applications would connect to the core software through standardized application programming interfaces (APIs). Salesforce launched its AppExchange marketplace for partner applications 2005 and quickly saw increasing numbers of partner applications [16].

In contrast to Salesforce and other could-native entrants in the enterprise software industry, such as ServiceNow (for workflow management, founded 2004) and Weclapp (for enterprise resource planning, founded 2008), incumbent companies such as SAP, IBM, Oracle, and Microsoft had to undergo a significant transformation to shift towards enterprise software provisioned in the cloud [17, 18]. This transformation entailed, first, redeveloping the core enterprise software as cloud services and, second, transforming the partner ecosystem so that partners would join in the effort to not only resell and consult on cloud services but also create innovative complementary products and services. The basis for the transformation was a cloud platform enabling partners to develop and distribute apps and services on the platform [7, 19, 20].

Given the importance of the partner ecosystems for the incumbent enterprise vendors, this ecosystem transformation was crucial for the success of their quest to shift toward cloud computing.

2.2   Governance of Partner Ecosystems

To manage partner ecosystems, the focal firm applies governance. Governance or organizational governance, in its broader sense in the field of management, refers to "a system by which an organization makes and implements decisions in pursuit of its objectives." [21]. The concept of governance has also been applied to interfirm relationships. For example, strategic alliances are managed through governance mechanisms such as contracts [22] and steering committees [23]. In outsourcing relationships between companies, both relational and contractual governance mechanisms are at play [24].

Expanding the concept of governance further, it has been applied to the management of platform ecosystems and referred to as platform governance [7]. Platform governance, in essence, captures how a focal firm (the platform owner) orchestrates an ecosystem of loosely coupled third-party developers [25]. It comprises governance mechanisms such as setting the optimal degree of openness for external third-party developers [26, 27], controls to ensure quality of third-party applications [28, 29], and the provision of boundary resources, i.e., resources such as application programming interfaces (APIs) that third-party developers can draw on to develop applications [30, 31].

While there is a significant body of literature on platform governance, this stream of work does not address all issues related to partner governance in software ecosystems. Platform governance applies when the ecosystem comprises a core platform run by the platform owner and a periphery of homogeneous third-party developers. However, in partner ecosystems in the software industry, there is often not one core platform but rather a suite of core products that can be extended through one or more platforms. Furthermore, the partners are heterogeneous, including partners that develop applications, partners that develop customer-specific solutions, partners that resell software of the enterprise software vendors, and consulting partners.

Furthermore, the literature on platform governance rarely addresses major shifts in the ecosystem's underlying technology—such as the shift of a partner ecosystem from an on-premises to a cloud-based setting. We address this gap by focusing on how enterprise software vendors can govern partner ecosystems during major transformations and how partners can adapt to this governance. Drawing on the case of Microsoft and the launch of its cloud platform Azure, we address how enterprise software vendors can govern significant transformations of their partner ecosystems and how partners can adapt to this transformation.

3   Research Method

Following Yin [32], we conducted an instrumental case study, selecting a case that would advance our understanding of ecosystem transformations, both from an orchestrator and a partner perspective. We had the opportunity to work with a practitioner at Microsoft, who is also a co-author of the paper, and observed the transformation of Microsoft's ecosystem following the launch of the Azure platform.

Data Collection. In addition to the practitioner's insights, we conducted fourteen one-hour semi-structured interviews with senior executives at Microsoft and one partner company. The interviewees were the Partner Sales Organization Lead, Head of Solution Sales Microsoft Azure, Azure Practice Development Unit Lead, Partner Business and Development Lead, ISV Program Lead, CSP Program Lead, two Partner Development Managers, two Partner Technical Architects, a Cloud Solution Architect, two Business Development Managers, and one partner representative. While our focus was on Microsoft's perspective on ecosystem transformation, all interviews considered the situation of ecosystem partners, allowing us to derive both mechanisms for ecosystem governance and partner adaptation. We conducted the interviews face-to-face or via Skype between late 2016 and early 2018 [33]. We recorded and transcribed the interviews.

In addition to the primary data, we collected publicly available data on the milestones of the Azure platform, use cases, and events. This material included annual reports, press releases, blog entries from the official Microsoft blog, tech blogs, video material on partner events, and websites. In total, we collected 59 documents. Furthermore, through the practitioner at Microsoft, we gained access to executive presentations on ecosystem transformation and partner strategy. These multiple sources enabled data triangulation [34].

Data Analysis. We adopted an iterative coding process to identify the challenges Microsoft and its partners faced during ecosystem transformation, governance, and adaptation mechanisms [35, 36]. First, we used open coding to identify any interview statements that would contribute to our understanding of Microsoft's partner ecosystem transformation. In total, we assigned 180 open codes to 193 quotations.

Then, we aggregated the open codes into sub-categories and categories (see Table 1 for analysis examples). Categories included "Challenges for Microsoft," "Challenges for resell partners," "Challenges for development partners," "Governance mechanisms," and "Adaptation mechanisms." Coding was performed by the first author and the co-author employed at Microsoft to ensure that the practitioner's perspective was also represented in the coding process. Thus, the resulting categories resulted from the bottom-up aggregation of open codes and the reflection of coding results in the author team. The complete codebook is available from the authors upon request.

Table 1. Illustrative excerpt from the coding scheme

Interview quotes and open-coded sections	Open code	Sub-category	Category
Nevertheless, we still have a very strong on-premises business at the same time. This means that we still have a classic client business, and we won't be able to get away from it anytime soon. (Principal IT Architect at SAP partner company, Interview 14)	Lion's share of revenue still generated in the established on-premises business	Reluctance of partners to transform	Challenges for Microsoft
We have to make sure that we transform our traditional partners. In other words, we empower them technologically and in the sense of a common go-to-market strategy. Ultimately, it is also a challenge for the partners to change the business model. (Partner Development Manager, Interview 8)	Resell partners must transform their business model	Business model becomes obsolete in the cloud	Challenges for resell partners
That was the central logic of the business transition. For an analysis of 80 scenarios and 30 markets, we picked out eight that we thought had the greatest potential. We have put a kind of start-up team on top of this, which has end-to-end capabilities, i.e., from partner recruitment to partner sales to marketing, research, and technical skills to build solutions and implement customer scenarios in one team, so that they can act sustainably end-to-end, a bit like a start-up, in an agile setup. (Independent software vendor program lead, Interview 6)	Establish teams that focus on one target market and build competencies in these target markets	Establish innovation clusters for specific target markets	Governance mechanism
The important thing is that you add value, that is, own IP, such as managed services. For example, you have a sensor that generates data that can be evaluated, and insights are gained from it. After all, you've developed a whole new business model where you don't implement the sensor once, and then you've sold three consulting days. No, you're saying, "You don't have to pay anything for implementation. Instead, I have to change my model so that, for example, I receive money from you for each successfully evaluated data set. You don't have to pay anything for implementation, support, maintenance, sensor, etc." (Business Development Manager, Interview 4)	Shift from projects to solutions	Develop own IP	Adaptation mechanism

4 Empirical Findings

4.1 Case Summary: Microsoft Azure

Founded in 1975 by Bill Gates and Paul Allen, Microsoft Corporation is a world leader in software and hardware development, with revenues of $198 billion in 2022 [37]. Its most important products and services include the operating system Microsoft Windows, productivity applications such as Microsoft Word and Excel under the umbrella of Microsoft 365, and hardware such as the Microsoft Surface products. These products and services target both end-users and businesses of all sizes. For example, more than 1 million companies used Microsoft 365 products in 2022 [38], and the combined number of paying private and end-users reached 345 million in 2022 [39].

To serve such large numbers of customers—particularly business customers—Microsoft relies on a global ecosystem of more than 400,000 partners [40]. Only a few of Microsoft's business customers directly interacted with Microsoft; this typically included large global corporations. All other business customers bought Microsoft products and services from partners. Beyond selling Microsoft products and services, partners offered services such as consulting, integrating products with the customer's legacy landscape, and developing new products and services. A partner manager at Microsoft underlined the importance of the partner ecosystem:

> For each employee, you can actually calculate 2.8 partners. For every employee, there are two to three partners. That's how Microsoft scales. Our partner ecosystem is the only way we can serve almost any company worldwide. (Senior Partner Development Manager at Microsoft, Interviewer 8)

Microsoft Deutschland GmbH, the subject of this case study, is one of the largest Microsoft businesses outside the US, with more than 2,800 employees. Its core business activities are product marketing, and customer and partner support. With more than 30,000 local German partner organizations, Microsoft Deutschland GmbH manages one of Microsoft Corporation's largest regional partner ecosystems to serve its 3.6 million German customers [41].

In the last decade, Microsoft has transformed from a business focused on selling on-premises products through traditional software licensing to a provider of services delivered in the cloud. This strategic shift is built on Microsoft Azure, Microsoft's cloud platform launched in 2014 that supports building, testing, deploying, and managing applications and services through a global network of Microsoft-managed data centers. It provides software as a service (SaaS), platform as a service (PaaS), and infrastructure as a service (IaaS), listing over 600 services such as identity management, AI and machine learning, security, integration, databases, and mixed reality [42]. In addition, it supports multiple proprietary and third-party programming languages.

However, given Microsoft's huge reliance on its partners, it had to transform its partner ecosystem and business model. In an address to 400,000 partners on the future of its new digital platform ecosystem in 2014, the CEO of Microsoft, Satya Nadella, acknowledged this strategic driver for the Microsoft Azure cloud platform and linked it explicitly to the partner support required for the success of Microsoft Azure:

*This company was built on enabling broad ecosystems and broad partner opportu-
nity. We now need to redefine what it means to build an ecosystem in a mobile-first,
cloud-first world. (Satya Nadella, CEO, Microsoft Agenda, 2014)*

In hindsight, Microsoft's transformation has been successful. After Microsoft
launched Azure in 2014 and started its transformation journey, its overall revenue stag-
nated and slightly declined until 2017 before strong growth rates kicked in (Fig. 1). The
strong revenue growth was driven by Microsoft's cloud business, which saw quarter-
over-quarter revenue growth rates nearing 100% each quarter in 2017 and 2018 [43, 44].
Furthermore, Microsoft's cloud infrastructure market share increased from 13.7% to
20% from 2017 to 2020, among harsh competition with global players such as Amazon
with AWS and Google with Google Cloud [45].

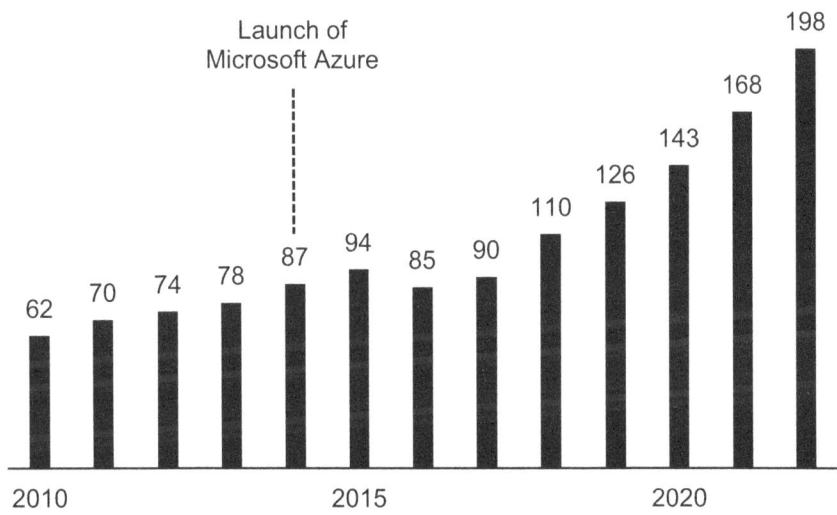

Fig. 1. Microsoft's global revenue 2010–2022 in billion $ [46]

To understand how Microsoft successfully transformed its partner ecosystem, we
conducted a case study of Microsoft Deutschland GmbH. We report details on our
methodological approach in the Appendix. Based on fourteen interviews and comprehensive secondary data covering a timespan from late 2016 to early 2018, we identified
the major challenge that Microsoft and its partners faced during the transformation.
Observing the reactions to these challenges, we establish four governance mechanisms
that guided Microsoft's successful transformation of its ecosystem and three adaptation
mechanisms that capture how partners successfully adapted to the changes of the partner
ecosystem.

4.2 Challenges During Ecosystem Transformation

The early phase of Microsoft's transformation was challenging both for Microsoft—as
highlighted by stagnating revenue (Fig. 1)—and for ecosystem partners.

Challenges for Microsoft. We identified three significant challenges Microsoft had to overcome: (1) reluctance of partners to transform, (2) shift of the point of contact at business customers, and (3) focus on short-term financial performance (Table 2).

Table 2. Microsoft's challenges during ecosystem transformation

Challenge	Description
Reluctance of partners to transform	• Lion's share of revenue still generated in the established on-premises business • Lack of in-house experience with cloud technologies • Security concerns
Shift of the point of contact at business customers	• Operational instead of IT departments become the point of contact for Microsoft • Access to operational departments is lacking
Focus on short-term financial performance	• Short-term revenue decrease in favor of stable long-term revenue and growth opportunities • Employees' incentives still aligned with short-term financial performance

First, many partners were reluctant to transform, that is, to shift their focus from on-premises products to cloud services. Reasons for their hesitation included that many partners still made the lion's share of their revenue with their on-premises business. As long as customers were not proactively demanding cloud solutions, there was no incentive for partners to promote them. Furthermore, many partners did not yet have sufficient expertise in-house to develop cloud solutions at the same level of quality as they did on-premises. In addition, partners raised security concerns concerning cloud services:

Some partners still claim that the whole cloud story is a big hype, a bubble that will explode tomorrow. And tomorrow is the moment when someone breaks through our security model and steals all the data. This has never happened before. But there are doubts that this will happen. They say: 'And what if someone steals all the customer/user data and sells it to a competitor?' (Partner Technical Architect, Interview 12)

In sum, this was a threat to speed to market and to achieving critical mass in the cloud, where Microsoft had become the second-largest player behind the Amazon Web Services offering [47].

Second, with the transformation towards an ecosystem enabled by the Azure platform, the point of contact at Microsoft's business customers changed. Microsoft and its partners have traditionally interacted with their customers' IT departments. However, with cloud services and related software-as-a-service offerings, the operational departments became the key actors. When end-users in the customer companies' operational departments became convinced of a specific cloud application, they would pitch that internally. The challenge for Microsoft was that it had only limited contact with customer companies, and those contacts were limited to the IT department.

> *The reality is that it works differently in the cloud market. Someone says, "I would like to have an application for order management!" Or for contact management, or whatever their problem is at that moment. This decision-maker is most likely not in the central IT department but somewhere else and wants to have his problem solved now, not in three years. This is satisfied by a digital buying process. (Independent Software Vendor Program Lead, Interview 6)*

Third, the revenue flow changes when shifting from on-premises products to services made available in the cloud. Instead of a significant up-front revenue for the sale of licenses, Microsoft would receive a smaller but recurring revenue for cloud subscriptions. While annual subscription revenues made Microsoft's overall revenue more predictable, this change also decreased short-term revenue. This was a challenge because many employees, particularly in partner management and sales departments, were still incentivized by their short-term revenue. Thus, the overall goal of "cloud-first" did not always translate into the individual incentives:

> *That's what I would say is the biggest challenge: How do you actually measure this success, which may come many months or a few quarters later? The best example is Thyssen Krupp: Now it starts, and there are real benefits of using the Azure platform. When we presented the whole thing at the HMI [1], we had a nice pilot, a showcase. We knew where it was going, but if you had looked at the numbers, it wasn't a case that would have been interesting for us in the short term from the licensing requirements. (Business Development Manager, Interview 4)*

Challenges for Partners. We first differentiate between two types of partners to identify the challenges Microsoft's partners faced following the introduction of Microsoft Azure (Table 3).

Resell partners focus on selling Microsoft products to their customers. In particular, they distributed software licenses and hardware and often offered value-added services such as help desk, training, and on-site IT support. Cloud computing would disrupt the business model of resellers, requiring them to reinvent their business models in the medium term. As customers could now access Microsoft services directly from the Microsoft Azure platform, the business opportunities for licensing software partners decreased. For example, Ingram Micro Deutschland, the German subsidiary of the US-based leading distributor of IT products, was one of Microsoft's largest resellers in Germany and had to expand its portfolio to be less dependent on on-premises products [48]. A transformation of the business model to become a provider of cloud services was challenging for resell partners because they often lacked the experience and skilled workforce to develop state-of-the-art cloud services:

> *Resellers are often large partners, very scaling partners. At the moment, however, they are not yet as successful as CSPs [cloud solution providers]. Of course, the*

---

[1] HMI or HM stands for the Hannover Messe, one of the world's largest industry trade fairs that takes place in Hannover, Germany annually.

Table 3. Challenges of Microsoft's ecosystem partners during the transformation

Partner type and activities	Activities	Challenges
Resell partners	• Software distribution • Hardware distribution • Hardware/software warranty support • Value-add services such as help desk, training, on-site IT support	• Business model becomes obsolete in the cloud • Proximity to customers becomes less important
Development partners	• Database development • Software development • Mobile applications • Web applications • Integration and customization of solutions from different vendors	• Shift focus from projects to products and services • Lack of skills

resellers have a lot of pressure to get out of this classic transactional business and into the managed service world, but they have a brutal hard time doing so. (Cloud Solution Provider Program Lead, Interview 7)

Development partners developed specialized software extensions (add-ons) or complete solutions that enhanced Microsoft products and services. The value of the partners' products for their customers was contingent on the Microsoft products and services to which they were connected. In addition, development partners offered installation, configuration, and consulting services to implement, maintain, and upgrade software. Some development partners focused on system integration. These partners advised on and integrated solutions from different suppliers. Primarily, these were customized services, including data migration, implementation, and support.

These partners' business models were built on individual customer projects, typically integrating Microsoft and other third-party solutions with the customers' on-premises legacy landscape. Thus, the major challenge for these partners was to shift their focus from projects to products and services. For example, T-Systems is an IT service provider based in Frankfurt that, amongst others, offers system integration services for all Microsoft solutions. T-Systems has expanded its partnership with Microsoft to leverage new business opportunities in the cloud [49].

Bringing about this change, taking partners with you, is already a major challenge for many partners. My personal experience is that the larger the partner, the harder it is to get out of the classic managed project world into the managed services world. (Cloud Solution Provider Program Lead, Interview 7)

In addition, partners faced the challenge of their employees requiring new skills. First, they had to get acquainted with the Azure platform and its functions. Second, the software development paradigm changed from on-premises to the cloud: Instead of developing independent software products, cloud applications would build on Azure's cloud infrastructure. Third, implementing new use cases with customers required a broad set of skill sets, for example, related to the analysis of data accumulated on the customer side:

> *The next thing to come: how can I develop new algorithms, for example? In the past, completely different people did this for completely different topics. Here, too, the partners have the challenge of needing data scientists. (Business Development Manager, Interview 4)*

In sum, for both partner categories, the transition from delivering on-premises products and services to providing cloud applications required significant changes to their business models, including the marketing and sales strategy, cost and profit calculation, the timing of cash flows, and the portfolio of products offered while coming along with uncertainty about adoption by customers [50]. These challenges explain why some Microsoft partners reacted negatively to Microsoft's transformation toward a cloud-based digital platform ecosystem: They perceived it as an attack on their business model rather than a novel business opportunity.

4.3   Governance Mechanisms for Ecosystem Transformation

Our case study allowed us to observe how Microsoft reacted to the initial skepticism between partners and internally. From these observations, we derived four mechanisms that Microsoft applied to govern the transformation of its partner ecosystem (Table 4).

Align Internal Partner Organization with Ecosystem-Level Goals. The first governance mechanism refers to aligning the internal partner organization with ecosystem-level goals. The internal partner organization proved to be crucial for implementing the transformation of the ecosystem. Before the ecosystem transformation, Microsoft's internal partner organization aimed to work with as many partners as possible who generate as much revenue as possible. During the transition, these goals proved counterproductive because the partner organization had to invest up-front in developing new markets with selected partners. It would take time before these new markets generated revenue. Thus, it was crucial for the partner organization that they got the flexibility and freedom they needed to develop new business:

> *But when you introduce great new projects to the top management, they expect to see an impact immediately. That means maintaining flexibility, freeing people up so they can think freely and proceed differently, getting higher management to ensure that you get these freedoms in the long term, freeing up resources, and having staying power so that the impact is visible and measurable in systems. I think that is the secret—that the partner channel transformation is doing well at the moment, but it's undoubtedly a new struggle every day.* (Partner Business & Development Lead, Interview 5)

To formalize the changes in its partner organization, Microsoft relabeled it as "One Commercial Partner" and restructured it into three areas: "build-with," "go-to-market,"

Table 4. Microsoft's governance mechanisms for ecosystem transformation

Governance mechanisms	Manifestations	Rationale
Align internal partner organization with ecosystem-level goals	• Decouple partner ecosystem performance measures from short-term KPIs • Establish startup-like teams with high degrees of freedom	• The internal partner organization is crucial for implementing the transformation of the ecosystem
Establish innovation clusters	• Establish teams that focus on one target market and build competencies in these target markets • Enter target markets with flagship projects • Form consortia of partners	• Innovative use cases draw customers to the platform • The orchestrator has to initiate the development of innovative use cases because partners are reluctant
Implement scalable partner enablement	• Offer resources to support the transformation • Provide funding for proofs-of-concept • Engage partners in the partner community • Offer new formats for co-innovation • Work with technology evangelists	• With an increasing number of partners, the orchestrator can no longer support partners individually • Interactions among partners can create synergies for partner enablement
Apply "carrot-and-stick" governance	• Implement goal-aligned financial incentives • Let the support of old, non-transformed business expire • Stop investments in relationships with hesitant partners	• Financial incentives are the most effective mechanisms to increase the number of partners that transform • Mid-term negative consequences for staying in the old ecosystem can incentivize partners that still have a sound business model in the old ecosystem

and "sell-with" [51]. Aligning the internal partner organization with ecosystem-level goals was a prerequisite for implementing further governance mechanisms because the partner organization ultimately implemented the governance and had to be incentivized to do so.

Establish Innovation Clusters. The second governance mechanism is to establish innovation clusters for particular target markets. Before the launch of the Azure platform, Microsoft had focused on making its products useful for as many markets as possible, and partners had then helped to adapt the products to customer needs. However, for the Azure platform to be successful, it had to offer innovative use cases because those would draw customers to the platform. Since partners were only starting to transition to the Azure platform or were even reluctant, Microsoft had to push innovation itself.

To establish innovation clusters, Microsoft established teams that focused on specific target markets and built expertise in these markets. Taking on an end-to-end perspective, these teams at Microsoft would systematically search for markets that could benefit most from use cases on the Azure platform. Once they identified a market, they had to understand the challenges of the customer companies. Thereby, they had to interact with people from the operational departments rather than with the IT departments, as the technology was no longer the central part of the conversation:

> When building a healthcare or sports business, I can use different technologies to make a business case. I take a different angle, and suddenly, I talk to people who understand something about healthcare or sports and use the relevant technology. This way, I shift the conversation to a customer-benefit conversation and away from a discussion about pure technology, which is then just a means to an end. (Independent Software Vendor Program Lead, Interview 6)

For example, Microsoft worked with Real Madrid, one of Europe's most famous soccer clubs, to create a virtual stadium application and further online services for Real Madrid's fanbase [52]. To do so, Microsoft had to build initial expertise in the sports and entertainment business.

Like with Real Madrid, Microsoft's goal was to enter markets with a flagship project, which would trigger further customers to adopt the Azure platform. Typically, Microsoft proactively involved partners in these flagship projects because the approach would otherwise not scale. Microsoft teams and partners formed so-called innovation clusters with a startup-like character and the goal of opening new markets for the Azure platform.

Implement Scalable Partner Enablement. The third mechanism refers to implementing scalable partner enablement. As more partners joined the Azure platform, Microsoft could no longer work with them individually as they became familiar with the platform. Furthermore, the increasing number of partners created more potential for synergies among partners as they would interact as well as share, and combine their experiences. Microsoft developed several mechanisms that helped partners to onboard the Azure platform and connect with other partners, depending on the requirements of different partner groups.

For example, Microsoft helped small and medium-sized partners develop cloud-based business models and services successfully by providing business, technical, and sales and marketing support, combined with transformation workshops, to help partners position themselves in the Microsoft Azure ecosystem and start a successful cloud business.

> We offer business transformation workshops for partners in various forms. There, privacy is still a big topic in cloud sales, so the customer brings objections and pretexts around privacy and the cloud. (Cloud Solution Providers Program Lead, Interview 7)

These workshops also help to reduce partner concerns and fears about moving to a cloud environment. Data protection and digital marketing emerged as the most important topics for discussion.

In addition, Microsoft established a marketing service portal to support digital marketing. The portal helped partners extend their reach with search engine optimization, develop a social media strategy, and guide website design and architecture. This portal aimed to provide partners with mechanisms to extend their potential customer base through a range of digital channels:

> *For CSPs [cloud solution providers] and, more generally, managed services, digital marketing, and especially social media marketing, are gaining importance; hence, we now also offer workshops for social media branding, which were very well received. (Cloud Solution Providers Program Lead, Interview 7)*

To help partners create innovative new solutions on the Azure platform, Microsoft increased and standardized its support for proof-of-concepts developed by partners.

> *We have various investment funds that support proof-of-concepts in projects. That means I have to set up a pilot and see if it works the way we imagined. We also have deployment support, which means we help all the way to the implementation. (Business Development Manager, Interview 3)*

Finally, as part of scalable partner enablement, Microsoft used technology evangelists to inspire partners about potential business opportunities.

Apply "Carrot-and-Stick" Governance. The last mechanism entails the application of "carrot-and-stick" governance to incentivize partners to transform, along with Microsoft's ecosystem transformation. Financial incentives were the most effective mechanisms to increase the number of partners that transform. However, partners with a sound business model in the old ecosystem would only consider going along with the transformation if they faced mid-term negative consequences for staying in the old ecosystem.

On the one hand, Microsoft designed direct incentive mechanisms for partners that adopted the Azure platform. First, financial incentives were contingent on partners delivering services in the cloud. For example, Microsoft rewarded licensing software partners with a fixed payment when cloud services were sold:

> *Partners get a revenue share from us for each EA [enterprise agreement] and a higher revenue share if there is a substantial cloud in the EA. Partners receive a relatively high revenue share programmatically from us for selling services in the Microsoft Cloud Germany. Partners get an extremely high revenue share for selling Azure high-end services such as Cortana, Analytics, or IoT. (Head of Partner Sales Organization, Interview 1)*

To fund these incentive mechanisms, Microsoft spent 4.3% of its commercial revenue in 2017 on partner incentives [53].

Second, partners received free licenses for services on Microsoft Azure, including software development, training, and marketing to boost business growth.

We give our partners internal licenses so they can use our technology independently without paying; we provide them with training vouchers, do roadshows with them, go to trade fairs, and so on. (Head of Partner Sales Organization, Interview 1)

On the other hand, Microsoft made the old, on-premises business less attractive for partners. Microsoft specified that upgrades to existing services and the launch of new products would be supported only on the Microsoft Azure platform and not in an on-premises environment. For example, using Microsoft Office on iOS without an Office 365 subscription and Microsoft Azure Active Directory was impossible. In this case, the end-users pull the Microsoft partners to the cloud and use the Microsoft Azure platform rather than Microsoft pushing them.

In addition, Microsoft clarified that support for a transition to the Azure platform was only available for a limited time. Partners had to show initiative to demonstrate their willingness to implement services for their customers in the cloud:

I like to invest time, money, and love in a partner, but I expect [the partner] to have the topic [of moving to the cloud] on the radar, at least after three or four months. (Program Lead, Cloud Solution Providers)

4.4 Adaptation Mechanisms of Ecosystem Partners

When Microsoft introduced the Azure platform and made it a strategic priority, it was clear that partners needed to adapt. However, many partners failed to do so because they still made sufficient revenue from their business model based on reselling and developing on-premises solutions. Still, many partners successfully adapted to the new ecosystem, and many new partners joined. From these partners, we can derive mechanisms for successful adaptation during ecosystem transformation (Table 5). We highlight how these adaptation mechanisms apply to resell and development partners.

Build Unique Experience in Relevant Target Markets. The first adaptation mechanism for partners during ecosystem transformation is to build a unique experience in relevant target markets. Microsoft's transformation showed that as an ecosystem orchestrator, Microsoft sought partners to help them create and offer end-to-end solutions to customers in specific markets—such as sports clubs or hospitals. Thus, for partners to remain relevant in the Microsoft ecosystem, they had to signal that they are well embedded in one or more such markets. Signaling such expertise helped partners become part of the innovation clusters Microsoft set up.

For resell partners, this transformation was particularly challenging because they often sold licenses across multiple industries without building in-depth experience. Still, they could leverage and expand their established relationship with both the IT and the operational departments of customers. Given that Microsoft often lacked direct contact with the customers' operational departments, it became crucial for resell partners to engage not only with the IT departments of their customers but also with the operational departments. These connections put them in a stronger position vis-à-vis Microsoft, granting them more time to shift to the Azure platform. Large resell partners had the additional opportunity to build market-specific expertise through acquisitions:

Table 5. Adaptation mechanisms of ecosystem partners

Governance mechanisms	Manifestations	Rationale
Build unique experience in relevant target markets	• Build and maintain relationships with both IT and operational departments of customers • For large partners: acquire specialists • Establish co-innovation with customers	• Only with expertise in relevant target markets will partners remain important for Microsoft • Such experience will help partners become part of Microsoft's innovation clusters
Develop own IP	• Shift from projects to solutions • Reuse modules across customer projects	• With their own IP, partners can offer software-as-a-service solutions, aligning their business model with the transformed ecosystem
Engage in partner communities	• Present use cases at partner events • Take on a role as an early mover in the community • Collaborate with partners	• Partners benefit from synergies with other partners • More innovative use cases can result from collaboration with partners

It's going to be really difficult for [resellers]. There's a range. There are the small resellers around the corner. I don't think we need them anymore. All the way to the big ones, the Large Account Resellers. They have the opportunity to invest; they buy new companies. I believe they have the opportunity to take this momentum with them through acquisitions and investments. (Head of Practice Development Unit, Interview 3)

For development partners, it was easier to draw on unique experiences from specific markets. These partners often had longstanding experience developing on-premises products and implementing complex integration projects in particular markets. These partners could then engage in co-innovation activities with their customers to create first use cases on the Azure platform. This approach would make partners highly attractive to Microsoft because Microsoft was looking for partners and customers to establish co-innovation clusters. For example, the IT consultancy Reply Deutschland SE engaged in co-innovation with Claas, a leading European agricultural machinery manufacturer. They jointly developed a platform that integrates data from the different machines, providing farmers additional services such as reviewing their machinery's position and driving tracks [54].

Develop own IP. The second adaptation mechanism refers to developing one's own IP. This mechanism applies to development partners even though resell partners, in the long run, would also benefit from selling their own products. With a focus on developing their own IP, partners could offer software-as-a-service solutions, aligning their business model with the transformed ecosystem.

Before the transformation to the Azure platform, development partners often implemented customer-specific projects, for example, to integrate their own or third-party products with the customers' legacy landscapes. The Azure platform allows partners to provide software-as-a-service to customers with little customer-specific implementation required. And even if some customer-specific implementation were required, partners would often be able to reuse modules of the solution across partners, as long as they kept the IP rights to the code. Microsoft highlighted the importance of partners focusing on developing their own IP early on in the transformation, but not all partners realized it:

> *We tell all partners to think about how they can get from their reselling and professional service to managed service and their own IP. That's a different discussion than 'How can we tackle the next customer with the following project?' We now say, 'What is your scaling solution for the future, and on which marketplace do you want to offer it?' Sometimes, managing directors of partners look at us and think, 'What is this person talking about?' because that's relatively far away for them. (Partner Business and Development Lead, Interview 5)*

The example of Aquia highlights how developing their IP could boost the growth of a partner business:

> *For me, Aquia is a prime example: They have an MSP [managed service provider] environment for Drupal. They offer Drupal as a service. But they don't just offer Drupal as a service; they have developed additional services, especially in the business intelligence realm. Thus, they have SaaS elements. In five years, they have grown abnormally and built a huge business on top of an open-source content management system. Doing something like this is an opportunity to evolve from a hoster to an MSP and from an MSP to a SaaS provider. (Independent Software Vendor Program Lead, Interview 6)*

Engage in Partner Communities. The third adaptation mechanism involves engaging in the partner community during the transformation. Bot resell and development partners could benefit from synergies with other partners in the partner communities, for example, through innovative use cases that result from the collaboration among partners.

To engage in partner communities, first, partners could present use cases they implemented with customers at Microsoft partner events. These presentations would increase the partner's visibility for Microsoft and attract more support from Microsoft. This effect was even more robust when the partner was an early mover in the community. Microsoft was actively looking for such early-moving partners, rewarding them with extraordinary resources and support. Second, engaging in the partner community created opportunities for collaboration. For example, resell partners could join forces with development partners—the resell partner benefited from the development partner's expertise in the target market, and the development partner from the reach of the resell partner. For Microsoft, such collaborations became increasingly essential, and it supported them with additional resources:

[Partners] also want to work with other partners because they know they can never cover everything. If we, as a company, still bring them together and orchestrate the ecosystem, i.e., bring several partners together to offer end-to-end solutions, then that is another added value for partners. (Head of Partner Sales Organization, Interview 1)

In sum, while the ecosystem transformation posed significant challenges for partners, it also provided opportunities for those flexible enough to adapt.

5   Discussion

Governing partner ecosystems has long been essential to enterprise software vendors' business [3, 55]. Over time, enterprise software vendors have established the capabilities to attract and retain partners in their ecosystems, for example, by providing resources for partners through partner programs or by certifying partner solutions [1]. However, the case of Microsoft illustrated that orchestrators and ecosystem partners need new skills when their ecosystem's underlying technology undergoes a significant transition—such as a transition from on-premises to cloud software [14]. We derived four governance mechanisms that help enterprise software vendors navigate ecosystem transformation and three adaptation mechanisms that partners can draw on as they react to such transformations (Fig. 2).

The model first illustrates the orchestrator's governance mechanisms. It shows that aligning the internal partner organization with the ecosystem-level goal is the starting point for a governance approach in an ecosystem undergoing transformation. Then, the orchestrator can engage in further governance mechanisms that, in turn, trigger adaptation by partners. First, the governance mechanism "establish innovation clusters" incentivizes partners to "build unique experience in relevant target markets." With this unique experience, partners can become indispensable parts of innovation clusters, strengthening their position to capture value from the ecosystem. Second, the mechanism "apply 'carrot-and-stick' governance" leads to partners engaging in partner communities—for those partners that go along with the transformation of the ecosystems. Some partners might drop out of the ecosystem due to the carrot-and-stick governance that tries to push them to the transformed ecosystem. The partners that remain in the ecosystem are more likely to engage in the partner community. Finally, the governance mechanism "implement scalable partner development" allows a more significant number of partners to develop their own IP, a strategy that helps, particularly former resell partners, to capture value from the ecosystem. In the final step, observing the partners' adaptation mechanisms provides essential feedback for the orchestrator on reconfiguring governance to further support the ecosystem transformation.

5.1   Contribution to Literature

Our work first contributes to research on enterprise software by shedding light on the transition towards cloud computing and its impact on vendors and partners. The findings add to previous work that has mostly studied partner ecosystems in the era of packaged

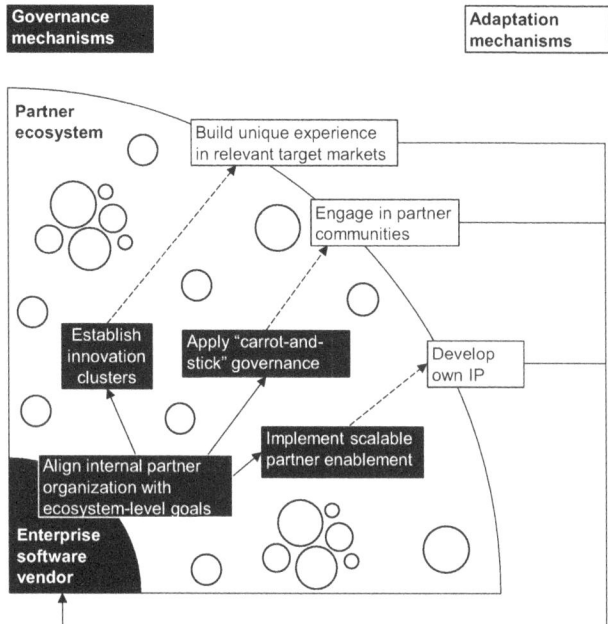

Fig. 2. Governance and adaptation mechanisms in ecosystem transformations in the enterprise software industry

enterprise software [e.g., 3, 4] and has not considered the effect of major shifts in the ecosystems' underlying technologies. We further contribute to work on the transition of software vendors to the cloud by taking on an ecosystem perspective, considering both the orchestrator and ecosystem partners [14, 15].

Second, we enhance the information systems literature on governance of interfirm relationships. While previous work has mostly studied the governance of close partnerships such as strategic alliances [22, 23] and loosely coupled third-party developers [7, 25]. In the first case, the number of partners is typically small. In the second case, the number of partners or third-party developers can be large, but they are treated as a homogeneous group. Our findings show that in partner ecosystems in the software industry, there is a large number of heterogeneous partners. Governing them during phases of ecosystem transformations is challenging, and our paper provides the first mechanisms for how ecosystem orchestrators can address that challenge.

Third, our work adds to the broader literature on digital platforms. This literature has mostly considered how orchestrators attract new third-party developers to a platform ecosystem rather than how to transform an existing ecosystem [7, 19, 20]. Furthermore, most studies focused on consumer-facing digital platforms such as app platforms for smartphones or gaming platforms. These studies' implications for literature and practice would not fully apply to more complex business-to-business settings such as enterprise software.

Future research could enhance our case study to evaluate generalizability. Qualitative case studies on other platforms launched by enterprise software vendors could underline and expand our findings. Quantitative analysis of partner reactions to ecosystem transformations could shed more light on the characteristics of partners that successfully adapt to these transformations. Data sources for this kind of analysis include curated industry data such as the ISVworld database [56] or data gathered from partner communities such as the SAP community [57]. Besides the characteristics of successful partners, it could be worthwhile to study why some partners continue to focus on the old ecosystem model and why. Such a strategy could be deliberate to become a niche player for developing and maintaining on-premises software and charge higher prices over time as the number of partners that still have these skills declines.

5.2 Contribution to Practice

We have derived these mechanisms from the case of Microsoft's Azure platform. However, we suggest that the findings can also be helpful for other companies in the enterprise software industry, for transformations other than those from on-premises to cloud software, and for some incumbent companies from industries other than enterprise software.

First, incumbent enterprise software vendors like SAP, IBM, and Oracle are still transforming their ecosystems toward cloud software [17]. For example, SAP extended its support for its popular on-premises ERP (SAP R3) until the end of 2027 with an option for extended maintenance until 2030 [58]. While many partners have embraced SAP's cloud platform, some still rely on revenue from on-premises business. Drawing on the adaptation mechanisms, these partners, for example, would benefit from developing their own IP on the SAP Business Technology Platform.

Second, the enterprise software industry will undergo further transformations as the underlying technology continues to evolve. While not every change might be as transformational as the shift from on-premises to cloud software, the governance and adaptation mechanisms can still be helpful. For example, advancing artificial intelligence tools in enterprise software affects the partner ecosystem. Enterprise software vendors have included numerous tools and services in their cloud platforms that customers and partners can use to implement AI-enabled use cases. Governance mechanisms such as establishing innovation clusters for specific target markets and implementing scalable partner enablement will help spread artificial intelligence offerings across the ecosystem.

Third, we suggest transferring the mechanisms to contexts beyond the enterprise software industry. For example, manufacturing companies have begun to invest in the industrial Internet, which requires the partners in their production network to become part of a new cloud-based partner ecosystem [59]. In the financial industry, banks have embraced open application programming platforms to allow existing and new partners to develop and distribute add-ons to the banks' core applications. Similarly, the healthcare industry has seen ecosystems of service providers transform as cloud platforms are launched to improve coordination among providers and allow the development of innovative new solutions [60].

6   Conclusion

In this case study on the introduction of Microsoft Azure, we shed light on the transformation of partner ecosystems in the enterprise software industry. With the advance of cloud computing technologies, the enterprise software industry has gone through a fundamental shift from on-premises software to cloud-based services. This shift challenged not only Microsoft as the ecosystem orchestrator but also partners that were already part of Microsoft's ecosystems. We first identified the challenges that Microsoft and its partners faced. A challenge for Microsoft was, for example, that the performance goals were focused on short-term results, while the implementation of the Azure platform would often not see revenues in the first years. To address these challenges, we derived governance mechanisms for enterprise software vendors during ecosystem transformation (e.g., establishing innovation clusters for specific target markets) and three adaptation mechanisms for ecosystem partners (e.g., developing their own IP). Our findings provide specific guidance for practitioners and contribute to the information system literature on enterprise software.

Acknowledgments. This work was partly funded by the Austrian Science Fund (FWF) [project no. I6567-G].

Disclosure of Interests. Author Thomas Schwaab is employed by Microsoft Germany GmbH. Author Tobias Riasanow is employed by SAP SE. The authors have no other competing interests to declare that are relevant to the content of this article.

References

1. Kude, T., Dibbern, J., Heinzl, A.: Why do complementors participate? An analysis of partnership networks in the enterprise software industry. IEEE Trans. Eng. Manage. **59**(2), 250–265 (2012)
2. Kude, T., Huber, T., Dibbern, J.: Successfully governing software ecosystems: competence profiles of partnership managers. IEEE Softw. **36**, 39–44 (2018)
3. Sarker, S., et al.: Exploring value cocreation in relationships between an ERP vendor and its partners: a revelatory case study. MIS Q. **36**(1), 317–338 (2012)
4. Ceccagnoli, M., et al.: Cocreation of value in a platform ecosystem: the case of enterprise software. MIS Q. **36**(1), 263–290 (2012)
5. Schreieck, M., Wiesche, M., Krcmar, H.: Capabilities for value co-creation and value capture in emergent platform ecosystems: a longitudinal case study of SAP's cloud platform. J. Inf. Technol. **36**(4), 365–390 (2021)
6. Nieuwenhuis, L.J.M., Ehrenhard, M.L., Prause, L.: The shift to cloud computing: the impact of disruptive technology on the enterprise software business ecosystem. Technol. Forecast. Soc. Chang. **129**, 308–313 (2018)
7. Tiwana, A.: Platform Ecosystems: Aligning Architecture, Governance, and Strategy. Morgan Kaufmann, Burlington (2014)
8. Cusumano, M.A.: Generative AI as a new innovation platform. Commun. ACM **66**(10), 18–21 (2023)

9. Moore, J.F.: Predators and prey: a new ecology of competition. Harv. Bus. Rev. **71**(3), 75–86 (1993)
10. Kumar, K., Hillegersberg, J.: ERP experiences and evolution. Commun. ACM **43**(4), 23–26 (2000)
11. Staehr, L., Shanks, G., Seddon, P.P.B.: An explanatory framework for achieving business benefits from ERP systems. J. Assoc. Inf. Syst. **13**(6), 424–465 (2012)
12. Chellappa, R.K., Sambamurthy, V., Saraf, N.: Competing in crowded markets: multimarket contact and the nature of competition in the enterprise systems software industry. Inf. Syst. Res. **21**(3), 614–630 (2010)
13. Stolinsky, P.: The IBM Software Development Platform Partner Ecosystem. IBM (2004)
14. Giessmann, A., Legner, C.: Designing business models for platform as a service: towards a design theory. ICIS **2013**, 1–10 (2013)
15. Xiao, X., Hedman, J.: How a software vendor weathered the stormy journey to the cloud. MIS Q. Exec. **18**(1), 37–50 (2018)
16. Baek, S., Kim, K., Altmann, J.: Role of platform providers in service networks: the case of Salesforce.com app exchange. In: 16th IEEE Conference on Business Informatics. Geneva, Switzerland (2014)
17. Schreieck, M., Wiesche, M., Krcmar, H.: From product platform ecosystem to innovation platform ecosystem: an institutional perspective on the governance of ecosystem transformations. J. Assoc. Inf. Syst. **23**(6), 1354–1385 (2022)
18. Beaulieu, T., et al.: Confronting, confirming, and dispelling myths surrounding ERP-in-the-cloud. AIS Trans. Enterprise Syst. **1**, 3–16 (2015)
19. Parker, G.G., Van Alstyne, M.W., Choudary, S.P.: Platform Revolution. W. W. Norton & Company, New York (2016)
20. Parker, G.G., Van Alstyne, M.W., Jiang, X.: Platform ecosystems: how developers invert the firm. MIS Q. **41**(1), 255–266 (2017)
21. International Organization for Standardization: ISO 26000 - Social responsibility (2010)
22. Reuer, J.J., Arino, A.: Strategic alliance contracts: dimensions and determinants of contractual complexity. Strateg. Manag. J. **28**, 313–330 (2007)
23. Reuer, J.J., Devarakonda, S.V.: Mechanisms of hybrid governance: administrative committees in non-equity alliances. Acad. Manag. J. **59**(2), 510–533 (2016)
24. Rai, A., et al.: Hybrid relational-contractual governance for business process outsourcing. J. Manag. Inf. Syst. **29**(2), 213–256 (2012)
25. Tiwana, A., Konsynski, B., Bush, A.A.: Platform evolution: coevolution of platform architecture, governance, and environmental dynamics. Inf. Syst. Res. **21**(4), 675–687 (2010)
26. Wessel, M., Thies, F., Benlian, A.: Opening the floodgates: the implications of increasing platform openness in crowdfunding. J. Inf. Technol. **32**(4), 344–360 (2017)
27. Ondrus, J., Gannamaneni, A., Lyytinen, K.: The impact of openness on the market potential of multi-sided platforms: a case study of mobile payment platforms. J. Inf. Technol. **30**(3), 260–275 (2015)
28. Goldbach, T., Benlian, A., Buxmann, P.: Differential effects of formal and self-control in mobile platform ecosystems: Multi-method findings on third-party developers' continuance intentions and application quality. Inf. Manage. **55**(3), 271–284 (2018)
29. Ens, N., Hukal, P., Blegind Jensen, T.: Dynamics of control on digital platforms. Inf. Syst. J. **33**(4), 890–911 (2023)
30. Ghazawneh, A., Henfridsson, O.: Balancing platform control and external contribution in third-party development: the boundary resources model. Inf. Syst. J. **23**(2), 173–192 (2013)
31. Eaton, B.D., et al.: Distributed tuning of boundary resources: the case of Apple's iOS service system. MIS Q. **39**(1), 217–243 (2015)
32. Yin, R.K.: Case Study Research: Design and Methods, p. 282. 5th edn. SAGE, Los Angeles (2014)

33. Myers, M.D., Newman, M.: The qualitative interview in IS research: examining the craft. Inf. Organ. **17**(1), 2–26 (2007)
34. Miles, M.B., Huberman, A.M.: Qualitative Data Analysis: An Expanded Sourcebook. Thousand Oaks, California: SAGE (1994)
35. Wiesche, M., et al.: Grounded theory methodology in information systems research. MIS Q. **41**(3), 685–701 (2017)
36. Urquhart, C.: Grounded Theory for Qualitative Research – A Practical Guide. SAGE Publication Inc., London (2013)
37. Microsoft Corporation, Annual Report 2022. Microsoft (2022)
38. Enlyft: Number of companies using Office 365 worldwide as of February 2023, by leading country (2023)
39. Microsoft Corporation: Earnings Release FY22 Q3. 2022 Microsoft (2022)
40. Clark, R.: Evolving Microsoft Partner Network programs for partner growth and customer success, in Official Microsoft Blog (2022)
41. Microsoft Corporation: Microsoft Deutschland – das sind wir (2023). https://news.microsoft.com/de-de/features/microsoft-deutschland-das-sind-wir/. Accessed 25 Sep 2023
42. Microsoft Corporation: Azure products (2019). https://azure.microsoft.com/en-us/services/. Accessed 8 Feb 2021
43. Levy, A.: Microsoft's cloud business is growing almost twice as fast as Amazon's, with Google far behind, in CNBC (2017)
44. Forbes: Microsoft's cloud services growth continues (2017)
45. Canalys; Statista. Cloud infrastructure services vendor market share worldwide from 4th quarter 2017 to 4th quarter 2022 (2023). https://www.statista.com/statistics/967365/worldwide-cloud-infrastructure-services-market-share-vendor/. Accessed 27 Sep 2023
46. Microsoft Corporation: Microsoft's annual revenue worldwide from FY 2002 to FY 2023. Microsoft (2023)
47. Gartner: Gartner says worldwide IaaS public cloud services market grew 37.3% in 2019 (2020). https://www.gartner.com/en/newsroom/press-releases/2020-08-10-gartner-says-worldwide-iaas-public-cloud-services-market-grew-37-point-3-percent-in-2019. Accessed 5 May 2021
48. Ingram Micro: Ingram micro news (2020). https://de.ingrammicro.eu/. Accessed 12 Mar 2021
49. T-Systems International GmbH: Into the Microsoft public cloud with T-Systems (2021). https://www.t-systems.com/de/en/partners/microsoft. Accessed 11 Apr 2021
50. Microsoft Corporation: Rentabilität für Cloudpartner (2020). https://web.archive.org/web/20170626103347/https://partner.microsoft.com/de-de/solutions/cloud-partner-profitability. Accessed 5 May 2021
51. Microsoft Corporation: Putting partners first (2017). https://blogs.partner.microsoft.com/mpn-canada/putting-partners-first/. Accessed 11 Apr 2021
52. Microsoft Corporation: Real Madrid brings the stadium closer to 450 million fans around the globe, with the Microsoft Cloud. 2015 Microsoft (2015)
53. Microsoft Corporation: Annual report (2017). https://www.microsoft.com/investor/reports/ar17/index.html. Accessed 5 May 2021
54. Reply. CLAAS: Cloud first for field logistics (2019). https://www.reply.com/en/cloud-computing/claas-cloud-first-for-iot. Accessed 12 Sep 2023
55. Huber, T.L., Kude, T., Dibbern, J.: Governance practices in platform ecosystems: navigating tensions between co-created value and governance Costs. Inf. Syst. Res. **28**(3), 563–584 (2017)
56. ISVworld (2023). https://www.isvworld.com/. Accessed 14 Sep 2023
57. Kauschinger, M., et al.: Detecting feature requests of third-party developers through machine learning: a case study of the SAP Community. In: 56th Hawaii International Conference on System Sciences. Maui, Hawaii, USA (2023)

58. SAP SE: SAP gibt erweiterte Innovationszusage für SAP S/4HANA und bietet Klarheit und Wahlmöglichkeiten für SAP Business Suite 7. SAP SE (2020)

59. Sandberg, J., Holmström, J., Lyytinen, K.: Digitization and phase transitions in platform organizing logics: evidence from the process automation industry. MIS Q. **44**(1), 129–153 (2020)

60. Choudary, S.P.: The state of the platform revolution 2021. Platformation Labs (2021)

Author Index

© The Editor(s) (if applicable) and The Author(s), under exclusive license
to Springer Nature Switzerland AG 2026
M. Schreieck et al. (Eds.): DSPE 2025, LNBIP 563, p. 205, 2026.
https://doi.org/10.1007/978-3-032-04512-6

The manufacturer's authorised representative in the EU is Springer
Nature Customer Service Centre GmbH, Tiergartenplatz 3, 69115 Heidelberg,
Germany. If you have any concerns regarding our products, please
contact ProductSafety@springernature.com

Printed and bound by CPI Group (UK) Ltd, Croydon, CR0 4YY

29/04/2026

02099461-0007